WEB PRESENCE

FT.com
FINANCIAL TIMES

books for the future minded

Welcome to the next generation of business

There is a new world which we can look at but we cannot see. Yet within it, the forces of technology and imagination are overturning the way we work and the way we do business.

ft.com books are both gateway and guide to this world. We understand it because we are part of it. But we also understand the needs of businesses which are taking their first steps into it, and those still standing hesitantly on the threshold. Above all, we understand that, as with all business challenges, the key to success lies not with the technology itself, but with the people who must use it and manage it. People like you – the future minded.

See a world of business.

Visit **www.ft.com** today.

WEB PRESENCE

creating an e-business out of chaos

Peter Small

FT.com
FINANCIAL TIMES

London / New York / San Francisco / Toronto / Sydney / Tokyo / Singapore / Hong Kong /
Cape Town / Madrid / Paris / Milan / Munich / Amsterdam

PEARSON EDUCATION LIMITED

Head Office:
Edinburgh Gate
Harlow CM20 2JE
Tel: +44 (0)1279 623623
Fax: +44 (0)1279 431059

London Office:
128 Long Acre
London WC2E 9AN
Tel: +44 (0)20 7447 2000
Fax: +44 (0)20 7240 5771

www.business-minds.com

First published in Great Britain in 2001

© Peter Small 2001

The right of Peter Small to be identified as author of this work has been
asserted by him in accordance with the Copyright, Designs and Patents Act 1988.

ISBN 0 273 65415 2

British Library Cataloguing in Publication Data
A CIP catalogue record for this book can be obtained from the British Library.

Library of Congress Cataloging in Publication Data
Applied for.

Many of the designations used by manufacturers and sellers to distinguish their products are claimed
as trademarks. Pearson Education Limited has made every attempt to supply trademark information
about manufacturers and their products mentioned in this book. A list of trademark designations and
their owners appears on this page.

Trademark notice
PowerPoint, Microsoft Office, Windows NT are trademarks of the Microsoft Corporation; Macintosh
and HyperCard are trademarks of Apple; OS/2 is a trademark of International Business Machines
(IBM), Novell R is a trademark of Novell, Inc.; NFS is a trademark of Sun Microsystems, Inc; VisiCalc
is a trademark of Visicorp, Inc.; Director, Flash and Lingo are trademarks of Macromedia, UNIX is
licensed through X/Open Company Ltd (in collaboration with Novell, Hp and SCO) and Lego is a
trademark of the LEGO Corporation.

10 9 8 7 6 5 4 3 2 1

Designed by Sue Lamble
Typeset by Land & Unwin (Data Sciences) Ltd
Printed and bound in Great Britain by Biddles Ltd, Guildford and King's Lynn

The Publishers' policy is to use paper manufactured from sustainable forests.

CONTENTS

ACKNOWLEDGEMENTS

No book can be created by an author in isolation. This book is no exception. Indeed, the feedback from so many people during the draft stages of the writing was a major influence on the content. Listed below (in alphabetical order) are the people who in one way or another contributed to the evolution of this book.

Ruth Arnold, Philip Ashman, Perry Barile, Vaughn Botha, Martin Burns, Yvan Caron, Stefano Cecere, Arthur Clemens, Garrett Coakley, Kate Cooper, Caio Barra Costa, Shawn Crispin, Scott Dexter, Barbara Edwards, Katherin Ekstrom, James Elbon, Bill Ethridge, Joe Evans, Pete Everett, Stewart Fallowfield, Nicholas Fish, Dave Gray, Vic Harper, John Helmer, Steve Howard, Dessislava Karoushkova, Vahé Kassardjian, Keith Kingsland, Hera and Garo Kurkman, Janet Laidler, Barbara Lamar, Donald C. Lawson III, Leonard Lewis, John Lyons, Chris Macrae, Matthew Murdoch, Wendi Murray, Tillman Pearce, Verne Pence, Joe Repka, Mary Rickman-Taylor, Bryan Rieger, Stephen Roberts, Richard Ross, Giles Rowe, Maninder Singh Kumar, Manuel Soler, Hubert Spall, Anette Standfusss, Aubrey Stanley, Dr. Stephen Thaler, Dr. Thomas Thum, Rainer Volz, Christian Wach, Skip Walter, Andy Webster, Dai Williams, Dan Winchester, Mikael Wirén, Martin Woollatt.

Thanks also to the team at Pearson Education who commissioned and edited this book for the FT.COM series of books on e-commerce: Richard Stagg, Steve Temblett, Katherin Ekstrom, Annette Abel and Marilyn StClair.

Especially, I'd like to thank my wife, Dalida, and my two sons, Elliot and Oliver, who have had to make so many sacrifices to allow me the time to spend writing this book.

INTRODUCTION

lessons learned from the dot-com bubble

The paradox of the internet is that it offers so many opportunities to create wealth yet so many e-business pioneers lost money. What went wrong?

It is easy to criticize the pioneers of the Information Age. Although they made every kind of mistake possible, these were only seen as mistakes in retrospect. The truth is that throughout the dot-com bubble nobody really knew what would work and what wouldn't.

I started to write about e-business in 1999, just as the dot-com bubble was approaching its zenith. The publication of the first book in this trilogy, *The Entrepreneurial Web,* coincided with the time the bubble burst. Although this first book explained many of the reasons for the dot-com failures, it hadn't been written because I understood e-business: quite the opposite, it had been written because I didn't understand e-business.

The book was simply a way of trying to wrap my head around the problems and implications of a massively connected world. This I managed to do not by creating an e-business myself, but by being in constant touch with developers and programmers who were at the cutting edge.

I'd been cautious about joining the enthusiastic rush into e-business ventures because I'd already been burned in one technology bubble: the CD-ROM bubble in 1993. At that time, I'd plunged in, confident that my past entrepreneurial experiences would put me ahead of the game. I was sadly disillusioned. I failed miserably and lost not only all of my capital, but my house as well. It was a very sobering experience.

From 1995 to 1999, determined to get back into the game, I plunged deep into the black arts of computer programming. My aim had not been to become an expert programmer, but to understand and appreciate the full potential of what the world of digital communication had to offer. I was surprised and delighted with what I found. I discovered a spectacular array of possibilities, matched only by the complexities found in the biological world. This four-year exploration into the world of lists, objects and intelligent agents is described in the two books *Lingo Sorcery* and *Magical A-Life Avatars*.

What amazed me, as I saw the dot-com bubble building up, was the number of people who were trying to create e-businesses based upon old-economy concepts. Certainly, the internet can be used to great effect by conventional companies to enhance their methods and procedures to bring about new efficiencies, but this is not what e-business pioneering is all about. E-business pioneering is about exploiting new opportunities that were impossible or unimaginable in the pre-internet world.

Reaching out, beyond the conventional and into the unknown, is not something that can be done with standard business models and methods. It requires the mind of a scientist and the skill of a games strategist. It requires conceptual models that allow solutions a freedom to evolve beyond a designer's imagination: not be limited by it. This was the main problem with the dot-com failures. They had predetermined business models that had limited scope to adapt and evolve. What couldn't be visualized beforehand couldn't be part of their plans.

The trick is to create a business that can self-organize: a business that is self-adapting and able to escape from the limitations imposed by human imagination and knowledge. This can only be done by using the techniques of Mother Nature: the all-powerful mechanisms of evolutionary biology.

I'd intended to write a single book on e-business, a book that explained how to think differently about the new implications of the internet. It couldn't be done with a single book. All I could do was expose the problems this new business environment was throwing up and provide some of the basic conceptual models to be able to think about the internet in a different way.

The first of these problems I encountered was the exploding volume of information that had to be dealt with. Every area of technology was fragmenting and expanding. Despite having had eight years of direct involvement, there was no way I could keep up with the developments in so many different areas.

What gave me encouragement was that everybody else was in the same position. Nobody could ever hope to know it all. This thought gave me a new perspective. It wasn't about learning all the technology, it was about learning how to proceed when you didn't know everything that needed to be known. This called for a game theory approach rather than a solution based upon organization and planning.

My visualization of this situation was to see e-business as a game of chess, where parts of the board and many of the pieces are invisible, such that most of the playable moves cannot be realized. As different people will have different areas of knowledge and different kinds of knowledge gaps, this chess board representation of e-business would look different to different people. They'd each see only parts of the board and only some of the pieces.

Seeing the situation in this way, it is obvious that a game can only be played if a mixture of people combine so that between them they can see all the pieces on the board. This took the emphasis of e-business strategy away from the technology and on to finding and working with an appropriate mix of collaborators.

The second problem seemed to be even more difficult to solve: technology is continuously evolving and changing. If seen as a game of chess, it would be the equivalent of a capricious imp, continuously moving the pieces around while you are not looking, sometimes removing some or adding others. This makes the game unpredictable and it is therefore impossible to use a strategy that involves forward planning.

Seeing e-business in the light of this Alice in Wonderland game of chess, I was totally amazed to see people playing the e-business game as if it were a straightforward game of chess. Entrepreneurs were presenting ideas and business plans as if they knew how things would turn out. Venture capital companies were supporting them with finance, as if the ideas and planning were reasonably reliable. Investors were encouraged to back these ideas and plans, on the basis that everyone knew what they were doing.

My second book, *The Ultimate Game of Strategy*, dealt specifically with these two major problems. It devised strategies to create and cultivate a suitable group of personal contacts and cope with the problems of a rapidly expanding and changing knowledge base. This put my thinking out of line with practically every conventional business strategy being recommended by most of the consultants and advisers to the e-business pioneers.

Using a game theory approach, I'd concluded that using capital investment in e-business pioneering ventures was not the way to proceed. Business planning was too unreliable to be of any better value than guesswork. Even more controversially, I'd come to the conclusion that the provenly successful concept of a managed team would be unsuitable for pioneering e-business ventures.

Not surprisingly, my first two books in this trilogy were treated with derision in many quarters. They asked, 'How can you create a business when you have no business plan, don't know what the results will be, have no capital, lead no team and have no management structure?'

This book is about answering those questions. I started off exactly in this position and the book is a record of the strategic thinking over a nine-month period that saw me getting into a position to create an e-business.

Most books on business strategy are based on historical events. They tell you how others have succeeded or failed. They are written for people who already have a set business idea and just want to know how to be more successful than their rivals or competitors. Few business books cover the area most difficult for entrepreneurs – the time before a business is born. This book covers this enigmatic but crucial period.

the entrepreneurial checklist
Every e-business entrepreneur must begin a venture with research and much preparatory work before

taking positive action. It is like being an explorer: setting off into the unknown. It needs months of preparation, to make sure there are sufficient resources available to complete the journey. Both e-business entrepreneurs and explorers will be acutely aware that, having once set out, there is no turning back without having to abort the mission.

Preparations take a long time. To make sure nothing has been forgotten, an explorer will have to compile a checklist of everything that will be needed for the journey. Different kinds of explorers will have different items on their checklists; an explorer venturing across the Antarctic wastes will have a totally different list to an explorer heading for the Amazon jungle.

Similarly, wise entrepreneurs will spend much time in preparation before they start on their ventures. They too will have checklists, to ensure their preparations have covered all possible contingencies.

The checklist of any entrepreneur, explorer or adventurer will be grouped into main categories. For an e-business entrepreneur these categories would include:

1 credibility;

2 a suitable communication strategy;

3 an array of conceptual components;

4 adequate experience;

5 a sound conceptual framework;

6 proof of concept;

7 a number of key contacts;

8 sufficient funding.

This final book of the trilogy describes the thinking processes behind getting this important checklist together. However, it is not neatly arranged in this order – nor even in these categories – because in practice the categories are highly interdependent. Worse still, the dependencies are circular. For example, funding will be dependent upon credibility, credibility will often be dependent upon proof of concept, and funding will be necessary to produce the proof of concept.

It is such circular dependencies that give rise to problems in mathematics. Circular dependencies cause computer programs to crash. In the world of e-business they cause breakdowns that lead to failure: promising ideas and projects being stillborn or abandoned at an early stage. The way out of this circular dependency trap is to have a firm grasp of the fundamentals: an abstraction of the business as part of a wider system.

This book is concerned mainly with such abstract models because they allow entrepreneurs to rise above detail to facilitate rapid change and adaptation without losing control. They provide the entrepreneur with the confidence needed to be able to act boldly and decisively without having to count on luck.

Fundamental to all business progress and success is cash flow. It is as important to a business as blood circulation is to a mammal. For this reason, the first part of the book sets up a conceptual framework for considering funding and finance. Although the issue of funding may be the final stage of getting a business up and running, the requirements necessary for funding cash flow will affect all other aspects of a business, particularly in the early stages. It is vital, therefore, that this critically important area is mastered first.

flexible business ideas

Probably the most difficult concept to grasp is that an an e-business entrepreneur cannot work with any firm idea as to how the future might unfold. An astute entrepreneur will realize that all business ideas are vulnerable to unknowns and uncertainties: partners or associates might let them down; funding bodies might change their minds; new technology might outdate proposed schemes, methods or processes; competitors might produce something cheaper, better, or both, maybe even copying their ideas and coming up with better innovations.

With such a range of unpredictable problems, a business based upon control and organization is not reliable. The alternative is to create a business that is self-organizing and self-funding: a business that evolves and adapts in an organic way to whatever the future might come up with.

Such a business will consist of a system of components, comprising many different ideas and human associates that can be reconfigured to meet any contingency. Instead of a plan that sets out a course of action, there is a set of guiding rules that steer the business through the minefields of danger.

It is this game theory approach to e-business strategy that is brought out in this book. It is not about being able to execute a business plan, but about being able to survive and prosper in a chaotic environment of change and uncertainty.

don't read the last chapter first
The reader may be tempted to read the last chapter first, to see what business has been created during the writing of this book. Try not to do this because you'll miss the value of the constantly changing directions the book takes before a viable business opportunity comes along. It must be appreciated that the business idea hadn't even been thought of until about halfway through the writing. Indeed, it was only in the final part, the last three chapters, that the business idea emerged as a real possibility.

Like a good murder mystery, it is best to read the book through sequentially, from page one to the end, evaluating the clues as they turn up, living with the author during the explorations, the dead-ends and the red herrings. The value is in the journey – not the final result.

THE FOUNDATION

THIS FIRST PART OF THE BOOK CONTAINS some seemingly arcane financial considerations. Originally, I'd planned to end with this material, as it is a disconcerting way to start a book and might put readers off. However, it soon became clear that the strategies described in the later chapters only make sense if the fundamentals of finance and investment are taken into consideration.

It is only too easy to get carried away with exciting technological solutions when working in a vacuum. Too often, great new ideas flourish in the conceptual and design stages only to founder disastrously when they meet the harsh realities of the competitive world.

It may be a new economy, it may be an unprecedented technological revolution, but this does not change the reality that success and progress are about doing things more efficiently. Creating clever solutions and highly sophisticated systems is nothing more than a waste of time, money and human resources – if the end product doesn't produce value for money.

For this reason, it seems worthwhile to tackle the financial considerations first. Ultimately, these will provide the practical restraints that guide an e-business to profitability. Without these restraints, technology can easily lead a business into a quagmire of irreconcilable cash flow problems – from which there is no escape.

Beginning with a little background, the first chapter explains that the object of the book is to go through the various thought processes that might be involved in the creation of an e-business.

It is not about techniques, methods or procedures. It is about acquiring a mindset that can use abstract models to cope with the rapidly changing, competitive environment of the internet. In a world where there is too much information to absorb, it is essential to build up a varied group of useful contacts to overcome the problem of unavoidable knowledge gaps.

Chapter 2 looks at the lessons that can be learned from the pioneers of the Information Age. As the internet is evolving so fast, there is little to gain from studying the winners to try to emulate their successes. The situations they found themselves in were quite different from what we would now expect to encounter in the newly emerging future. Instead, we need to learn from the mistakes of the failures, to make sure we don't fall into similar traps.

The new economy is totally unpredictable. There may be a boom or a recession ahead and we need to be able to cope with any extreme that emerges. The only way to do this is to have a clear grasp of the fundamentals of business economics. For this purpose, Chapter 3 provides a basic grounding in the essentials of funding and finance. Whichever way the Information Age takes us, it must always be based on the pragmatic realities of shrewd financial decision making.

1

FIFTY COLLABORATORS

how it began

My entry into communication technology began in 1989, when, after 15 years' experience as an entrepreneur in the world of fashion and entertainment, I saw a potential in multimedia. At that time, CD-ROMs were emerging as 'the next big thing'. Like many others, I saw this as a great opportunity to be a first mover in a new area of technology and become a pioneer in what seemed to be a field of unlimited opportunity. As I have described in *The Entrepreneurial Web*, despite producing an award-winning CD-ROM, this venture came to a sad ending – as did similar ventures for so many others, who joined that first mad rush into the new CD-ROM technology.

What I did gain out of the experience, though, was an appreciation that along with the unlimited possibilities offered by this new world of information technology, there also came unprecedented pitfalls and dangers. I discovered it to be a world of constant and unpredictable change. This taught me to think carefully before plunging into any new business venture connected with the technological world of information.

Like a diver, who tests the water to see how deep it is before diving in, I decided to investigate the complexities underlying communication technology. I'd learned the hard way that it isn't sufficient just to have good ideas, it is first more important to learn what makes an environment tick. This led me into the black arts of computer programming. I figured that if I was going to work with computers I should begin by learning how their power could be harnessed and controlled.

Learning computer programming is something like opening Russian dolls. Just as you think you have acquired an understanding, a new level of awareness comes into view. It is like entering a cave to find an opening into yet another cave and in this cave is an opening to yet another. The whole experience is a never-ending process of discovering new levels of awareness.

This progress through these levels of awareness is evident in the two books I wrote on computer programming: *Lingo Sorcery* and *Magical A-Life Avatars*. First came the discovery of syntax and the thrilling experience of being able to write code that made the computer actually respond to the user and do things. Next came the discovery of objects and object-oriented programming where highly complex systems can be constructed out of relatively simple modules that can be placed into the RAM (random access memory) space of computer memory.

Next came the revelation of the synergy that can be created between a human and a computer: the understanding that a computer can be used to enhance the limited powers of the human brain. As if this wasn't momentous enough, the internet emerged. It is an all-consuming entity that connects vast numbers of people and computer programs into a vast conglomeration of unimaginable complexity.

As hundreds of millions became connected and millions of websites were built, I looked for some order and stability in this seething, chaotic environment. Where could I fit in? How could I benefit? What sort of business could I create that would be able to exploit the opportunities that this phenomenon so obviously contained? I envisioned a virtual world that existed partly in computers, partly on CD-ROM and partly in the minds of the users. An enigmatic world where boundaries were continually changing and merging into one another.

My computer programming books reflected this view of the new electronic world that was emerging. I explored the potential of using intelligent agents, of software that extended and enhanced the human brain. Software robots with simulated emotions – surely these would lead me into a successful e-business venture?

For many months I worked at these exotic software creations. I produced a system that could clone a user's character and personality onto an intelligent agent. It was designed to seek out other clones on the internet and, with simulated emotions, choose those clones whose owners were likely to be compatible with their own owners.

When I'd solved most of the technical problems and made working prototypes, I decided to introduce these ideas to the world. Surely everyone would wonder at these creations and I'd have investors queuing up at my door? Then I hit the reality of the newly emerging information environment – it wasn't what I had been expecting to find. I discovered I wasn't the only one with a brilliant idea. Hundreds of thousands, maybe millions of others also had brilliant ideas. I was just one voice in an unimaginably vast crowd of people waving their hands to seek attention.

I did get to speak to several funding institutions, banks and venture capital companies. I tried to explain my ideas and showed them demos of the software, but they weren't interested in technical details. They were more interested in tangible concepts they were familiar with and could understand. To them, this new technology was a foreign world where they had no way of knowing whether or not they were dealing with genuinely breakthrough products or cranks with weird ideas.

The banks wanted to see securities to back up loans. Funding bodies wanted to see impressive records of past academic or commercial success. Venture capital companies wanted to see a business plan, a cash flow forecast and a strong management team. I couldn't satisfy them on any of these counts. When I explained the uniqueness of my agents – cloning personalities, simulated emotions, able to search the internet for compatible partners – I fitted neatly into the category of 'the crank' and was quickly shown the door.

the world of finance, funding and investment

When I came up against these attitudes, I was neither annoyed nor frustrated. I'd had a long experience of being a pragmatic entrepreneur where broad commercial principles and practicality came way before technical detail. It made eminent sense to me that these financiers should filter out my kind of proposition. They weren't in the business of being experimenters or pioneers; their overriding concern was return on capital investment or a substantial capital gain.

I understood and appreciated their position because in the early 1970s I'd spent some time in the City of London with brokers and professional invest-ment managers. I'd even written an educational course to explain the prin-ciples of investment and financial strategy. It wasn't the financiers and funding bodies who were being short-sighted – it was me, because I hadn't taken into consideration the practical criteria upon which their investment decision making would be based.

The realization struck me that I was faced with a classical 'chicken or egg' problem: which comes first, the chicken or the egg? To get these ideas into operation, I'd need capital. To get capital I'd need to get these ideas into operation to illustrate their practical viability.

I decided to put my intelligent agents on hold, while I tried to work out a way round this dilemma.

the reality of the e-business world

Getting my head out of the box to take a wider view of the e-business environment, I found a confusing world of complexity; a world where knowledge constantly increased and nothing was certain or stable. Yet people were plunging into this chaotic environment, many of them succeeding and making obscene amounts of money. I wanted to dive in myself and join in the free-for-all, but I was cautious. I'd seen the hidden depths. I'd experienced the dang-erous underlying currents. I needed to think before taking the plunge.

This thinking process lasted nearly two years; it is recorded in the first two books of this trilogy: *The Entrepreneurial Web* and *The Ultimate Game of*

Strategy. The broad conclusion I came to during this time was that I would be wasting my time if I used conventional business methods. Instead, I should be concentrating primarily on the two most difficult problems: (1) dealing with knowledge gaps and (2) handling the dynamic complexity of a chaotic environment. I concluded that it would be the ability to deal with these two crucial problems that would sort out the winners from the losers.

Fortunately, I'd had 15 years' experience working in an environment with these kinds of problems – the London fashion scene. Although this may seem to be a million miles away from communication technology and e-business, there are some remarkable parallels. Fashion is constantly changing in unpredictable ways and the fashion industry has evolved to cope with such volatility. Just like e-business, current trends can suddenly change direction, causing whole design ranges and manufacturing practices to become obsolete. Current success is no indication of success in the future, and historical design and strategy have no place other than in the history books.

There is no way you can plan fashion. Being successful is about creating an effective information network that can recognize changing trends as early as possible. It is not about predicting customer needs, it is about responding to them at the same moment as the customers themselves become aware of them. These comparisons between e-business and the fashion industry were fully covered in *The Entrepreneurial Web*, and will be the inspiration behind many of the strategies to be described later in this book.

The Entrepreneurial Web was largely theoretical. It used the technique of abstraction to provide a practical framework in which to think about the problems involved in e-business. In an environment devoid of reliable case histories to provide useful examples, this is the only effective way of obtaining guidance and exercising any control over direction. Building upon this framework, the second book, *The Ultimate Game of Strategy*, provided a toolbox of concepts that might usefully be applied in the creation of practical e-business strategies.

The final conclusions of these two books were totally at odds with conventional business thinking. Business plans and planning were seen as useless, even counter-productive. Management and managed teams were seen as being inefficient. Having a single good idea was seen as being the wrong way to start off any e-business venture. Not surprisingly, these conclusions were seen by many as being ridiculous, especially as they were couched in terms of arcane theory.

The only way to confound the detractors and prove these conclusions valid would be to demonstrate their use in creating a strategy which leads to a viable business. This, then, is the main purpose of this book.

a seemingly illogical sequence

Throughout the writing of *The Entrepreneurial Web* and *The Ultimate Game of Strategy*, the conclusions pointed again and again to e-business being about people rather than ideas or technology. This suggests that the first concern should be to find people to collaborate with.

This may seem an odd way to go about creating an e-business. Conventional business theory always assumes that you start with the business idea – then go on to find suitable people to help put that idea into practice. Yet the implication is that a better strategy for creating an e-business might be to reverse that sequence: first find people to collaborate with and then look for the business opportunity.

This is not such an outrageous proposition as it might first appear, if you take into consideration that the internet environment offers a huge variety of ways in which wealth can be created. It is easy to think up ideas and identify probable profitable situations; hundreds of thousands of people are doing this all over the world all the time. The problem is to be in a position to take full advantage of an opportunity when it is recognized. To be able to do this you would need to have the right combination of contacts and skill sets at hand.

which contacts to choose?

A strategy that starts by simply acquiring contacts and then waiting expectantly for an opportunity to come out of the blue would seem to be hopelessly naïve. But, this is not taking into account object-oriented design philosophy. In essence, this philosophy says that your skill sets, knowledge and experience are not limited to your own abilities and knowledge – they are the sum total of your own plus those of all the friends and acquaintances you can call upon for information, help or guidance. Even in the world of bricks and mortar this philosophy has credence, but in a massively connected world this is a powerful way of thinking.

Compare the strategies of 17 hypothetical graduates who decide to spend the two years following their graduation predominantly in one of the following ways:

1 Learning about the creation and distribution of music in the digital world

2 Learning how to create multimedia presentations

3 Learning how to create video productions

4 Learning to be an expert computer programmer

5 Learning about networks, servers and communication protocols

6 Learning how to be a graphic designer

7 Learning how to create front-end website designs

8 Learning about databases and back-end website technologies

9 Learning about web-specific sales and marketing techniques

10 Developing a product that would be sellable from a website

11 Learning about e-business investment valuations

12 Learning about logistics and order fulfilment techniques

13 Learning about e-money and payment systems

14 Learning about legal matters relating to websites and e-commerce

15 Learning about taxation aspects over a universal domain

16 Learning a small amount of each of the above 15 topics

17 Establishing close relationships with the other 16 graduates

Which of these 17 graduates would be best placed to create an e-business at the end of the two years? Wouldn't it be number 17?

In the world of bricks and mortar it would be nigh on impossible for anyone to establish relationships with such a wide range of contacts. In the world of the internet it may take a little time but it is not impossible. This would see graduate number 17 as being strategically best placed to take advantage of any opportunity that came along – even if it meant being reliant on many of the others to be able to take effective action.

I came to this realization after being in the position of firstly number four, learning to become an expert programmer, then in the position of number two when I learned how to create multimedia presentations, and finally number ten when I developed a product. That took six years of my life, but even so, I wasn't in a position to create a viable e-business because I didn't have sufficient knowledge or expertise in any of the other categories.

At first, I made an attempt to get up to speed with all the other knowledge I would need to be able to create an e-business. I learned enough HTML to create a website. I learned some Javascript to add a few clever tricks. I dabbled in graphics and tried to pick up information on as much as I could in the various other categories. The more I learned, the more I discovered I needed to know. Instead of getting more confident as I progressed, I got less confident.

I had been aware of the well-known metaphor that likened obtaining information from the internet to drinking from a fire hose (i.e. however much time is spent acquiring information it is possible to taste only an infinitesimally small fraction of it). What I hadn't been prepared for, though, was the over-abundance of 'luck' I had in finding vitally important snippets of information. It seemed as if every discussion forum I joined, I arrived at a fortuitous time when a discussion thread was focused on a topic that was essential to me. Time and again I thanked my lucky stars that I had joined in at just the right moment.

The same thing happened when I looked at website articles that were mentioned in discussion forums. The few I had time to read more often than not contained invaluable information. It was the same with e-newsletters; it was uncanny how often they contained some point of view that gave me a radically new insight into e-business.

Having at one time owned a gaming club and also spent some time as a professional poker player, I was more than familiar with the phenomenon of lucky runs. They never last indefinitely and, if they ever did, it was usually the result of some anomaly, which involved factors other than chance. Checking with friends, I found they were also experiencing amazing runs of luck in discovering new and exciting information that seemed to apply specifically to them and their problems.

The startling inference was that these discoveries of new and exciting information were not down to lucky dips into the fire hose. It became apparent that there was so much vital and interesting information available that it would be almost impossible to miss important information wherever you choose to look. This has a downside: if everywhere you seek information you usually make exciting discoveries, what are you missing in the other 99.99 per cent of the places – those that you haven't the time to visit?

It then became obvious that learning and seeking new knowledge and information is like trying to explore a bottomless pit. It could go on for ever and never reach any definitive conclusions. Surely, there had to be a more efficient way to become successful in creating an e-business opportunity? The only answer was to rise above the detail and con-centrate on fundamental principles. This is what I aimed for in the previous two books: looking for broad concepts that could get me out of the syndrome of trying to absorb more and more information from an infinite sea of 'need to know' knowledge.

> ONCE YOU COME TO REALIZE HOW MUCH VITAL 'NEED TO KNOW' INFORMATION THERE IS AND TO APPRECIATE THAT YOU CANNOT HOPE TO LEARN IT ALL, IT BECOMES OBVIOUS THAT A SPECIAL STRATEGY IS NEEDED

Once you come to realize how much vital 'need to know' information there is and to appreciate that you cannot hope to learn it all, it becomes obvious that a special strategy is needed. This strategy would need to be such that it would allow you to compete successfully in an environment when you are severely handicapped with huge knowledge gaps. It would obviously have to involve collaborating with others, who will have specific areas of knowledge that can fill the gaps.

The problem then is to find some way you can get people to share their knowledge with you. You don't want them to teach you what they know. You just need to be able to call upon their knowledge and expertise on demand: whenever it is needed. But why should people want to do this?

The clue to the solution is that everyone else is in the same boat. Everyone has vast knowledge gaps. Wouldn't they be willing to give you help and knowledge on demand if they could get a reciprocal similar benefit? The trick then is to nurture a number of relationships where such an understanding can be established. The solution I came up with was the virtual café. This was a conceptual device that everyone can use as an efficient mechanism to facilitate the exchange of vital information on a 'need to know' basis.

finding collaborators

Having experimented with the virtual café idea over a couple of years and used it successfully for the previous two books in this series, I now have to put it to the ultimate test: to find out if it can be instrumental in the creation of an e-business. First I had to find collaborators.

There were three sources I could use:

1 people I knew and had already had dealings with;

2 people who had visited my website and expressed an interest in my work;

3 people selected from discussion forums.

Most of the people who visit my website go there out of curiosity because they have either encountered me in a discussion forum or have read one of my books. I also have a few articles on the website that bring people there through referral or recommendation.

On this website I invite visitors to subscribe to a newsletter that I send out from time to time. This provides a small but steady stream of new contacts (currently at the rate of about one per day). Over time, this has built up to several hundred people who are aware of me and my work.

When I have need of any assistance I can appeal to this group and because they know me I have more chance of a response than appealing to a group of complete strangers.

More difficult is getting collaboration from complete strangers in e-mail discussion forums. I've tried several times to explain what I'm doing by posting to a forum as a whole, but this seldom elicits any response. A regular feature of almost every discussion forum I've participated in has been propositions by different members of the group to join in something they are organizing. As far as I can tell, these appeals are seldom successful; it seems that discussion groups get so saturated with offers of this kind that responses are always very low.

The only way that seems to work is to spend some time in a forum, contributing to the discussions to establish some kind of identity. By initiating discussions in the area of interest it is possible to discover people who might make suitable collaborators.

As I know I'm going to work with an unconventional strategy, I usually initiate a discussion by making what would seem to be an outrageous statement. Usually this is something along the lines of 'planning is not appropriate in e-business' or 'managed teams are not an efficient organizational structure'. Such propositions immediately polarize opinion and it is easy to identify those who would be inclined towards my way of thinking. Once identified, I can then contact them off-list and explain the nature of the collaborative project I have in mind.

In this way, I assembled a group of about 50 people to collaborate with me in this project. Between them, they represent a far-ranging variety of fields and interests. Here are some of the items taken from their bios they sent to me when agreeing to join the group:

▶ a teacher of web authoring from Melbourne in Australia;

▶ an American engineer, experienced in management of linguistic schools, specializing in technical translations from Japanese to English;

▶ a Spanish telecom engineer writing a doctoral thesis on business and applying game theory to digital satellite pay TV;

- ▶ an expert on workflow in new media companies;

- ▶ a director of a web design company in South Africa;

- ▶ an American business consultant who advises companies on setting up e-businesses;

- ▶ a nuclear physicist who has set up company intranets and has a strong interest in electronic art and video, now freelancing as a web designer;

- ▶ a programming and web design guru from Scotland who is just setting up an e-consultancy service;

- ▶ a graduate in Biological Computation, whose dissertation and present specialization is on web-based decision support systems for farmers;

- ▶ a college programme manager for a fine arts course who has just received funding to research new media applications in fine art;

- ▶ an Oxford University graduate in philosophy and economics who is now running three micro businesses and doing consulting work in public relations and marketing;

- ▶ a marketing manager for a company supplying web-based applications;

- ▶ a multimedia developer, a principal in a company providing ISP (internet service provider) and web-hosting services, responsible for site development, deployment and maintenance, business support systems and promotion;

- ▶ a specialist in intelligent agents and evolutionary systems, working out of Santa Fe;

- ▶ a manager of a multimedia design company;

- ▶ a lecturer and researcher from a university in India;

- ▶ a graduate from the Netherlands, specializing in information studies, information management and document retrieval systems;

- ▶ an ex professional saxophone player, now specializing in web-based multimedia productions;

- ▶ a senior systems analyst with a prominent New York bank;

▶ an Italian consultant, experienced in IT project management within the financial services industry;

▶ a transport system specialist, now migrated to the web;

▶ a cross-media technology designer, working with one of the most powerful media corporations in Italy, providing new business solutions linking the internet/TV/radio/mobiles/paper/... worlds;

▶ an engineering consultant, helping the chemical and food processing industries design and optimize manufacturing and logistics processes as well as realizing and improving plants and factories;

▶ a German IT consultant;

▶ a managing editor for an international publisher of books on e-business and information technology;

▶ a Canadian systems analyst, specializing in databases and server-side programming solutions;

▶ an investment analyst with a large firm of brokers who bring many dot-com IPOs to the market;

▶ an eccentric entrepreneur, one-time accountant, now studying plants at a mountain retreat in Texas;

▶ a principal of a group of freelance web designers, specializing in back-end solutions;

▶ a website designer employed by a large company in Amsterdam;

▶ a German specialist in virtual communities and customer relationship management tools.

It is not difficult to see how such a varied assembly of collaborators can be of great assistance in a quest to find and establish an e-business. They are valuable contacts in a world of mind-numbing complexity. They won't have all the answers, but I'll be a lot better off with their help than I would be trying to find and develop an e-business opportunity on my own.

Obviously, it wouldn't be wise to force a single idea onto this group. It would be better to sow a few seeds and see which take hold. Even more likely, an idea will emerge out of the discussions in the virtual café – ideas which I wouldn't even be able to imagine at the commencement of this project.

a collaborative strategy The idea of setting off alone to explore
the environment of the internet looking for a suitable e-business opportunity might seem hopelessly naïve, especially with a limited amount of knowledge and technical skills. However, setting off in the company of 50 others, whose combined experience covers a wide variety of knowledge and skills, is a more credible situation: especially if everyone is agreed on creating an atmosphere of mutual collaboration.

Here it is necessary to make a distinction between cooperation and collaboration. If this group were cooperating, a common goal would need to be established. Everyone in the group would contribute their speciality knowledge to help achieve this agreed goal. The problem is that it would almost certainly be impossible to get an agreement on a common goal. Certainly I couldn't expect 50 people to concentrate selflessly on a goal of my choosing.

Collaboration, on the other hand, doesn't require a common goal; everyone can have their own goal. Collaboration allows people to interact with each other, yet still have independent viewpoints. This can be appreciated by considering the way collaboration takes place in e-mail discussion forums. In these forums, there is usually a common theme, perhaps a niche speciality area of technology. Everyone subscribing to the discussion is free to ask questions, put forward propositions or just listen in.

When a subscriber asks a question, there is usually someone in the forum who will give an answer or provide a pointer to where a solution might be found. This has the effect of providing everyone who belongs to the forum with a source of knowledge and information. It is almost the equivalent of every subscriber to the discussion forum having the combined knowledge of all subscribers. This is a very powerful asset.

In a highly technical, constantly changing environment such as the internet, these discussion forums are absolutely essential because it is impossible for anyone to know all there is to know. The forums allow members to obtain knowledge on a 'need to know' basis: information on tap, eliminating the need to have to know absolutely everything in order to act competently.

Upon first encountering these collaborative e-mail discussion forums, it seems amazing that so many people act altruistically to take so much trouble to help each other. It seems too good to be true. However, when the motives of the helpful posters are examined, they are nearly always found to be benefiting from the helpful contributions they make. Three of these are of interest here:

1 **Collaborative learning.** They might be interested in the nature of the problem and this gives them an incentive to work out a solution. It gives them an opportunity to test their knowledge or skills. Usually, several people come up with answers or solutions, illustrating different ways of approaching the same problem. They then have a chance to compare their answer with others. Or, if there is a degree of uncertainty about an answer, the range of uncertainty might become apparent.

   Wrong or inferior answers or solutions are almost always corrected. In this way, anyone providing answers or solutions can very quickly get feedback on their thinking or approach, allowing them to gain experience or knowledge that might otherwise be difficult to obtain.

2 **Acquiring a reputation.** Just as in the world of bricks and mortar, people have more credibility if they can give evidence of their knowledge or expertise. This also applies to personality and character. It is this kind of information about posters that comes across in e-mail discussion forums when posters take an active part. Those who are helpful and freely give others the benefit of their knowledge and experience become group personalities, who are more likely to be able to get cooperation or collaboration from others on the list. This quite often leads to beneficial business propositions and associations.

3 **Making new friends and contacts.** Discussions in e-mail discussion forums often lead to further private discussions off-list. In this way,

posters who are active in discussion forums can build up a list of personal contacts to whom they can go directly for information or advice. Quite often, these relationships develop into collaborative business associations.

These three reasons alone illustrate advantages for people who contribute to e-mail discussion forums. The people who merely listen in, without contributing, miss out on these three highly valuable benefits.

discussion forums for strategic issues

Asking questions and getting answers works extremely well for tactical subject matter, i.e. activities involving skills, techniques, methods or procedures. This is because answers are usually of a type that have a recognizable best solution.

However, when it comes to strategic issues, there are often no definitive answers or right solutions. In such cases, discussion often results in much disagreement and antagonism as different people try to put their own particular point of view across. This is readily observable in forums where there is competition between several subscribers to be recognized as 'the authoritative voice'. In order to protect their reputations, they will argue most forcibly, even though there can be no certainty that they hold the only correct answer or solution.

After writing *Magical A-Life Avatars*, I set up an e-mail discussion forum for readers who might be interested in exploring the ideas presented in the book. The principal theme of the book was that software agents could be created as extensions of human capabilities. In other words, intelligent agents would be constructed as systems that included a human as part of the system rather than as separate autonomous entities. The theme proposed for the forum was that many of us could work together to create such a system of intelligent agents, based on the programming environment provided by Macromedia's Director runtime engine.

It would seem that an e-mail discussion forum would be an ideal framework within which to facilitate this cooperative project; unfortunately, it proved to be a total disaster. Instead of a cooperative effort, it produced a confusion of irreconcilably different viewpoints. Some people wanted to use programming environments other than the Director runtime engine. Others wanted to create autonomous agents that were independent of human controls. It disintegrated into a confusion of animosity.

However, what emerged out of this was the idea of creating much smaller groups, which contained people with compatible thinking. By selecting specific people from the main forum discussion, who were more attuned to the idea I had in mind, I could have more productive discussions that might make more progress.

It wasn't long before I realized that this method of creating discussions was seriously flawed because I was deliberately choosing people who were attuned to my own way of thinking. The larger discussion forum may have been unproductive but I'd benefited considerably by being made aware of the different ways in which people looked at the kind of problems I was trying to solve.

This presented a dilemma. I needed people who had the same train of thought as myself to make progress with a project, but I also needed the input of the people who would disrupt progress because they could introduce contradictory thinking that would prevent the project becoming biased or too narrowly focused.

I then began experimenting with the creation of small groups that included a mixture of people with conflicting viewpoints. Unfortunately, these small groups had no more success than the large discussion forum. They also quickly disintegrated into irreconcilable arguments.

It was then that I turned to evolutionary biology for a solution. At an abstract level, Mother Nature had solved this very problem. Biological organisms make progress through the simple expedient of creating many different groups of genes (individuals) that come into existence for short periods of time (lifetimes). At the end of each period (generation) the genes are reorganized to create different groupings (birthing new individuals). In this way, combinations of genes that make progress are preserved, but it also allows new combinations to be created that could prompt alternative evolutionary directions to take place.

Looking at a discussion forum as a biological system, this strategy of nature could be adopted by dividing the forum up into many small groups which come into existence for short periods of time. At the end of each period, the people in these groups could be changed around in much the same way as genes are changed around in a biological system at the end of each generation. In this way, the discussion could be allowed to make progress yet allow for the continuous input of fresh ideas and influences.

the concept of the café
This idea corresponded to a technique I'd used in the fashion business. The world of fashion is similar in many ways to the world of e-business because it consists almost entirely of information. Fashion is about the wearers transmitting an impression of themselves to others through their choice of clothes. To be successful in this business you don't have to be an original designer, simply a successful communicator who can find out the latest ways for people to identify with a group.

Much of my time was spent in discussions with small groups of people, mostly in cafés, talking to designers, retailers, wholesalers and various groups of people who were representative of my target customers. It was a daily ritual that provided useful information and feedback needed by the workshop to be able to produce sellable, up-to-the-minute fashion clothes. In a sense, these informal meetings could be considered as part of a creative engine driving the business.

With this scenario in mind, I thought of small e-mail discussion groups as conversations around a table in a virtual café. They lasted for a short time and then reconvened at a later time when some of the same people returned and new people joined in the discussion.

It is only a short step from thinking about a single discussion around a table in a café to thinking about a café full of tables where there is a discussion going on at each table. In a café in the real world, it would be possible to sit at only one table at a time. In a virtual café, with e-mail discussions around virtual tables, it is possible for the host to sit at every table.

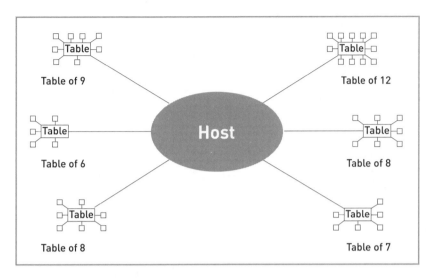

FIG 1.1 The initial 50 collaborators are split into six groups. Each group is set up as a separate short-term e-mail discussion forum where the host is a participant in each group. This can be likened to a café with six tables

Let's look at this in terms of the 50 people involved in the project of this book. They might be split up into six separate e-mail discussion groups as if they were sitting at six different tables in a café having a discussion. This is illustrated in Figure 1.1.

From Figure 1.1, it is easy to see how the 50 initial participants could be split up as if they were on separate tables in a café. This separation into six separate groups allows discussion to take several different directions. If there are any strong but biased viewpoints dominating a discussion at a particular table they wouldn't be able to spread to them all.

This was the method used to write the first two books in this trilogy. As each chapter in the book was written, it was submitted to each of six tables in a virtual café. They would comment on the content and compare it with their ideas on e-business. These comments would then strongly influence the direction and content of the following chapter. This process is illustrated in Figure 1.2.

Using this technique, the books could evolve without any pre-planning

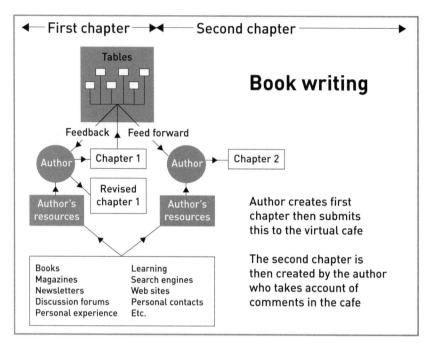

FIG 1.2 As each chapter is written, it is given to each of six tables in a virtual café. This produces six separate discussions regarding the content and these discussions influence the content of the next chapter

on the author's part. The content and direction were kept on track by the feedback and feed forward from the café discussions. In this way, the book was a result of the synergy between the author and the café of readers who could apply their combined thinking to the problems involved in creating e-business solutions. The progression of the process from chapter to chapter is illustrated in Figure 1.3.

A full description of using the café to write a book is described in *The Ultimate Game of Strategy*. It was provided as an example of how customers can be instrumental in designing products.

It was also used as an example of using the strategy of a genetic algorithm to optimize searches for solutions to problems where rational thinking cannot come up with the answers. It was proposed that this

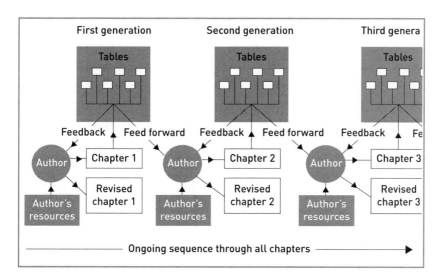

FIG 1.3 By submitting each chapter to the café for opinions and comment before writing the following chapter, the entire content of the book is guided and influenced by the many different points of view of the people in the café

technique might be equally useful for searching for viable e-business opportunities. This is explained in Figure 1.4.

what's in it for the other collaborators?

Before jumping straight in to start looking for an e-business opportunity, let's take a closer look at this concept of a virtual café. It certainly isn't as simple as it appears. Most people, when they take part for the first time, assume that it takes the form of a cooperative discussion group: people working together to arrive at some kind of mutually agreeable solution.

It comes as quite a surprise that the idea is for everyone to think about their own problems and solutions. They are in the café mainly for their own benefit and are there to gain something positive from the experience. The proposition is that the host provides an interesting situation from which the participants can benefit through learning something worthwhile and meeting potentially valuable contacts. In return, the participants

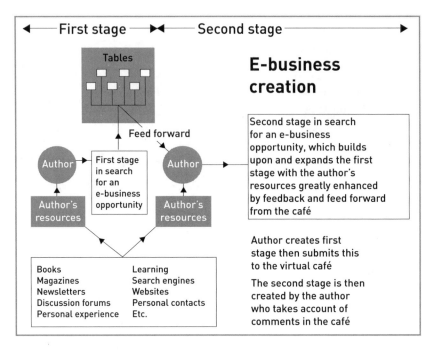

FIG 1.4 Similar to the way in which the virtual café was used to create books, it should be possible to use the same technique to search for viable e-business opportunities

must provide value. This they do simply by offering intelligent and informed comment and opinion.

The participants are in absolute control of their own situation because if the café isn't providing them with sufficient benefit or stimulation they can leave at any time. They don't have to announce they are leaving, they simply cease giving comments and opinions. As the café is reconfigured at regular intervals (every one or two weeks) the non-contributors are automatically excluded. This ensures that the café continues only with people who are benefiting from the experience. The onus then falls on the host to try to ensure that the people in the café are benefiting, otherwise the café will empty out.

To see this in perspective, let's imagine a wealthy entrepreneur deciding to create an e-business. She has much experience of business in the conventional world of bricks and mortar but the environment of electronic communications is too complicated for her to understand fully. To compensate for her lack of knowledge she asks 50 people who are experienced in the ways of the internet to advise and comment on her progress as she tries to find a business opportunity. For their helpful comments and opinions she gives them $200 a week for every week they comment on her ideas and progress.

She would reason that if she did this for a year, it would cost her half a million dollars for this advice, but the value of having 50 experienced people commenting on her progress in finding and establishing a viable e-business would probably result in her being able to create a business that would be worth considerably more than half a million dollars. This expenditure could thus be justified.

Being a rational person, she would like to see some value for the money she is paying out each week. If she finds any of her consultants not bothering to make comments or contributing towards her progress, she would discontinue their services and find somebody else to take their place who might give better value for the $200 a week. In this way, she could ensure that not only did she get full value for her weekly expenditure of $10,000 a week, but the value she was getting would improve as she continuously replaced the non-performing consultants. Or, if she didn't replace them, she'd be getting the same value for a reducing cost.

Realizing that it would take all of her time to correspond with 50 corres-pondents every week and then having the bother of trying to sort out whose opinions were valid and whose were not, it would make a lot of sense for her just to explain her current thinking to them each week and then let them discuss it amongst themselves. She could then listen in to the discussions for confirmation or otherwise of her thinking and for inspiration and future directional pointers.

Besides saving the correspondence time, she would also have the added advantage that the comments and opinions, when combined in discussion environments, could be challenged and corrected where appropriate. This would greatly reduce the harmful effects of bias or lack of knowledge. Discussion would thus provide a greater accuracy plus an added synergy as different ideas and viewpoints were combined.

It would also make sense to divide the 50 consultants into a few small discussion groups, rather than have them all in a single discussion forum. This would allow several different directions to emerge rather than have the group become dominated by a few strong opinions. Remixing the groups from time to time would prevent group viewpoints becoming locked into particular narrow mindsets.

the consultants' viewpoint

It would probably be a very good arrangement for the consultants. It would involve reading the entrepreneur's ideas as they were evolving and being able to have interesting discussions with a peer group regarding the subject matter. Their contributions would require no more than a few posts a month and, if the subject matter was of interest to them in their professional capacity with their own business dealings, the discussions could provide them with valuable knowledge and information.

This would be particularly valuable if the discussions enabled them to raise their own problems and get opinions themselves from the discussion groups. Looked at in this way, a consultant not only gets a fee, but also the benefit of having their own opinions checked out by a peer group. In addition, they will be exposed to a variety of new ideas and inspirations.

Now consider what might happen if the entrepreneur suffered a serious setback in her financial situation such that she was no longer able to pay the consultants the $200 a week. Would it be rational for all the consultants to pull out immediately? Certainly they would not be getting the original incentive, but by pulling out they would also be losing the benefit of the knowledge and experience they were gaining from being part of this collaborative group. They may well decide that despite the loss of the $200 a week, the effort of participation was amply rewarded by the benefits they were getting from these discussions.

They might take the same view as the entrepreneur when she set up this discussion in the first place. They might look at the loss of income as a lump sum – which might amount to $10,000 in a year – and consider that the benefits they were getting from the discussions would probably result in their own earning prospects being improved by at least as much as this. If this were so, then although they weren't actually being paid this amount of money, by participating they would in effect still be earning it.

After all, this was the way in which the entrepreneur would have seen it. Having the advantage of the opinions and comments of 50 consultants would greatly enhance the prospects of eventual success. It was highly likely that along the way several e-business opportunities might emerge, in which any of the collaborators might become actively involved.

Looking at the café from this viewpoint, they would see it as a non-zero-sum game where everyone can gain. As everyone can benefit from this situation, it becomes one of those enigmatic sources of wealth generation that we are looking for in the environment of the internet.

Everyone contributes a little effort for little or no commitment and everyone can gain far more than they are putting in.

AT ODDS WITH THE CONVENTIONAL WORLD

four important questions In Chapter 1, it was explained that the idea behind this book is to use the concepts described in the previous two books of this trilogy to create an e-business and write about the experience as it happens.

A few of the readers were asking for specific business ideas to concentrate on. As one reader put it, 'You seem to be dancing around the fire rather than getting on with the job of creating a real e-business.'

Another frustrated reader wrote:

Peter's feeling is that 'going into the details of a particular business at this early stage of the book will slant the content in a narrow direction'. But, it is precisely when he decides to go in a narrow direction that he'll get our support and experience. In wanting to stay with the concepts he prevents me and maybe other sympathizers contributing in a meaningful way.

←snip→

Without some element of governance from the top, bottom-up control will freeze when there are too many options. Without some element of leadership, the many at the bottom will be paralyzed with choices. Numerous small things connected together into a network generate tremendous power, but this swarm power will need some kind of minimal governance from the top to maximize its usefulness.

These expressions of exasperation are typical of many who have yet to come to grips with a bottom-up approach to creating e-business systems. They feel moribund without any central idea or business plan to focus on: incapable of taking action without guidance or direction. Oddly enough, people often dogmatically maintain this attitude even when they agree that ideas, guidance (management) and business plans are of very little value in a highly volatile and unpredictable business environment.

The way to get over this conceptual hurdle is to think of the strategy used by Sherlock Holmes when he was faced with seemingly unsolvable problems. He would conclude that if an explanation could not be found through rational reasoning then rational reasoning had to be abandoned, because the answer must lie within the realm of the irrational.

In the context of e-business, this would mean abandoning the rationality of using initial ideas, management and planning and looking for a different kind of strategy that doesn't require them. The eureka moment comes as soon as it is realized that there are such strategies available – and that they are extremely efficient for creating robust e-businesses suitable for an unpredictable and highly competitive environment.

It is just such a strategy I'm pursuing here. No preconceived ideas, no business plans: I'm simply starting with a blind search in a solution space until a viable e-business opportunity emerges.

To the mindset of the Industrial Age, this will evoke four questions:

1 How can you start to create a business with no initial ideas?

2 What is a solution space?

3 How do viable systems emerge without planning?

4 With no visionary idea, no business plan and no strong management, how can you possibly attract investment funding?

Over the course of the next few chapters I'll attempt to provide answers to these four questions. Only then will it become clear that the apparent vagueness of this approach to establishing an e-business is a necessary requisite that will avoid the problems that have been encountered by most of the early dot coms that failed to survive.

anyone can have a great idea

Most successful e-businesses appear to have succeeded through someone having a great idea and then following through with it. But during the dot-com boom at the turn of the century, it seemed that just about everybody had a great idea for an e-business. In almost every office in the world, people were plotting and planning websites. Not only was this happening in business offices, it was happening in all kinds of social gatherings, pubs and clubs, universities and colleges and even school playgrounds. Even people who hadn't used a computer before were suggesting ideas for e-businesses.

With millions of people coming up with ideas, it is a statistical certainty that some of them will succeed, just as it is a statistical certainty that someone with a lottery ticket will win the lottery. And, just like having a lottery ticket, a good idea may get you into the game, but it doesn't guarantee success.

With so many people and businesses coming up with ideas, it is pretty hard to come up with something completely original. Anyone who has made any serious effort to follow through with an e-business idea will soon tell you how true this is. A quick search around the web will almost certainly uncover somebody already working on any good idea you can come up with, however original it might appear to be.

If it really is a great idea, then there are likely to be many different people working on something similar; maybe even e-mail discussion forums discussing its implementation in various forms. This can be very disconcerting and depressing for newcomers to the world of e-business.

It might seem that the key to success is in putting an idea into operation faster than anyone else: by being the first to market. However, this is a fallacious argument because if an idea is seen to work, others are likely to copy and improve on it, leaving the originator disadvantaged because they will have carried the cost of the pioneering and the test marketing.

Common sense tells you that with millions of people trying to think up great ideas for e-businesses, and millions of others looking for ideas to copy, it's no good relying on originality as being a key ingredient of an e-business formula for success. There will almost certainly be many others with similar ideas that you will have to compete against.

This puts the emphasis on the competitiveness of the position, not on the idea itself. Any idea must be accompanied by circumstances that provide a strong competitive advantage. Without this, a great idea is about as useful as an arrow without a bow.

the business idea has to emerge later

A business idea has the best chance of being brought to fruition if it is born into the right environment (where a suitable infrastructure and the necessary contacts are in place). Surely then, it would make sense to wait until these conditions are in existence before firming up or going ahead with any specific e-business idea?

The situation can be likened to a game of poker. Does it make any sense to have a plan or an idea to win a game of poker before the cards are dealt? Isn't it more sensible to wait and see what cards turn up before making any play decisions? In this way, you wouldn't be forced to play with a weak hand: you could wait for a really good set of cards to come along before making any strong bets. The play would then be determined by the emergent situation: responding to what is, rather than what might be.

This is what e-business should be about, waiting until you have developed a competitive position with a strong hand. Then, like a poker player, you make opportunistic plays according to a developing situation. In other words, setting up a position of strength before deciding what business moves to make.

With this mindset, it becomes pertinent to think about the timing of the

> WITH MILLIONS OF PEOPLE TRYING TO THINK UP GREAT IDEAS FOR E-BUSINESSES, AND MILLIONS OF OTHERS LOOKING FOR IDEAS TO COPY, IT'S NO GOOD RELYING ON ORIGINALITY AS BEING A KEY INGREDIENT OF AN E-BUSINESS FORMULA FOR SUCCESS

main business idea. Should the idea come before or after a position of competitive strength has been established? This order is vitally important because it determines the whole nature of the e-business strategy.

The intuitive assumption is that the main business idea would have to come first because otherwise you wouldn't know which infrastructure to design or what appropriate contacts to make; you wouldn't know the kind of web presence that is needed or staff to employ.

Stop to think about this for a moment. You are going to enter a fast-moving, highly changeable, competitive environment. Would you have the time to set up contacts, hire and train staff, arrange associations of cooperation and collaboration, design a website with all the necessary back-end organization – before the idea goes out of date or the competition moves on to something better? What if the idea goes stale before the business infrastructure is fully operational? Wouldn't it mean that much of the custom-made preparation work has been wasted, losing time and haemorrhaging capital?

" IF ANYTHING IS PREDICTABLE ABOUT THE E-BUSINESS ENVIRONMENT IT IS THE CERTAINTY OF CONTINUOUS CHANGE "

If anything is predictable about the e-business environment it is the certainty of continuous change. No ideas are viable for very long. This means that if a competitive position is constructed according to the demands of a business idea, the infrastructure would have to be continuously changed and updated. This would see the business spending more time working on the infrastructure than implementing the idea.

Here is where a conventional business mindset has to make a large conceptual leap because in a volatile business environment it would be necessary to arrange for the infrastructure to be a solid, stable base and to view any business ideas as transient and changeable (a nightmare scenario for a managed team with a business plan).

This is counter-intuitive because it would seem that building an infrastructure before any definite business idea had been decided on would be hopelessly inefficient. Surely, it must seem, much of the work would be wasted if you didn't know how the infrastructure was going to be used?

However, in a fast-changing, competitive environment this strategy makes a lot of sense because from the position of a stable infrastructure, you can wait for an opportunity to emerge that exactly matches the facilities and skill sets at your disposal. Instead of a delay between having a business idea and being able to put it into operation, it would be possible to act instantly, capitalizing on an idea while it is still hot.

It would seem, then, that the most efficient strategy will be to create and maintain a position of competitive strength and search for suitable business ideas that can be handled from that stable base. It is for this reason that 'dancing around the fire' is a necessary first step in the creation of an e-business. Core strength, credibility and appropriate contacts have to be established first. Only then, when these cards are in your hand, can you start to look for ideas or opportunities that match the cards. This situation is illustrated in Figure 2.1.

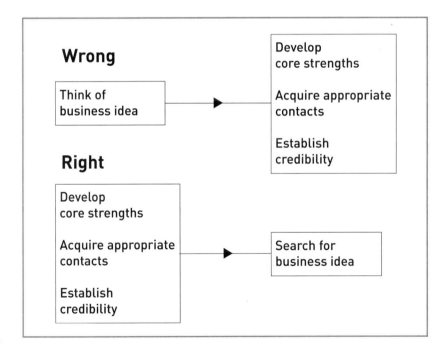

FIG 2.1 An e-business venture should start by establishing a core strength, acquiring contacts and establishing credibility before even contemplating a business idea. The business idea should then be selectively chosen to match these assets

By using this strategy of establishing a stable base first, it is possible to act immediately and efficiently when any opportunity presents itself because you don't have to change your contacts and rebuild your infrastructure.

Naturally, the contacts, the infrastructure and the assets to hand will limit the number of opportunities that can be taken advantage of – but these are some of the parameters that help define the boundaries of the search space when looking for e-business opportunities.

two different mindsets
The concept of the business idea coming last is not easy for Industrial Age business strategists to get their heads around. Their mindset is to work out what is wanted and then to organize a way to get it. They need to have a target or goal to aim for: this provides the focus for their strategy. Without this goal or target they are lost.

In the Information Age, a completely different mindset is required. Instead of having a business idea and creating an organization to carry it out, you start with the organization and then search for a business idea that is ideal for the organization to handle.

The situation is illustrated in Figure 2.2 where the conventional, Industrial Age business strategy is shown at the top, with the bottom-up strategy necessary for a highly volatile environment shown underneath.

Industrial Age business thinking would expect a business to descend into total chaos and gross inefficiency if there is no planning or guidance. However, the overwhelming evidence seems to suggest that it is the conventional approach that is more likely to go off course and become unstable. This is because goals and plans seldom survive for long in the harsh realities of the information environment.

Unpredictable events are constantly occurring, necessitating plans having to be altered. As fast as contingency plans are drawn up, new technology, a change in customer expectations or surprising competitor innovations throw any new planning into total disarray. Frequently, this results in the

> 66 INSTEAD OF HAVING A BUSINESS IDEA AND CREATING AN ORGANIZATION TO CARRY IT OUT, YOU START WITH THE ORGANIZATION AND THEN SEARCH FOR A BUSINESS IDEA THAT IS IDEAL FOR THE ORGANIZATION TO HANDLE 99

Conventional approach – planning for viability

Visionary goal   Control exercised
Business plan   by aiming at
Managed teams   pre-determined goals
Guidance and direction

Bottom-up approach – searching for viability

No fixed goal   Control exercised by
No plan   restricting the system
No management   to within restraining
No guidance or direction   parameters

FIG 2.2 Summary of the two different approaches to e-business. The conventional approach aims at planning a solution. The bottom-up approach aims at searching for a solution

rapid burn-up of investment capital – killing an enterprise stone-dead before it has achieved either stability or viability.

Perversely, when e-businesses fail through using an outdated Industrial Age approach, the Industrial Age mindset seldom recognizes that it is the approach that is wrong. Nearly always, the blame for failure is placed on the Industrial Age methods not being applied strictly enough.

To understand how conventional Industrial Age strategies can produce spectacular failures it is worth looking back at the history of some of the early dot-com start-ups that came into being at the end of the last century.

a little bit of history The internet revolution couldn't have arrived at a more appropriate time. Not only was it at the end of a century, but it

was at the end of a millennium. This allows history to place a nice neat date on the start of a new period in the history of civilization – the year 2000 – the beginning of the third millennium, the end of the Industrial Age and the start of the Information Age.

Decades from now, this revolution will be seen as an instantaneous transition from one system of civilization to another. Few will dwell on what happened during the transition itself. It will be treated more like the metamorphosis of a caterpillar into a butterfly – a mysterious transformation, where the details of the transition processes are far too complex to be explained.

However, science does have some idea as to how these complex system transitions occur. They may not know every detail of a transition – such as the exact sequence of chemical events that occur when a caterpillar changes into a butterfly – but the generalities of the process can be explained in terms of a mathematical concept known as Chaos Theory.

This theory explains how complex systems can self-organize and then, perhaps through a seemingly trivial event, become totally disorganized and then spontaneously reorganize themselves into a completely different state of organization. It happens when a caterpillar changes into a butterfly. It happens when a revolution overtakes a civilization. It is happening now as the Industrial Age gives way to the Information Age.

Observing and experiencing the rapid changes that are taking place, as the Industrial Age gives way to the Information Age, is the business-world equivalent of being present in the cocoon of a caterpillar while the mysterious events – which turn the caterpillar into a gooey mess and then turn that gooey mess into a butterfly – are occurring.

At the turn of the century, the caterpillar was the social and business organization of the Industrial Age. The butterfly is the new kind of business organization that is emerging in the Information Age. The gooey mess in between is epitomized by the failures of hundreds of early dot-com start-up companies as they struggled to cross the divide between the Industrial Age and the Information Age – handicapped by knowing only the methods and strategies appropriate for the pre-transition age.

These pioneers were the first to be exposed to the unprecedented changes brought about by the new communication technologies.

It is easy to put the failure of the early dot coms down to poor management, unrealistic business plans and lack of proper control and organization – as so many business commentators did at the time of their demise. But this is to ignore something more probable: the use of totally inappropriate business strategies.

Consider for a moment the decision making of the various funding bodies responsible for providing the billions of dollars of venture capital to all those hundreds of failed dot coms. Wouldn't the financiers have critically assessed the ideas, looked carefully at all the business plans and made sure that the principals had suitably impressive track records? On what other grounds could they have justified the handing over of billions of dollars to those early pioneers?

There were so many errors of judgement, on such a grand scale, that it was unlikely to have been a result of incompetence alone. It is much more probable that the criteria used for making investment decisions were at fault. This calls into question the value of basing investment decisions on the quality of ideas, plans and managerial competence.

calculating the value of a dot com

Most of the early dot-com start-ups that met a rapid demise during the era of the dot-com bubble probably started out with great visions, detailed business plans and impressive management teams. Yet the reality was that they had been brought to market on the basis of speculative ideas, which were given unrealistic prospects for successful profitability. Even respectable brokers had been presenting IPOs (initial public offerings) based on self-fulfilling speculations.

By concentrating on ideas, business plans and management skills, the fundamental wisdom that value is based on assets, earnings and dividends was pushed under the carpet. Traditional concepts of discounting for risk were forgotten as brokers rushed companies with unproven ideas to market. All emphasis was placed on scaling factors, the reasoning going something like this:

The worldwide market for widgets is $100 billion. If half of this can be expected to migrate to the web, a company with a 10 per cent share of this market would generate sales of $5 billion. A bricks and mortar company with this order of turnover would be valued at $10 billion. As the efficiencies of trading online would be expected to halve sales costs, the profits should be double. This would value the company at $20 billion. Even discounting this value back through a build-up time of five years would still see a present-day value of $15 billion, so the valuation at the time of the IPO will be a bargain at $12 billion.

These calculations assumed that a sound management would be able to capture and retain 10 per cent of the market, perhaps even more if the company was a first mover. This gets investors falling over themselves to invest in such IPOs, pouring millions of dollars into the hands of 'sound management' (but who had never before been exposed to the unpredictable and chaotic world of e-business).

With the comfort of knowing that the start-up was not expected to make profits from day one, most managements looked to the future and set their goals on market share and maximum revenue instead of profits and dividends. Attracting web traffic and directing customer eyeballs became the sole focus of strategies.

A madness crept into e-business equity markets: an online airline ticket ordering company saw its equity value rise at one time to a point where it was worth more than the value of United Airlines, American Airlines, British Airways and KLM put together. Investors were pouring money into dot-com companies without any idea of what the basics of the business were, let alone the technology involved.

Companies were being floated on the basis of creating some kind of portal (an entry point on the web for customers to link to a range of products or services) and these portals were being sold as dot-com businesses on the strength of the future purchases that would be made by the people using these portals. Yet, in essence, these were no more than glorified mailing lists – with each name being valued by as much as $1,000 each. In such crazy times, free computers were given away, just to get a name on a list.

At the time, I spoke to a friend of mine who was an analyst for one of the big London brokers which had brought many of these dot coms to market. He had the job of calculating the launch price of shares when the equity of a company is first offered to the market. He told me that these valuations were based on the discounted value of the profit that can be earned from customers over a period of several years.

When I raised the point that these customers would have many alternative ways to spend their money on the internet and would have the choice of an almost unlimited number of alternative portals and places to buy, he told me that these calculations were made on the basis that most people have a reluctance to change from a familiar source once they have become customers.

Unfortunately, like so many other people involved in these kinds of calculations and valuations, he had very little experience of being on the internet himself. If he'd had, he would have known how easily and quickly people can chop and change around. This tendency to stick with the familiar is a characteristic applying specifically to the world of bricks and mortar and isn't valid in the fast-changing world of e-business. It is a world where change is familiar and frequently rewarding.

On the internet, as soon as people learn from others where they can get a better price or a better service – just by making a few clicks with the mouse – they start to shop around and the concept of customer loyalty becomes redundant. In this situation the only justification for expecting to retain a customer base is by providing exceptionally competitive products or services. This thought didn't seem to enter the calculations of many investment advisers and analysts.

The discussion got around to a recent dot-com offering, where the IPO equity share price had valued the dot com higher than the current valuation of the huge multiple retail business of the bricks and mortar company that had initiated it. The dot com was providing little more than a 'free' connection to the internet, something any other company could do (and subsequently did). How could the equity in this new dot-com business, with virtually no assets, be worth more than that of a long-established, successfully trading company which had stores in nearly every town in the country?

My friend pointed out that the company had more than just this list of customers; it also had the vast sum of money that it had gained by selling its equity shares (less the not inconsiderable costs of the launch and the broker's fees). 'They will be able to buy out the shares of other dot coms,' he explained.

This conversation then opened my eyes to what the dot-com boom was really about. It was a gigantic zero-sum game, winners winning only what the losers were losing. It was all smoke and mirrors. It was almost as if they were all sophisticated scams that were dragging in investment funds to create more scams with the scams feeding off each other – with the poor investors, who were financing this free-for-all, getting sucked in deeper and deeper.

It wasn't that most of the people involved were dishonest (although frauds and deceptions abounded), the main fault was that it was a totally new business environment, which nobody understood and where traditional valuations and business practices couldn't be applied.

the strategy of a venture capital company

At the peak of the dot-com boom, there was a much-publicized national competition being run in the UK by a major venture capital company. The winners – who would be judged as having the best e-business proposition – would be financed with up to £2 million (about $3 million) of capital, with the venture capital company taking only 25 per cent of the equity in return.

It sounded like the venture capital company was being altruistic and supportive of entrepreneurs – benefactors, who were helping young hopefuls to get a start. But, after working with financiers and investors in the City of London, my reaction to this competition was perhaps somewhat more cynical: I presumed they were running this competition to make a profit.

As venture capital companies make their money from capital gains rather than income, it is reasonable to assume that their primary interest is in what is going to look appealing in the documents for an IPO when they take the company to market. In this respect, convention holds that you need an experienced management team and a detailed business plan before offering equity to investors. Investors will expect this. This is what they will want to base their investment decisions on.

It was only to be expected, therefore, that the judges were said to be looking for 'strong management teams and realistic financial projections as well as products that have sustainable growth possibilities and the chance of competing in the global marketplace'. The big question, though, was whether or not these requirements actually had any relevance to the eventual success of the company that would be financed. Strong management with business plans seemed to me to be a handicap rather than an asset in the volatile e-business environment and the idea of 'realistic financial projections' totally ludicrous.

The competition reminded me of an experience I'd had a couple of years previously, when I'd received a telephone call from a venture capital company. They'd been told, by one of their associate companies, that I might be someone who could have some good e-business ideas – this was on the strength of two books I'd written on computer programming and intelligent systems.

I was invited to the venture capital company's offices for a discussion. When I arrived, I was somewhat surprised when the first thing the interviewer did was to have me sit through a computer presentation showing me how great their company was.

When it was finished, I started to explain my idea of a strategy to create an e-business but the interviewer wasn't interested. He wanted to know what fully developed products I had (none), what patents I had (none), what management structure I had (none), what my business plan was (vague). At that point, a secretary came over (probably at a pre-arranged signal) and told the interviewer that his next appointment was waiting for him.

However, during the interview, I'd managed to get in a few questions myself and discovered that the interviewer, who was a principal of the firm, had originally been a pop record producer. I'd asked how much he used the internet and he'd told me he didn't have time to use it himself. Then I clicked. He wasn't interested in my ideas; he was only interested to know if I had anything that would look good in a prospectus for a flotation on the stock market.

The whole thing rang a bell with me. I'd had a similar experience when I'd applied for a patent on a method for mixing different types of secure information on a CD-ROM. Soon after the application had been applied for, I'd had a phone call from a company claiming they could market my patent for me.

Full of hope and excitement, I went to their smart offices in central London and was surprised to find that they had no interest in the details or potential of my product whatsoever. All I got was a computer-generated description of how good their company was and a hard sell to get me to part with £750 for them to act as agents for me. It didn't take much figuring out that they weren't interested in selling my product at all: only in the fee that they could get out of me.

As a postscript to the interview I had with the venture capital company, it was only a year later that I read in the press that the company had grouped together a promising-looking selection of start-ups and gone to market with a valuation of $3 billion. Out of curiosity, a year later I looked at the price of their shares after the dot-com bubble had burst – they'd fallen to less than a tenth of their initial offer price.

the dilemma

Here is my problem. I want to create a business but my whole approach is at odds with the conventional requirements for obtaining funding:

► I don't want to start with a great idea.

► I don't want to have a detailed business plan.

► I can give no realistic financial projections.

There is also a paradox to be resolved. How can I create a business with a stable base when the need will be for a very flexible base, which can adapt and evolve in response to continuous technological developments and constant competitive initiatives?

entrepreneurial businesses

Businesses created by entrepreneurs have to be generated from business ideas that come from within a solution space the entrepreneurs create for themselves: a short list of ideas that match the resources available to the entrepreneur. To be worth pursuing, these ideas must have a realistic chance of creating and maintaining a profitable income even if the intention of the entrepreneur is to make a capital gain.

It is common to think of these ideas as arising through an entrepreneur's imagination or from the shrewd reading of a market's needs. These will certainly be factors in the creation of an e-business, but the most dominant influences will be the ability to put ideas into practice and the capital investment needed.

As soon as investments come into the picture it becomes pertinent to start thinking about the returns that would be expected by the investors who make these investments. This puts the spotlight on the financial gains that an idea might be expected to produce. In other words, ideas will have to be given a value to determine whether or not they will justify the amount of investment needed to turn them into reality. This should be the overriding consideration in determining whether or not an idea is allowed into an entrepreneur's solution space.

Obviously, the value of any idea in the solution space would have to be greater than the amount of capital needed to finance it. Additionally, the activity of putting the idea into effect will carry a minimum overhead – due to the running costs – which will set a minimum value for any of the ideas that can go through the gate. This scenario is illustrated in Figure 2.3.

From this viewpoint, the boundary conditions of the business idea solution space can be defined as:

1   The idea must be within the capabilities of the business.

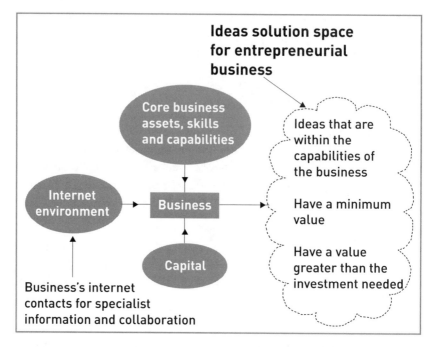

FIG 2.3 The ideas within an entrepreneurial business's solution space are limited to those that the business is capable of carrying out – and by the value of the idea in relation to the investment needed to put it into operation

2   The value of the idea must be greater than the amount of capital needed to finance it.

3   The idea must have a minimum value determined by the running costs of the core business (or the running costs of a section of a large business if the idea is assigned as a project).

What is not always obvious is that a similar model is used by funding bodies. They will also have a solution space where they have gates designed to let suitable application proposals in and keep unsuitable application proposals out. However, most funding bodies will have traditional attitudes towards funding and their solution space will almost certainly be static and top-down. This is illustrated in Figure 2.4.

Funding bodies will not want to waste their resources on investigating

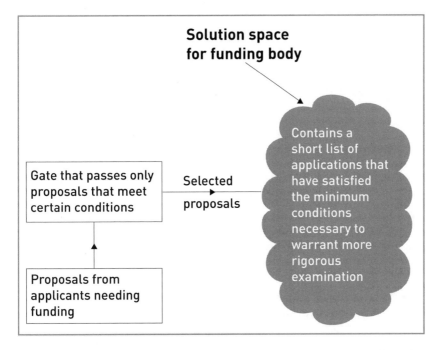

FIG 2.4 Funding bodies have a static, top-down solution space that contains only proposals that meet certain criteria. It is only these that are given serious consideration

every proposal that comes along (most funding bodies receive 40 or 50 times as many proposals as their analysts can handle), so they use a series of tests that eliminate all but the most promising. It is the funding body's skills in constructing such tests that determine the success or otherwise of their own business strategy.

Any sensible applicant for funding will make sure they know what tests are being made on the proposals they submit to a funding body to ensure that their proposal gets through the gates. This raises a number of important questions:

1 What are the tests that funding bodies apply to proposals?

2 What if the tests are not compatible with the proposer's business strategy?

3   What if the funding body's tests are wrong, such that the most promising business proposals are excluded and the least promising included?

To answer these questions, we'll need to know some of the technicalities involved in financial and investment valuations.

current price versus fundamental value

In the early 1970s, I wrote a course on investment strategy for a London firm of investment advisers who were setting up a college to teach students the art of investment. The approach I took was to start by explaining to the students how to calculate fundamental investment values so that they could use these theoretical values to make judgements on current market prices of stocks and shares.

NOTE The value of any income is calculated by discounting all future income payments back through time to the present day. It's like compound interest in reverse where each payment in the future is given a value according to what sum today would reach that payment amount through compound interest at the time the payment is made.

This technical method of valuation involved calculating expected future earnings and comparing the value of those earnings to the current price of annuities (fixed incomes that continue into perpetuity).

By suitably discounting for risks and inflation, this appeared to be a logical approach to investment valuations because it was comparing like with like, i.e. one income stream with another. However, when I came to apply this valuation to current equity prices at the time I wrote the course, I found it gave answers widely off the mark. Equity share prices were two or three times the value my calculations were indicating they should be.

At first I thought I'd made some silly mistake in my formulae or was missing some important factors, but despite a month of going over the calculations and methods I could find no obvious errors. So, with great trepidation, I let my recommended calculations stand, fearing that as soon as the course went out to the students someone would spot the fault and expose me as a charlatan.

Much to my surprise, I had no adverse comments even though the valuations remained way out of line with current prices for four years. Then, in 1974, the Arab oil crisis occurred. Within a few months there was a stock market crash, and prices on the London stock exchange fell by over 70 per cent. When the market eventually recovered, the equity share prices recovered only to their fundamental values: the values calculated by the methods I'd proposed in the course.

What I hadn't realized at the time I'd written the course was that it was at a time of a stock market boom. Illogically, the equity prices of all shares had risen to unprecedented levels, way beyond their fundamental values.

I never did get to understand how the prices could have been out of alignment with fundamental values for so long, or why it had taken a special event to bring them back into alignment. However, the experience gave me a healthy respect for fundamental valuations and a lack of trust in current market prices.

fashion trends in stock market valuations

Logically, equity stock market valuations should always be based on fundamental reasoning and calculation, but the way these calculations are made can be greatly influenced by currently fashionable trends in business strategy.

Until the late 1950s, equity valuations were based on the actual returns a company was likely to provide in the way of dividends to the share-holders. No account was taken of profits used for future business. Equity share prices were based solely on the discounted value of actual incomes with allowances made only for any risks that dividends might not be maintained.

This put the onus on the directors and executives of a company to do everything in their power to maintain the profitability of the company to the extent that dividends were fully supported by earnings and with sufficient reserves to give confidence that dividend payments would be maintained every year into the foreseeable future.

This worked fine while dividend yields from equities were greater than the yields from fixed interest bonds, but then IBM came along. The price of IBM shares started to increase substantially without the company paying any dividend at all. This shocked investors into realizing that the value of a company was not based solely on what it was paying in the way of dividends in the present, but, also account must be taken of the potential for increased dividends it may be able to pay at a future date.

This realization totally transformed the model for evaluating businesses. No longer was the emphasis put on a company's ability to maintain a steady and reliable dividend payout; instead, valuations were based on an assessment as to how successful a company might be in finding and developing new projects where the results would realize a substantial profit over the expenditure.

This changed the emphasis of company management from that of preservation to that of expansion. The payment of dividends became of lesser importance than the ability to invest earnings into new projects. This trend eventually reached a stage where the payment of dividends was seen almost as a sign of failure by the company to find new opportunities to expand.

This change in the investment model made the dividend yield an irrelevant ratio for estimating equity share values. Accountants decided that the true value of equities needed to be based on the bottom line: the net profit that a company was making. This was known as GAAP (Generally Agreed Accounting Principles), which saw earnings per share as the principal basis of a company's true value.

The problem with GAAP, though, was that any investments in future projects would be deducted from the bottom line, effectively writing them off as if the projects were doomed to failure. It allowed no valuation for the effects of strategic marketing plans that gave long-term benefits, it attributed no value for expenditures on research and development, and it placed no value on branding or goodwill. In effect, the GAAP valuation of a company was the liquidation or break-up value.

The smarter investors soon spotted these anomalies and there were many highly profitable takeovers before accountants woke up to the fact that they were undervaluing their companies in some way.

To compensate, the accountants started to add a nebulous component to a company's value, known as 'intangible assets'. This figure included all the expected future benefits that could be realized through current advertising and marketing, employee training, goodwill, branding, research and development, etc. No provable evidence could be supplied to support the valuations given to these intangible assets, but their addition certainly provided a more accurate valuation of a company as a going concern.

The problem, however, was that this nebulous asset allowed all manner of discretionary additions to be included in company valuations. It led to much 'creative accounting' where a company could be given any kind of value according to how the directors and accountants measured the intangibles and the elements of risk associated with them. This led to the bizarre situation where companies could show continuous losses on their balance sheets while their equity share prices continued to rise.

Until the advent of the internet and the world wide web, intangible asset values, although not precise, were usually based on some kind of generally accepted, common-sense reasoning. Most of the factors and their consequences were more or less understandable; outcomes and risk were predictable within a reasonable degree of accuracy.

The coming of the technological and communication revolution threw these valuations of intangible assets into confusion. It involved dealing with a technology that few, if any, of the investment analysts, accountants or investors understood. Valuations involved unknowns and unknowables, unpredictable events and technological changes. Effectively, this made the valuation of intangible assets a matter of total guesswork, allowing the imagination to run riot.

The problem was that the promise of potentially huge profits that might be made in a massively connected world had fired the imagination of investors. The potential for profit seemed to be without limit. Fantasy started to creep into the valuations of intangible assets. All common sense was thrown to the wind, with equity share valuations changing rapidly from being based on earnings per share to being based on dreams per share.

The most surprising feature of the dot-com boom was the way in which many respectable and long-established stockbroking firms subscribed to the dreams per share method of calculating values. They could almost have been prosecuted for fraud and misrepresentation for some of the IPOs they put together. However, allowance has to be made for the fact that stockbrokers are in business to give clients what they want and, with such a huge demand for technology stocks, they had to provide them.

The buying and selling of equities is purely a zero-sum game where winners win what the losers lose. As such, there is no strong pressure to keep prices at fundamental levels. There is no convincing argument that an equity price is too high if somebody is willing to buy it at that price.

If some stockbrokers were basing IPO prices on dreams, others had to do the same to be able to maintain their share of the new-issue market. Although traditional methods of evaluation indicated that these valuations were incredulously large, there were so many takers of the equity offerings coming onto the market that IPO equity prices expanded beyond all reason.

When these initial public offers were being bid up as much as several times their offer price by the market, the brokers assumed that they must be doing something right and continued to value IPOs at increasingly unrealistically high values.

But, of course, it couldn't last.

the pricing of the dot-com bubble

In the first few months of this century, the shrewder investors began to realize that all was not well with the dot coms (the name given to the internet start-ups that were being rushed to market after receiving massive amounts of venture capital funding). After a few spectacular failures, analysts began looking more closely at the accounts. What they found was truly alarming.

Most were burning up capital so fast that they were almost certain to run out of cash before reaching profitability. Advertising and marketing weren't working for them. They could get the eyeballs, but it wasn't translating into profitable income. It wasn't uncommon for marketing costs to be multiples of the profits on sales and in some cases even multiples of the gross sales revenue itself.

One company, Pets.com, had to fold even though it had received $85 million of funding and had acquired a customer list of 500,000. Conventional marketing strategies had produced totally unexpected poor results. This was a situation that had no parallel in the Industrial Age world.

Analysts started to look more closely at the accounts of the e-businesses. They found many irregularities and misleading accounting practices. For example, where a company had low or non-existent trading incomes, it could find ways to create artificial sales or assets to falsely boost the apparent value of the company. One such trick was where companies exchanged banner advertisements with each other: back-to-back arrangements where each charged the other the same huge sum of money for running the other's banner advertisement on their site. This can artificially boost the sales revenues of both companies, to make it appear in the accounts that they have large turnovers.

Although this does not generate any real profits, the accounts of the companies involved in these back-to-back arrangements can be made to show a net gain because the payments (by each company) for the banner advertising are charged to marketing instead of writing these costs off against profits. In this way they can legitimately (but falsely) claim that these costs are additions to the intangible assets of the company: on the basis that marketing usually leads to increased value of a brand name and to future sales.

Similarly, many companies were selling goods at huge price discounts, but entering the sales into the accounts at full retail values. This allowed them to treat the discounts as marketing expenses that could boost the intangible assets valuation of the company, on the pretext that the discounts were being employed profitably to build a customer base.

Without being aware of such tricks, it is easy for an investor to see what appears to be a healthy balance sheet that, although not showing a trading profit, is reflecting the results of a rapidly expanding business with a growing potential to become profitable.

Trying to ascertain a 'true' value for those early dot-com companies was fraught with many such difficulties. Websites, some of which had cost millions of dollars to build, were being treated as if they were permanent buildings in the world of bricks and mortar. Site-building costs were being included in the accounts as assets, even when it was patently obvious that the sites were transitional and temporary structures, often failing at what they had been designed to do and proving to be more of an expensive liability than an asset.

Complicating and clouding the valuations was the question of where corporate incomes and expenditures were booked. A company could be set up anywhere in the world, and its websites could be distributed all over the planet. Product design and manufacture could be fragmented and outsourced to a variety of contractors and subcontractors in a variety of countries. If the product was software it could be dispatched from anywhere. It was impossible for even professional investment analysts to discover where profits were being taken or removed. Sorting out such accounts and investment valuations can be impossibly complex.

Perhaps the biggest conundrum for investors was in puzzling out the meaning of a dot-com's burn rate (burn rate is the term used to describe the haemorrhaging of capital as a company spends money in its efforts to become profitable). Burn rate, or negative cash flow, is not alarming in itself as most dot-com companies were set up with the expectation that real trading profits would not materialize immediately. Nearly always, the start-ups had business plans that indicated profits would appear only after a substantial infrastructure had been set up and a customer base established – which could be several years away from the date of funding or market launch.

So, in the absence of a conventional profit and loss account based on actual trading, investors had to work out whether the outgoing cash (the burn rate):

▶ was being used by a business to build a profitable company, or

▶ was merely symptomatic of a company that had lost its way and was trying to spend its way out of trouble.

In most cases, the answer to this question was found out too late – after all the money had gone.

funding problems after the dot-com bubble

After the dot-com bubble burst, the dreams started to be taken out of the valuations for the intangibles added to e-business company accounts. New regulations curbed many of the accountancy tricks. The huge numbers of failures gave an indication of the true risks involved; these were seen to be unacceptably high.

Investors became more sceptical and started to look for real evidence of income and profit. Brokers, fearful for their reputations, stopped bolstering claims and glossing over practical realities, thus reducing the attractiveness of market offerings. This drastically reduced the number of IPO opportunities.

Without a large pool of gullible investors and with much stricter conditions being placed on high-tech companies coming to market, the venture capital companies ran out of steam. Profitable situations were much harder to come by; more expensive and extensive expert analysis work had to be carried out. With the costs rising and the profit opportunities reducing, the boom times for the venture capital companies were over.

In short, the investing public became disenchanted with dot-com companies when the risks were fully exposed; opportunities for funding were much reduced and, where capital was available, it came only after much closer examination and with more stringent conditions attached.

In the wake of the dot-com boom and the drying up of indiscriminate funding, many e-businesses were left floundering. Whereas in the boom times companies could rely on going to the market for new funding whenever they ran out of funds, this source dried up as the market became increasingly sceptical of companies that were not showing a trading profit.

With the hazards of speculative risk capital exposed, investors became cautious and started to look at fundamental values such as real assets and actual income and profits. Potential start-ups began to find it hard, if not impossible, to raise venture capital and many market flotations were postponed or abandoned altogether.

It is in this post-dot-com boom environment that I now have to consider creating an e-business to serve as an example to include in this book.

the increasingly difficult problem
This chapter began with a problem common to all bottom-up business strategies – how do you obtain funding when you have no business idea, no business plan and no management structure? Now the problem has worsened because it seems as if funding has practically dried up altogether.

3

THE HARSH REALITIES OF FUNDING AND FINANCE

exasperation and despair On Thursday 15 February 2001, a London-based organization, NETPROZ (formed for the purpose of bringing e-business entrepreneurs together with funding organizations), held a special event. The event, called the Equity Food Chain, was part of a unique collaboration between six business networks based in London: NETPROZ, The National Business Angel Network, Netimperative, HRNet, Simplesite and Wave2. The idea was that members of these various communities could come along to the event to ask a panel questions relating to the funding of e-business start-ups.

It was a particularly apt time to hold this event because in the wake of the many recent dot-com failures, enthusiasm for investment in e-business ventures had fallen off dramatically. It wasn't hard to see why. Only the day before this meeting, an article had appeared in the London *Evening Standard*, by the city editor, Anthony Hilton, highlighting the problem.

The Nasdaq index of high-tech stocks had fallen to half the value it had reached at its peak in March 2000. At the time of this market high, the average price to earnings ratio of the top 100 stocks had stood at an incredible 165. With stock prices falling to half their former values, it would have been expected that the price to earnings ratio would have followed suit and fallen to around 82. Instead, the price to earnings ratio had risen to an unprecedented 811 – due to the low earnings and the losses reported by these top 100 companies during the year. It was these kinds of figures that were dampening the enthusiasm of even the most optimistic of investors, so the e-business start-ups looking for funding had every right to feel concerned.

As one of the panel, I was sent a list of the questions that had been sent in for the panel to answer. These included the following:

Question 1

What is the best way to secure seed capital to develop a concept for a technology start-up?

Question 2

We are a start-up company developing a product that could revolutionize the way data is handled over multiple platforms. We have interest and a great deal of help and support from a major technology company. We are still looking for funding. When we first started approaching VCs we thought that our offering would be received with delight as it has the potential for fantastic growth and enormous financial return. We were hugely disappointed, however, to be frequently told, 'Oh well, it hasn't been done before, we prefer tried and tested products.'

They all seem so afraid of looking at something new, preferring either something conventional, a mild revolution by somebody who has already tried once and failed, or something being developed by a tribe of Microsoft employees! Even the angel investors we have spoken to say that they are only interested in investing in serial entrepreneurs. Bearing in mind we have secured technological (and later marketing) support from one of the biggest companies in the business, where can we find an investor who is prepared to put the venture back into capital or at least give us a proper look?

Question 3

We are entrepreneurs currently at funding stage and looking at business angel/VC opportunities. Taking into account the recent reduction in value of tech stocks, what factors need to be addressed/altered (if any) when preparing a business plan for potential investors to review?

Question 4

The investor market seems so scared of investing in start-up technology companies and is demanding a level of development often impossible for companies looking for their first round of funding. With fewer start-ups finding funding and fewer companies reaching maturity as a result, surely the pool of companies requiring funding for second round plus (which VCs seem to be looking for) will eventually dry up. Is it any wonder, when investors show such lack of faith in the industry, that stock market values fall and the general public lose faith in what should be an industry of tremendous growth? What can be done to break this cycle?

Question 5

We all welcome a return to sensible valuations and the application of 'normal' commercial logic, but let's not forget that venture capital is still about risk taking. That requires vision and leadership, as well as analysis and clever financial engineering. Does the panel agree that these qualities are now in short supply among the investor community and that the winners will be those with the guts to lead deals rather than follow 'safe bets'?

Question 6

We have huge confidence in our business proposition, and are very ambitious about its worldwide relevance. But we're humble enough to recognize that the world around us will change, and things just won't turn out the way the business plan says they will. How much thinking about this do your investors expect to see in a business plan? What do the panel think are the critical success factors for funding bids going forward, particularly in emerging areas such as content for mobile devices?

Question 7

Are investors, on the whole, more risk averse today? Are there differences between the UK and US?

Question 8

I am particularly interested in corporate venturing, and would like the panel to comment on their thoughts on whether there is evidence that corporate investors are increasingly willing to seed early-stage businesses. As a follow-up, I'd be interested to know if the panel agrees with me that the efficiency of this process can be greatly increased if corporates work in parallel with VCs. (It's our view that more corporate money will free up if larger organizations can be reassured that there are good processes in place for deal evaluation, deal structuring, and ongoing support once the businesses have been funded.)

Question 9
Given the change in the VC role for funding seed/start-ups, what will fill this gap, if anything at all?

Question 10
The question I have and the problem we face is to recover our business (both on and off-line) after funding 'fell through' at the last minute through no fault of our own. The business is still viable and potentially very profitable and dominant; however, we have a short-term funding crisis to deal with and the prospect of starting the funding search again. Where are the investors who can look at a business opportunity as a 'real business' rather than talk in acronyms and look for the latest technology?

Question 11
Were all the VCs who appeared in the last couple of years really professionals or were they merely gamblers?

Question 12
What are the three key elements investors look for in a business plan? In what ways have investors changed their approach to finding suitable start-ups over the last six months? Given that VCs are less likely to invest in unproven start-ups, what is the best way to find appropriate angel investors? How critical to investors is having key staff in place, despite the problems in recruiting people to theoretical jobs?

Question 13
With reference to the provinces and funding, business angel networks tend to be a waste of time. Members are old fuddy-duddies, who like the prestige of attending meetings but with no intention of funding. What can be done to support entrepreneurs in the provinces?

Question 14
I believe that current tech-stock pessimism is the flipside to misplaced tech-stock optimism: IT was set up for a fall, and now it's being dismissed

prematurely. My main question for the panel is: How can businesses in the IT community convey their value in a realistic and convincing manner, so that investor expectations never have to be frustrated on such a scale again?

These questions reflect the general air of exasperation and despair that afflicted so many of the entrepreneurs who attended that event. They'd gone there with the hope that somebody would be able to tell them how to get the necessary funding to finance their business plans. They didn't get the answers they were looking for.

To most of these hopefuls seeking finance, investment decision making appears as a black art, driven by ignorance, prejudice, bias and lack of vision. Yet, if they applied the fundamental basics of investment calculation, together with a grain of common sense, they might be able to answer their own questions and have a more realistic approach to their business strategies.

looking from the financier's viewpoint
In contemplating a business venture that involves selling a product or service to a client or customer, it is obvious that it is necessary to build the product or service around what the customer or client actually wants. As obvious as this basic tenet is, it is often completely ignored when it comes to seeking funding or finance for a business venture.

Seeking finance is much like selling any product or service; a profitable revenue stream is being offered for sale in return for a capital sum. It makes sense, therefore, to see what a financier wants the revenue stream for and to know how it will be valued by the financier.

Start-up or business development financing can take several different forms depending on the stage.

preliminary stages
The preliminary stages are during the birthing process of a business venture, the time when there are mainly ideas with no clear directions as to how to proceed. Most ventures at this stage are stillborn and proceed no further.

NOTE I'm using the term 'financier' here as a general expression to cover all types of funding bodies that an entrepreneurial business, or a new business project within a large company, might need to provide exploratory or working capital before it is in a position to generate its own funding needs from earned profits.

Birthing usually begins with some inkling of a possible business situation that occurs as a result of recognizing an opportunity or seeing the possibility of a unique or better solution to a problem or a need. At this stage it will be necessary to do some market research, make a prototype, develop a proof of concept, etc.

This stage will require much time and skilled effort, but financing can only be provided on the basis of hope and faith. This is often provided by the instigator or instigators themselves, their friends and families, but more often is directly or indirectly financed by an employer.

Although the stereotyped start-up business venture is romantically thought of as beginning in a garage, most start-ups originate within companies. Even many private business ventures are birthed within a large company, often where a project is cancelled before coming to fruition and the frustrated employees working on the project leave the company to continue working on the project themselves.

Many ventures also start from within companies when employees recognize an opportunity before the management. They might then develop a business venture to the birthing stage while still working for the company; using the company's time and resources in place of seeking finance. Not a particularly honest way to go about starting a business, but very common in the world of e-business.

Some start-ups are birthed from the dying embers of a failed company, where there has been a basically sound, core business idea which has not been successfully brought to fruition through poor business strategy, burdensome overheads or cash burn-up. After the company goes into liquidation, the core idea might be taken up by the original initiators, or by the employees, who can then make a fresh start without debts or onerous liabilities.

This phoenix-like phenomenon is observed in the fashion industry, where sudden changes in trends or fashion can wrong-foot a company, causing bankruptcy. Such companies are quick to restart from new beginnings, after their debts have been wiped out through an official liquidation process. This same pattern is starting to emerge with dot coms.

There are unlimited ways in which the need for capital at the birthing stage can be circumvented, without the principals having to apply for professional financing facilities. This is mostly a necessity because few financiers will ever bother to spend time investigating investment opportunities that consist mainly of speculative ideas and broad assumptions.

In general, financiers don't like uncertainty or unknowns. They prefer to have strong justification for any investments, particularly as most funding bodies have to account to others for their decisions. This practically eliminates all sources of professional funding for the birthing stage of a business.

start-up stage Many small service businesses can be started without the need for finance. They can bootstrap themselves up into profitable operation through charging for services rendered. Most expert services and consultancies can start this way, where overheads are minimal and stage payments can alleviate any cash flow problems.

For the more ambitious start-ups, there will be a need for seed capital to get the business up and running to the point where it is either self-financing or developed sufficiently to attract serious investment capital.

Seed capital can come from two sources: angels or venture capitalists. Although the distinction between these two sources of finance is very blurred, it may be useful for the purpose of this chapter to treat them as being black and white caricatures. The exaggerated difference we'll define as being the difference between gamblers and business packagers.

The angels will have an interest in the success of the business, taking a gamble on their own judgement as to the viability of the proposition and the ability of the initiators to create profits. Most often, angels will not need detailed business plans and cash flow projections. They will be calling on their own business experience to recognize talented people and potentially viable situations and will usually have some kind of interest or control to ensure that the venture keeps on track towards profitability.

Venture capitalists, on the other hand, usually have very little interest in what a company does or how it does it and sometimes are even

THIS RATHER CYNICAL CARICATURE of a venture capital company is not typical of all venture capital companies. It is meant to apply only to the situations involving the financing of e-businesses where there is no way in which a venture capital company can be in a position to predict accurately the future viability of the business. This would apply to practically all e-businesses because of the chaotic and changeable nature of the world of digital communications. They can only be guessing and the failure rate of venture-capital-financed dot coms has proved this point.

In fact, most venture capital companies will go to considerable lengths to investigate the prospects of profitability for the companies they finance. They do make judgements on whether or not a business is likely to be successful because failure reflects on their ability to pick winners, which in turn affects their credibility with investors.

Basically they provide a service for a particular group of investors who are putting up the capital to finance young and promising companies. These investors will be looking for a return on their capital of something like a 25 per cent compound rate of interest – but this profit comes from selling on, not from the profitable returns of the companies they are financing.

A venture capital company will not be looking for just any attractive proposition that comes along; they will tend to specialize in particular technological niches where they have contacts and inside knowledge. They will have a profile as to what to look for in a company, which will limit selection to the areas of business where they have special knowledge. This profile will also include the particular preferences of their own group of investors.

Many start-up companies seeking venture capital finance are unaware that different venture capital companies have different profiles with which to select companies to finance and will waste much valuable time and effort approaching those which do not cover their particular area of business.

The important point to note is that venture capital companies are not looking for long-term results. They are creating a vehicle that they can sell on at a profit for themselves and their investors. This they can do even if a company eventually fails.

The uninformed hysteria of the dot-com bubble resulted in hundreds of thousands of investors clamouring for high-tech shares simply because they were in fashion and the prices were rising. Some venture capital companies responded to this need and made enormous profits for their investors by feeding this share-buying frenzy. Many of the investors who ended up with those shares when the music stopped weren't so lucky.

unconcerned as to whether or not it will eventually become profitable. They are not gamblers, neither do they put up money based on their own judgement as to whether a business is likely to be successful. They simply look for suitable situations that can be attractively dressed up to sell on to investors.

serious business stage Once a business has passed the start-up stage and shows either an actual or reasonably certain expectation of a profitable revenue stream, it can start to look for investment capital. Investors providing investment capital, for a business coming out of a start-up stage, might have several motivations that cover a spectrum of different needs:

1   There is the long-term investor looking for the potential for steady growth or a reliable dividend income. It is unlikely that this kind of investor would be attracted to internet businesses because they will not have a long track record and the volatility of the e-business environment could see them being overtaken by events, losing their way or meeting superior competition that emerges out of the blue to crush them out of existence.

    However, many long-term investors assign a small proportion of their portfolios to speculative investments, sometimes to add a little excitement to their investment strategy, sometimes as a way of keeping in touch with new and unfolding events in new and up-and-coming markets. These funds may be used for investment in high-tech new issues.

2   There is the type of investor who would be looking for a short-term capital gain. These are the investors who are particularly attracted to high-tech companies. They gamble on a company's trading expectations being fully realized. Effectively, their investment strategies involve discounting the risks less than the more cautious investors.

3   There will be the speculative investors, who ignore the risks and the fundamentals and act on spurious information or doubtful reasoning and buy on the basis that they think a share price will rise sufficiently

to be able to sell again for a quick profit – presumably to an even more optimistic gambler. All booms are led by this kind of investor.

getting financing into perspective

Not counting the speculative investors and the various kinds of capital that might be introduced at the birthing stage of an e-business start-up, all other forms of financing need to have some basis in rationality.

This basis must, in some way, be related to the four cornerstone concepts of finance and investment calculation:

1 discounting through time;

2 turning an income into a capital value;

3 turning a capital amount into an income stream;

4 discounting for risk.

It is worth noting that all banking, insurance, pension and investment industries are based solely on these four important concepts. All financiers, and anyone seeking finance, should fully understand the conceptual mindset they represent.

discounting through time

Discounting through time is the calculation necessary to be able to turn income into capital and capital into income. Its basic premise is that a sum of money in the future is worth less than that same sum of money in the present.

The best way to imagine this is to think of a visual image. Up close it appears large. As the image moves further and further away it gets smaller and smaller. Substitute money for the image and distance for time and you have a good visualization as to how the value of a sum of money shrinks the further away it is from the present day.

It may seem impossible that a sum of money can reduce in value as it appears further away in time. After all, if you put $10,000 under the mattress and fetched it out after ten years, it would still be the same $10,000.

However, the factors influencing present and future values are:

1 inflation, which can cause the actual value to shrink;

2 the risk of some unexpected disaster occurring whereby the money gets lost;

3 the money in the present can be profitably invested so that it will increase in value by a future date due to compound interest.

This can be imagined by thinking of two people, each with $10,000. One puts it under the bed for ten years, the other invests the money in safe securities that pay an interest of 7.2 per cent per annum which adds each year to the total amount (compound interest). What happens to the values of their respective savings is detailed in Figure 3.1.

$10,000 left under mattress Inflation rate 3%		$10,000 invested at 7.2% Inflation rate 3%	
After	Worth	After	Worth
Year 1	9700	Year 1	10420
Year 2	9409	Year 2	10858
Year 3	9127	Year 3	11314
Year 4	8853	Year 4	11789
Year 5	8587	Year 5	12283
Year 6	8330	Year 6	12800
Year 7	8080	Year 7	13337
Year 8	7837	Year 8	13898
Year 9	7602	Year 9	14481
Year 10	7374	Year 10	15090

Two ways of saving $10,000

FIG 3.1 Showing how the value of money changes over ten years according to how it is saved

As can be seen from Figure 3.1, money not put to work can decrease in value due to inflation. Money invested can increase in value due to compound interest. With inflation at 3 per cent (affecting both ways of saving) and the investment paying 7.2 per cent per annum interest, after ten years the invested money is worth about double the money put under the mattress.

All financial business decision making is based on being aware of these differences between a present-day value and a future value of money. The concern is not only with how much a sum of money will grow to at some time in the future, but also how much a future sum is worth in the present. For example, the table in Figure 3.1 tells us that a sum of $15,000 in the future is worth $10,000 today, because $10,000 will turn into $15,000 over ten years.

Being aware of the way in which a future value seems to shrink as it is brought back to the present allows an important financial calculation to be made. It allows incomes to be given capitalized values. This is illustrated in Figure 3.2, where an income of $100 per annum stretching over the next 100 years can be given a value by adding up all the payments discounted through time back to the present day.

From Figure 3.2, it can be seen that an income over one hundred years has a finite value because the present-day value of future payments gradually reduces to zero. In this example, where the interest is assumed to be 7.2 per cent, it can be seen that the capitalized value of an income of $100 per annum approximates to just under $1,400.

Similarly, an income of $10,000 per annum would be valued at $140,000. An income of $100,000 per annum would be valued at $1.4 million. It is through this kind of calculation that the value of a company's equity shares can be valued. If you can estimate the rate of earnings, you can get an idea of the basic value of its shares and therefore its share price.

Of course, it is not quite as simple as this because there is an element of guesswork in assuming the correct percentage to use for the discounting. There is also a guess that has to be made as to what the rate of inflation will be. This allows wide differences in opinion as to the correct value of

Income of $100 per annum discounted back to the present day at 7.2%	
Present-day value of each annual payment of $100	Total accumulated value of all payments discounted back to the present day
After 1 year, $100 is worth $93	(Acc. total 93)
After 2 years, $100 is worth $87	(Acc. total 180)
After 3 years, $100 is worth $81	(Acc. total 261)
After 4 years, $100 is worth $76	(Acc. total 337)
After 5 years, $100 is worth $71	(Acc. total 408)
After 6 years, $100 is worth $66	(Acc. total 474)
After 7 years, $100 is worth $61	(Acc. total 535)
After 8 years, $100 is worth $57	(Acc. total 593)
After 9 years, $100 is worth $53	(Acc. total 646)
After 10 years, $100 is worth $50	(Acc. total 696)
After 11 years, $100 is worth $47	(Acc. total 742)
After 12 years, $100 is worth $43	(Acc. total 786)
After 13 years, $100 is worth $41	(Acc. total 826)
After 14 years, $100 is worth $38	(Acc. total 864)
After 15 years, $100 is worth $35	(Acc. total 899)
After 20 years, $100 is worth $25	(Acc. total 1043)
After 25 years, $100 is worth $18	(Acc. total 1145)
After 50 years, $100 is worth $3	(Acc. total 1346)
After 75 years, $100 is worth $1	(Acc. total 1381)
After 100 years, $100 is worth $0	(Acc. total 1388)

FIG 3.2 The value of an income can be calculated by discounting the value of each payment back to the present day and totalling up these discounted values

any particular income: according to what values are assumed for the discount and inflation rates. Figure 3.3 shows how an income of $100 per annum might be valued assuming different discount rates.

discounting for risk Simply discounting back the value of income payments according to the interest expected from a safe investment does not allow for the element of risk. The discount rate has to be suitably

---

Valuations of $100 per annum income using different discount rates

At 5% – after 100 years, $100 is worth $1 (Acc. total 1985)

At 7.2% – after 100 years, $100 is worth $0 (Acc. total 1388)

At 10% – after 56 years, $100 is worth $0 (Acc. total 995)

At 15% – after 38 years, $100 is worth $0 (Acc. total 663)

At 20% – after 30 years, $100 is worth $0 (Acc. total 498)

At 50% – after 14 years, $100 is worth $0 (Acc. total 199)

At 100% – after 8 years, $100 is worth $0 (Acc. total 100)

FIG 3.3 The value of an income will be valued differently according to what discount rate is used. A discount rate of 5 per cent will value a $100 per annum income at $1,985, but at a discount rate of 50 per cent the value will be only $199

NOTE Any risk of loss can be allowed for in this way, simply by adjusting the future value. The fact that there is a risk of the money being stolen means that any expectation as to its future value cannot be as great as if it were locked up in the vaults of an impregnable bank. This lesser value is calculated by multiplying the future value by the probability that the money will not be stolen. So, if there is a 10 per cent chance of the money being stolen, there is a 90 per cent chance that it won't be stolen. The future value is then determined as being only 90 per cent of the full value of the money. It is these kinds of calculations that are used to calculate the future values of revenue streams and share price valuations.

chosen so as to allow for all possible risks in the particular investment under consideration.

Consider the example above, where there are two ways of saving money for ten years: under the mattress or safely invested. For the invested money, the risk will be minimal if the funds are put into safe and secure bonds. For the money put under the mattress there is the risk of theft or burglary. If there is a 10 per cent chance of the money under the mattress being stolen during the ten years, the effective value will be reduced by 10 per cent because there is only a 90 per cent chance of realizing the anticipated future amount at the end of the period.

Investors always have a standard on which to base their income valuations. This usually takes the form of a current market valuation placed on an income which is more or less guaranteed, i.e. long-term bonds of a large and stable government. This provides them with the market value of a relatively risk-free investment. Knowing the price of a risk-free investment enables them to adjust this price appropriately downwards to discount for any perceived risks in any riskier investments.

Risk can also be allowed for by adjusting the expectations of an income. As capital amounts can be converted into income equivalents, risks can be discounted by increasing the income required to justify a particular amount of investment. In other words, a higher rate of return would be needed to compensate for any added risk. This effectively increases the discount rate needed to be applied to the calculation of future values.

For example, if there were twice the risk, the investor would be discounting any projected income back at twice the rate. This can be seen from Figure 3.3. If an income of $100 per annum from a safe bond returning 5 per cent is valued at $1,985, then an investment with a 5 per cent risk would have to be discounted back at 10 per cent. So, the value of a $100 per year income with 5 per cent risk would be worth only $995: about half as much.

If the risks were judged such that there might be a 15 per cent chance of the projected income not being realized, then the discount rate for the projected income would need to be raised from 5 to 20 per cent, reducing the value of this riskier income to $498. It is by using this kind of calculation that an investor can look at the projected income of a business, assess the risk and so be able to give a valuation to the business.

This has great relevance to an investor's or a business angel's expectations of the returns they are looking for in an e-business venture. For example, the early dot coms that went on to be listed on the market had a failure rate of 80 per cent. If this risk factor is taken into account it would be madness for the valuation of any new dot com's projected earnings to be based on a 5 per cent discount rate. A more sensible view would use a discount rate of between 20 and 50 per cent. This would see an investor valuing a business with projected earnings of $1 million per annum at only between $5 million and $2 million. That is a P/E ratio (share price/ earnings ratio) of between 5 and 2.

It is these realistic valuations that would see venture capital companies and business angels appearing to be extremely greedy when it appears that they want to see their money returned within only two or three years. The fact is they are not being greedy at all; they are simply discounting appropriately for the risks involved in the investment. After all, if venture capital or angel finance didn't allow for the risks involved they would be far better off investing their money in safe government bonds.

the fallacies of conventional funding requirements Most

of the entrepreneurs who attended the NETPROZ event had gone there with a conventional idea of business start-ups and the requirements necessary to obtain funding.

The usual starting place for an e-business venture is with an idea. An idea is proposed and, like most ideas in e-business, would seem to have great merit with the potential to create much revenue and profit. The idea is fleshed out in outline with sufficient technical detail to provide credibility. A plan of action is described and the anticipated returns summarized.

Backing up this plan is a list of key personnel who will be responsible for carrying it out. This will include a strong management team with a sound previous track record of management, cost control and business organization.

On the strength of the plan and the pedigree of the key personnel, a sum of money will be allocated. The management team are then left to use this money to bring the project to fruition. This they will do by allocating various sums to the various components of the plan in order to complete the project within the specified time.

> THE DOT-COM BOOM AND BUST IN THE YEARS 2000 AND 2001 PROVED CONCLUSIVELY THAT GOOD IDEAS, CAREFULLY WORKED OUT BUSINESS PLANS AND STRONG MANAGEMENT IN THE VOLATILE WORLD OF E-BUSINESS DO NOT PRODUCE GOOD RESULTS

It all sounds so reasonable and logical, but the dot-com boom and bust in the years 2000 and 2001 proved conclusively that good ideas, carefully worked out business plans and strong management in the volatile world of e-business do not produce good results. Although there were several spectacular successes, there were even more spectacular failures.

It wasn't simply that some were doing it right and some were doing it wrong. The problem was that a new and rapidly evolving environment is totally unpredictable. Such dynamic complexity is chaotic and defies all logical attempts to predict or control events. Just like the fashion industry, people follow each other in chasing trends and fashions and when a trend or fashion peters out, it gives rise to a different trend or fashion. Whichever way you look at it, investing in any business venture in the field of e-business can be nothing more than a gamble.

Let's look more pragmatically at the criteria on which conventional funding is based.

business plans These cannot be anything other than totally unreliable guides as to the way in which an e-business will progress. There is too much uncertainty involved in the e-business environment, there are too many unknowns and unknowables. Technology is changing at such a fast rate that what seems a sensible plan can be rendered completely useless at any time by a competitor unexpectedly applying some new technology to come up with something cheaper or better.

Isn't it reasonable, then, for an astute investor to treat any future plans with extreme caution and heavily discount any projected earnings and profits?

proven strong management As fully explained in *The Ultimate Game of Strategy*, conventional managerial methods and techniques are totally inappropriate in a volatile, fast-moving environment where the necessity is to take advantage of change, rather than to try to control it. Executives and managers who have established their reputations in the more predict-able old-world economy are liable to hamper the necessary quick reactions and rapid changes that are needed to compete in a fast-changing techno-logical world.

This has been proved time and time again, as can be evidenced by the high proportion of dot-com failures. Despite most of them being funded on the basis of sensible-sounding business plans and apparently experienced managers and executives, the failure rate has been unacceptably high.

The fact is that many of the failures resulted from the business plans becoming irrelevant and the managers and executives being put into the position of the blind leading the blind. When things start to go wrong, panic sets in and vast sums of money are thrown to waste in desperate moves to try to regain control of the situation. Typical were the high expenditures on lavish but totally ineffective websites and the vast sums spent on inefficient advertising and marketing campaigns.

As with business plans, wouldn't an investor with the knowledge of the limitations of experienced management teams (to control the unpredictable events that are continuously being thrown up in an e-business environment) heavily discount for the probability of failure?

two kinds of player

There are two types of gamblers: the naïve punters and the professional players. The difference between the two is that the naïve punter tries to predict a winner and the professional player knows that prediction is impossible.

The naïve punter will sometimes back winners, but this will invariably be more by luck than judgement although they will be convinced that their astute ability to pick a winner gives them a special edge. Usually, their next plunge sees their vision and insight evaporating due to 'unforeseen circumstances'.

The professional player knows that it is impossible to pick winners, so will use a strategy that will allow for failure. Downside risks are limited and risk is spread over a number of options. More importantly, the professional player will allow for unpredictable change. The trick is to be in a position to take advantage of sudden and unpredictable events and not be exposed or vulnerable to them.

The professional poker player does not expect to win every hand; winning comes about through a statistical result of making the best of winning opportunities and not losing too much with the failures. The professional poker player does not make the best gains through being lucky with the initial cards that are dealt, but through taking advantage of favourable situations that develop during the course of the game. It is this 'professional gambler' mentality that is needed by both e-business investors and entrepreneurs.

Unfortunately for entrepreneurs seeking funding, the ability to change and adapt rapidly is not something that can be described in a business plan. It can only be identified after events have taken place. This is perhaps why the person who asked question 2 at the NETPROZ event had noticed that investors prefer to back serial entrepreneurs rather than placing their trust in first-timers.

looking for a sensible way to invest

Let's look for a moment at the more regular world of business funding, to see how investment decisions are made when working in a fairly stable and predictable business environment. In this world, business is about rational decision making; doing the right things. The strategy is concerned mainly with reducing risk and eliminating uncertainty. Monitoring and control are the main methods for keeping a business on track to meet targets and reach designated goals.

In a reasonably predictable environment, it is possible to estimate roughly how long it will take to complete a project and how much it will cost. In this way a funding body can have an idea of how much they will have to invest and what gains are possible. By suitably discounting for time and risk they can make an investment decision to fund or not to fund.

This situation is illustrated in Figure 3.4, where funding or investment decisions are founded on facts and figures based on experience and carefully researched projections. The ability to make reasonably accurate future predictions means that the risk of failure does not have to be heavily discounted in estimating future profitability.

In a stable and predictable environment, where future projections can be made with some degree of accuracy, a company does not need to forecast exceptional profits to attract funding. All that matters is that there is enough future profit forecast to cover any possible downside risk. The more predictable the environment, the less are the risks and the less the anticipated future profits need to be to cover those risks.

However, in the volatile and unpredictable environment of e-business, the risks associated with reaching an intended goal are much greater. There are too many unknowns. This means that there has to be a far greater allowance made for the risks, and in most cases the discounts that

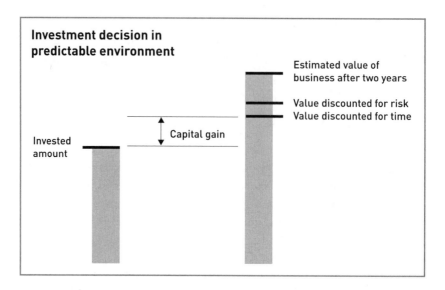

FIG 3.4 In a reasonably stable environment, the value of the anticipated future value will not have to be too heavily discounted. This lessens the pressure on a business to produce exceptional earnings

have to be applied to estimates of future earnings reduce the estimated future value of a business so much that, although on paper the investment would appear to be profitable, the realities of the investment decision process make it an unsound investment. This is illustrated in Figure 3.5.

Figure 3.5 shows graphically how a business that would appear to offer an investor a chance of a very handsome capital gain would actually be a poor investment choice – once the risks and time to realize the gain are taken into account.

The reason why it should be rated as a poor investment decision is not obvious. So, it's worth pausing a moment here to go through a few pragmatic, investment decision calculations.

calculating an investment decision

While visiting California in January 2001, I decided to call in on a company that I'd learned had a

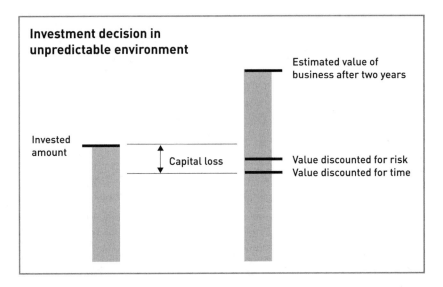

FIG 3.5 The added risks associated with an uncertain and volatile environment can reduce the value of a seemingly promising business venture to a point where it would be considered a loss-making investment

neat little product that supplied an excellent messaging and bulletin board system. Expecting the company to consist of a handful of dedicated technologists, I was amazed when I walked into sumptuous offices with hordes of employees.

What I'd discovered was one of the fabled dot coms, a company that had acquired $10 million of venture capital funding within a year of start-up. From the original two founding partners, the company had expanded to a staff of around 50 people that now included some very high profile sales and marketing executives together with many illustrious technical experts. The company looked very busy and were justifiably proud of their growing customer base. To all the world it looked like a successful company that seemed likely to be satisfying the requirements of the venture capital company that had organized their funding.

However, if we go back in time to when a decision was made to fund this company, we can go through some of the calculations that might have been made. Firstly, we'd look at what the $10 million might have returned as a less speculative investment. Let's say it could have been invested fairly safely by spreading the capital around many different established companies to provide an average return of 7.2 per cent. That is $720,000 per annum.

The investors would be looking to better this return significantly to be able to justify the risk in investing in an unproven venture. However, it would be accepted that such profitability would take some time to materialize. Let's say this time would have been estimated to be three years: not an unreasonable projection.

With the investment not expected to reach this level of profitability for three years, the value of the investment at that future time would have to be discounted back to be able to compare it with the present-day value of the $10 million. From Figure 3.2, we can see that every $100 is reduced by 19 per cent when discounted back at 7.2 per cent over three years. This would mean that the value of an investment of $10 million must rise to $12,345,679 in three years' time just to keep pace with a fairly safe investment.

In terms of an earnings target for the company, it would mean that the break-even profitability of the company would have to be increased from $720,000 per annum to $890,000 per annum – just to equal the returns from a safe investment.

As the investor would be looking to see a reasonable gain by choosing to invest in risky ventures, it is most likely that the aim would be more like a minimum of $1.2 million per annum earnings – increasing the value of the investment by about a third. However, this extra return would be an acceptable target only if the profitability actually materialized. In reality, the company might fail, so the risk of the company failing to make this profit has to be taken into consideration.

At the time the $10 million was invested in this dot-com company in California, investors were investing in hundreds of other similarly promising e-business start-ups – each of which the investors might have been confident in expecting to succeed in reaching a suitable level of profitability.

As was subsequently revealed, the failure rate of the dot-com start-ups was of the order of 80 per cent. Only one in five was reaching profitability before their capital ran out. If this risk element had been factored in when the decision was made to invest $10 million in this Californian start-up, the investors would have been looking to see a profitability of five times that $1.2 million: about $6 million per annum to sensibly justify their investment decision.

To make sense of this $6 million figure, imagine the investors spreading their risk by investing not in a single company but dividing up the $10 million to take shares in many dot coms. With four out of five dot coms failing, $8 million of the $10 million would have been lost, so the remaining $2 million of surviving investments would have to earn five times as much to make up for the lost earnings of the losers.

In theory, it may seem possible for a company to earn $6 million per annum in profits. However, the reality is that any business that is making substantial profits will attract competitors. This competition will compete aggressively for clients, not only winning clients over to them but also raising the cost of attracting new clients. This competitive activity effectively puts a cap on the profitability that any company can realistically expect to achieve.

It is like any market situation. If a store starts to earn huge profits by selling a particular item, it won't be long before other stores will be selling it. As they compete with each other for customers, the price will be driven down so that the level of profitability gradually gets in line with all other items that are on sale.

After visiting the dot-com start-up in California, I used various search engines on the web to trace the company's activities as they had been reported in various news media. I found a brief history that explained how the core product had grown out of a university bulletin board system that one of the founders had created. Another of the founders was an experienced deal maker, who had wide connections with venture capital companies in the USA.

The company had acquired an impressive list of executives that included

Vice President of Marketing/Operations, Vice President of Engineering, Vice President of Sales, Director of Business Development, Director of Product Management, Director of Quality Assurance. The board of directors included an impressive list of CEOs from the many different companies that had syndicated in the funding. At a guess I'd say this company was running with an overhead of something like $4 million per annum, in which case they would have to be trying to obtain an income of at least $5million a year – which runs out at about $420,000 a month.

When I read through the impressive-looking list of executives and directors, the thought that ran through my mind was 'too many fingers in the pie'. It certainly didn't look like the lean and adaptive kind of organization that was needed in a rapidly evolving, massively connected information environment. Sure they had a great product, but it wasn't so great that it couldn't be copied by hundreds of other competent companies that had far fewer overheads and without the ball and chain of $10 million worth of investment that needed servicing.

They may have had a great sales team, they may have had hundreds of current clients, but they were highly vulnerable to other companies being able to offer a similar product – at far less cost – to a market that their $10 million of funding had created. What hadn't seemed to have been realized was that the internet isn't like the world of bricks and mortar where a product is established only by a strong sales force. The competition is just one click away and the ease with which the knowledge of less costly solutions can so easily diffuse through the internet community means that everyone will soon know where that click is.

❝ THE COMPETITION IS JUST ONE CLICK AWAY ❞

This is not to predict that the company I visited will fail, but it's not one that I'd be queuing up to invest in.

a more realistic strategy for e-business funding
In light of fundamental investment calculations, it becomes clear that investments in early-stage e-business ventures involve risks that are unlikely to be compensated by even the most optimistic return expectations. Without a bubble situation, where a naïve speculator can sell to an even more

naïve speculator as equity prices increase beyond reason, investment cannot be justified.

This situation calls for a radical rethink about the funding of e-businesses that are in the early stages of development. A way has to be found where the funding body is not exposed to such high risks. Such a way is possible if we start out with the premise that an investor's capital is sacrosanct and must be preserved at all costs.

This would give an entirely different perspective to funding e-business start-ups. How, though, could an investor's capital be totally preserved when used in such a high-risk situation, where fast-evolving technology and predatory competition make life so uncertain and unpredictable?

Let's consider the question of the preservation of capital first. The only way capital can be preserved is to invest it in safe securities. So, let's start with this idea. Instead of putting a capital sum into an e-business venture, why not invest the money safely and then let the e-business use the returns from the safe investment to fund its cash flow while it is trying to establish profitability?

Let's take an example of an investment company with $100 million to invest, which wants to use 10 per cent of this money to have an interest in e-commerce. We could imagine that all the money is invested safely to provide 7.2 per cent earnings, but 10 per cent of those earnings are allocated to financing the cash flow of an e-business start-up.

If we take the same figures as the investment in the Californian dot com described above, the $10 million earmarked to finance the cash flow of an e-business venture would provide $720,000 per annum of cash flow to finance the business. This works out at $60,000 per month, as illustrated in Figure 3.6.

This arrangement preserves the capital base and gives control to the investors who can limit their losses at any time by terminating the cash flow injection if the e-business isn't showing signs of meeting expectations.

This dramatically changes the situation, not only for the investment company but also for the e-business venture. The e-business may lose the

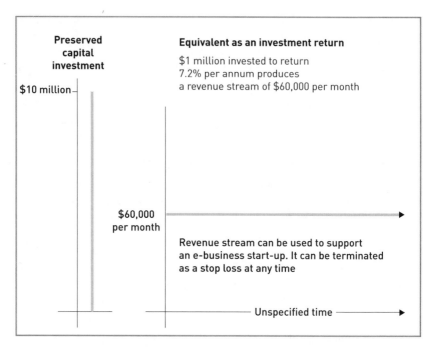

Preserved capital investment

$10 million

$60,000 per month

Equivalent as an investment return

$1 million invested to return 7.2% per annum produces a revenue stream of $60,000 per month

Revenue stream can be used to support an e-business start-up. It can be terminated as a stop loss at any time

Unspecified time

FIG 3.6 A capital sum of $10 million can be invested safely to preserve the capital and the income generated from the earnings used to fund the cash flow of a start-up e-business venture

strategic advantage of having a large sum of money to play with, but it also means that they are no longer accountable for the safety of a large sum of money. This allows for a more efficient management structure that is concerned only with developing a profitable situation – eliminating the need for the kind of costly executives that would be needed purely to safeguard the large capital base. This cash flow funding arrangement is illustrated in Figure 3.7.

Notice from Figure 3.7 that the cash flow input, needed to finance the business, starts to reduce as soon as the business begins to generate its own revenue. When critical mass is reached, where the profitability can cover the outgoings, no further input from the funding company will be needed. Any further profitability will generate an income which will create a capital gain. As soon as the capitalized value of this profit

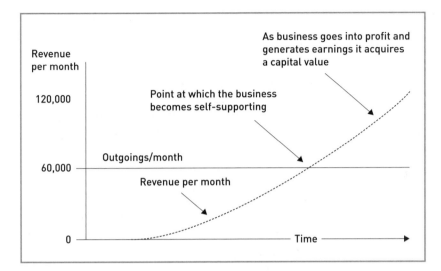

As business goes into profit and generates earnings it acquires a capital value

Revenue per month

120,000

Point at which the business becomes self-supporting

Outgoings/month

60,000

Revenue per month

0

Time

FIG 3.7 Where a company is having its cash flow financed, any revenues generated will reduce the amount of funding needed. All being well, revenues will increase to where the company reaches a stage of overall profitability and acquires a real capital value

exceeds the cash that has been injected into the company, the investing company will start to make real gains.

comparing the two ways of financing a start-up

Providing a company with $10 million of capital needs an experienced and professional team to handle the finances. This will greatly increase the overheads without necessarily improving a company's ability to reach profitability. Mistakes can be costly and if the company loses its way, it can easily start wasting large sums of money on inappropriate strategies while it is seeking to recover its position. This was a notable feature of the many failed dot coms, where huge sums were spent on ineffective advertising and marketing.

With a large capital available, companies are tempted to design grandiose schemes that might be found to be fatally flawed only after most of the capital has been burned up. Again this was a common occurrence among the dot-com casualties.

Working with a limited cash flow concentrates attention on inputs and outputs. Any large-scale project or extensive advertising and marketing would have to be financed out of earnings. This may seem restrictive, but with so many unknowns and so much unpredictability in the world of e-business, gambling on outcomes would expose the company to risks that would not be adequately covered by the probability of gains.

Let's take the company in California as an example. They have been forced to take on board a large number of chief executives. Their burn rate is so high that they are forced to go for ambitious sales targets. Perhaps it will pay off for them before their cash runs out, but the statistical odds against their survival are high.

Far better if the team had been kept small, limited to an overhead of $60,000 a month until success brought them profitability and gave them the cash flow to expand through their earned income. Then their target would have been to produce a revenue better than $720,000 per annum rather than the $5 million they were being forced to aim for when I visited the company.

Maybe they could argue that they would have a better chance of achieving a revenue of $5 million a year with a large staff and greater overheads than a more compact organization could have of achieving a revenue of $720,000 per annum. This brings us to the question of efficiency. E-business is not only about having great ideas: more importantly, it is about increased efficiency. In other words, it is about reducing the cost of getting something done. This must be the overriding consideration at the heart of all e-business strategies.

The speed with which people and businesses can learn about more efficient ways to satisfy needs makes it imperative for e-businesses to be able to respond, change and adapt. This can be taken to mean that the e-business will be in a continuous process of dynamic change as cheaper, more efficient ways to achieve goals emerge. This can be done more efficiently with a small group that is not encumbered by a top-heavy management structure.

Many companies rely on patents and intellectual rights to safeguard them against competition. However, the idea that a company can rely on patents in technology and business procedures is a fool's paradise in a rapidly evolving environment where new technological breakthroughs are occurring all the time. In a provocative article in *New Scientist*, 20 January 2001, Robert Matthews described the work of John Koza at Stanford University who is using genetic algorithms not only to evolve solutions to difficult design problems but also to evolve better ways to think about solving them.

The principle of using genetic algorithms for design solutions is to break up all previous solutions into components. Then, from the results achieved by these previous solutions, choose the best and combine their various components in different ways. These hybrid solutions are then tested and the components of the best of these are combined yet again. This process is continuously repeated until a superior product emerges. In numerous instances, in various companies in various industries, this technique is regularly delivering solutions to problems that are surpassing anything that humans have come up with before.

This is the way biological evolution works, where superior genes of successful organisms are selected for and recombined in different individuals. This has been the driving force behind all industrial and technological progress, as people take the best ideas of what others have done to come up with superior solutions.

This is happening all the time in the environment of e-business where the best of some ideas are combined with the best of others for a business to leap ahead of its competition. The internet and the web thus provide a vast environment where genetic algorithms are unconsciously being used by millions of people in their competition with each other to produce superior e-business solutions.

Of particular interest in Robert Matthews' article was his warning to inventors that they will no longer be protected by their patents as genetic algorithm design techniques become more widespread. Normally, a designer will check with patents to make sure that any design they come up with does not include features that have been patented by somebody else. For a genetic algorithm this is not a problem because details of patented ideas can be programmed into the selection process so that they are not included in selected solutions which are used to breed new ideas. In other words, genetic algorithms skirt round patented ideas and seek superior solutions that make these patented ideas redundant.

Now it may be stretching the imagination somewhat to imagine contrived genetic algorithms being designed to do this on any large scale just yet, but if one looks at the millions of people involved in e-business, each looking at each other's best ideas and combining them with their own in a multitude of different ways, it becomes obvious that the whole evolution of the internet environment consists of a vast number of genetic algorithms at work: seeking more and more efficient solutions to problems and bypassing any patents that stand in the way.

> IT BECOMES OBVIOUS THAT THE WHOLE EVOLUTION OF THE INTERNET ENVIRONMENT CONSISTS OF A VAST NUMBER OF GENETIC ALGORITHMS AT WORK

It is this picture that any person involved in e-business has to have in mind. It is the picture the business angels, venture capitalists and investors have to think about when they think about backing any particular venture based on what seems like a good idea.

The fact is that e-business is a dynamic environment, where survival and success can only be achieved through being able to change and adapt continuously. For this, ideas are very secondary; what is more important is people: people who are able to use the internet to make contact with others to share information and knowledge and to collaborate and combine.

So, my advice to anyone wanting to invest in e-business is to look beyond ideas and knowledge and to concentrate on the super individuals who have developed superior abilities and techniques of communication. As is so often true in business: it isn't what you know but who you know that counts.

the efficient structuring of an e-business
This insight into the arcane world of investment decision making allows us to approach the creation of an e-business in a more professional manner. It might be

of benefit to the reader to read through once more the questions presented to the panel at the NETPROZ event. How would you answer those questions now?

From the point of view of the purpose of this book, these investment considerations tell us that it is no good devising involved and detailed schemes that require massive funding. Even in the unlikely event that it will be granted, the business would be laden down with an inappropriate management structure that will demand excessively high targets and reduce flexibility.

What we need to look for is a way to create a highly flexible system that has minimal overheads. We must seek situations and opportunities that can quickly produce revenue streams. We must construct a business based on expendable components that can be selected from, mixed and matched in different ways to deal with new emerging opportunities and rapidly changing circumstances.

Above all, we should be looking to create many strategic contacts, who can be brought into play when and where needed.

In my experience, as a life-long entrepreneur, the solution to the funding problem is not to look for funding, but to let the funding look for you. The moment you start showing signs of making a profit, the financiers and investors will appear like magic – out of the woodwork.

ABSTRACT
CONCEPTUAL
MODELS

THIS PART OF THE BOOK DEALS WITH the most hazardous area of the Information Age: the vast amount of changing technological knowledge and information. This causes knowledge gaps, which impair the ability to use logical reasoning. It leads to fashions and trends where the blind are leading the blind. The only way of coping with this difficulty is to work within abstract conceptual models that can override all the technicalities that cloud strategic decision making – making it possible to maintain a firm grip on the fundamentals.

Chapter 4 looks at the way in which entrepreneurs explore opportunities. It explains why ideas are of much lesser importance than the means to implement them. It describes how business opportunities can emerge as a consequence of exploring the unknown.

In a world of too much knowledge and too much change, it is not what you know but who you know that is important. Chapter 4 also looks at the conceptual models necessary to create a personal community of useful contacts and to form strategic associations with people who can take care of situations outside your own areas of speciality knowledge.

To avoid the trap of getting bogged down with too much technological detail, web presence is viewed in the light of a useful mental model of the internet.

Chapter 5 visualizes the web as a system of interacting objects, where a website is seen as a tool that provides an efficient interface to the internet. It deals with the difficulty of getting noticed on the web, providing a conceptual framework that sees the environment of the internet as a system of interacting portals and vortals.

It stresses the need to be part of a system, describing the world of e-business as a self-organizing environment that is driven by constant competitive pressures.

Chapter 6 gives an even more abstract view of the e-business environment. Instead of seeing e-businesses in terms of structured forms, fixed physical locations, managed organization and definable assets, it sees them as more nebulous entities: as functions within a rapidly changing, universal dynamic system. From this perspective, it becomes apparent that the most likely route to creating successful e-business isn't through adapting new technology to established business practices, but through using the communication environment to produce solutions that have no parallel in the everyday world.

Visualizing activity within a space – a system space, or an information space – helps devise novel strategies of communication, organization and control to provide low-cost, highly flexible systems that can survive and prosper in highly competitive situations during volatile economic conditions.

4

SEARCHING FOR AN
OPPORTUNITY

a question of strategy The last chapter illustrated by way of
simple financial calculations that large sums of money thrown at the
problem of finding an e-business solution in the chaotic environment of
the internet are largely wasted. From an investor's viewpoint this is not
only off-putting, it can be a convincing argument for them not to invest
at all.

However, the advantages of finding and exploiting the enormous potential
of the digital communication environment are only too obvious. This
presents a paradox: it is not profitable to invest in e-businesses, but there
are numerous opportunities for making a profit. The resolution of this
paradox is to think in terms of strategies.

Most people, when asked to name a game of strategy, will answer,
'chess'. This fits in nicely with the conception of strategy as it was
envisaged in the Industrial Age. It is a game where there are many
options, each of which can be countered by an opponent, and the way to
win is to be better than your opponent at seeing ahead. Working out all
the possible moves that are available to both players over a sequence of
moves is the key to a winning strategy.

Computer programs designed to play chess use this strategy to win against human opponents. They can rapidly analyze the alternatives and consequences of millions of possible moves and thus keep ahead of a human who has far less ability to deal with so many possibilities.

The only reason why a computer can be programmed to beat a human at chess is because the environment of the chess game is unique. All the information that is needed to plan ahead is available on the board. Apart from competitive moves, all possibilities are known and, by assuming an opponent plays logically, even these competitor moves are predictable.

In the industrial world of the twentieth century, business strategies could be similar to chess-playing strategies. With the aid of statistics, probability and market research, business strategists could have a pretty accurate idea of what the future holds and be able to make optimum choices from a range of possibilities.

In the chaotic environment of the Information Age, the future is not predictable. Using conventional Industrial Age business strategies is much like a computer program having to play chess when it is only allowed to see the positions of a few of the pieces on the board. In such a situation, a conventional, chess-type strategy is totally useless.

Human brains have evolved to deal with uncertain and incomplete information. Unlike chess-playing computer programs, humans don't examine every possible alternative way the future can unfold. Unconsciously, the human brain ignores most possibilities and gambles on just a few of the most likely scenarios. This strategy relies on an ability to respond rapidly if things go wrong because logical reasoning cannot be used to anticipate and avoid unfavourable future events.

Philip Johnson-Laird, a psychology professor at Princeton University, has been working for over a decade to prove that humans do not naturally use logical reasoning and rational rules to make decisions. He concedes that humans are capable of using this method of deduction to think problems through and make strategic decisions, but he claims that this is only a relatively recent evolutionary feature brought about by the conditions prevalent in an ordered society.

Johnson-Laird believes it is more natural for humans to carry a rough model in their heads rather than pursuing every possibility through to its logical conclusion. To explain this, he devised a simple little puzzle:

Only one of these statements is true:

1   There is a king in the hand, or an ace, or both.

2   There is a queen in the hand, or an ace, or both.

3   There is a jack in the hand, or an ace, or both.

Is it possible that there is an ace in the hand?

Most humans would answer 'Yes', but a computer logically programmed to solve this puzzle would give the correct answer and say, 'No'.

Johnson-Laird explains that humans get the wrong answer because they have a limited space in what is called 'working memory', the area of the brain that deals with logical reasoning. When this memory is overloaded with too many possibilities, it leaves out part of the information, sometimes resulting in an inaccurate mental model.

The brain decides what to leave out by ignoring information that throws up ambiguity. For example, being told that the statement 'Oliver is clever and Elliot is stupid' is false throws up many alternative possibilities. The brain tends to ignore this kind of statement because the processing involved in examining all the possible meanings uses up too much working memory.

In the puzzle above, the brain unconsciously recognizes the complexity involved in considering falsities, so will ignore the fact that only one of the statements can be true. A more pedantic reasoning process would observe that if there is an ace in the hand the first two statements must be true, and as it was specifically stated that only one of the statements is true then it isn't possible for there to be an ace in the hand.

The observations of Johnson-Laird, based on testing many variations of this puzzle on students, seem to indicate that the human brain has evolved to sacrifice accuracy for the sake of expediency. When quick decisions have to be made there isn't time to consider the consequence of every action. In this process, falsity considerations are often ignored. This throws some light on the strategy preferred by evolution. Our brains would have evolved greater processing power if this had been essential. Instead, the survival of the most successful resulted in brain mechanisms that went for expediency.

It is this more natural strategy that is characteristic of entrepreneurs working in a new and changing environment. If they stopped to examine every possible consequence of their actions, they'd never progress. Instead, they ignore uncertainties and unknowns and make initiatives based on conceptual models that do not contain specific detail.

In one sense, the entrepreneur is in the same position as an investor: being unable to avoid mistakes and errors of judgement. But by using an appropriate strategy, the mistakes and errors can result in little cost that will be more than compensated by gains. The way an entrepreneur does this is to:

1   work with non-detailed conceptual models;

2   maintain low overheads;

3   create multiple opportunities;

4   establish a variety of strategic contacts;

5   not get locked into single fixed ideas;

6   think in terms of reconfigurable components that can be used in a variety of situations.

In this way, an entrepreneur can remain flexible enough to weave around any setbacks and misjudgements that would bring more carefully planned projects to a jarring halt.

To illustrate how reasoning and logical analysis can handicap an entre-preneur, we might consider two of the most important areas of business: ideas and trust. Ideas abound in a fertile entrepreneurial mind, but if every idea was thoroughly thought through, to examine every possible problem and consequence, none of the ideas would ever be put into practice. Similarly with trust. If an entrepreneur had to check up on everyone they had dealings with before forming an alliance or association, their progress would be too slow to be able to respond quickly to opportunities.

ideas and trust
The first chapter described the concept of the virtual café, which is a conceptual device for communicating and collaborating with a variety of contacts. One of the collaborators in the café commented:

A question about how the e-business ideas will develop. I'm sure every collaborator could come up with an idea right now, but if starting out with one good idea is not the way forward, will 50 ideas be better? Also (and this is very traditional business in thought) are we comfortable enough to offer ideas at this point? I mean, has a relationship of mutual trust been created yet?

Katherin Ekstrom

These two points have been covered in the first two books in this trilogy. Firstly, starting with specific business ideas is very limiting. Secondly, we have to assume that we can't trust anyone else. Let's recap here.

initial ideas
The first book in the trilogy, *The Entrepreneurial Web*, proposed starting any e-business venture with a green frog. This green frog is the business idea and the business plan. Of course, this represents something ludicrous. How can a serious e-business be started with nothing more in mind than a green frog?

The point is that it is better than having a fixed idea or a business plan because you have no preconceived notions. An e-business can emerge more easily out of a green frog because you are forced to start from first principles, allowing ideas and opportunities to emerge without the danger of being sidelined into dead-ends or handicapped by knowledge gaps.

Starting with an e-business idea and a plan is much like having a great design for a house and then trying to build it on quicksands. The sensible place to start is to look for solid ground and then build firm foundations. It is only then that the design of the house becomes relevant.

The idea of starting literally with a green frog is a way of being able to avoid a stereotyped way of thinking. Following what everyone else is doing or thinking either gives you unnecessary competitive pressure or sees you following the lemmings over the cliff. Stereotyped thinking is not the way to find a breakthrough into a novel way of doing business.

trust This was dealt with in the second book of this trilogy, *The Ultimate Game of Strategy*. The conventional notion of trust, as it is understood in the world of bricks and mortar, has no relevance in e-business. In its place is the notion of 'playing the game intelligently'. This means that although you might not have any basis for trusting somebody in the conventional sense, you may be able to trust them to act rationally in their own best interests.

> THE CONVENTIONAL NOTION OF TRUST, AS IT IS UNDERSTOOD IN THE WORLD OF BRICKS AND MORTAR, HAS NO RELEVANCE IN E-BUSINESS

By assuming that people are going to act selfishly, you know where you stand. You can predict what actions they should take to act in their own best interests and in this sense they will act reliably. This is much better than not being sure whether or not you can trust somebody.

This different form of trust assumes everyone will renege on a deal, steal a march, take your ideas for themselves, copy what you are doing, etc. if it is beneficial for them to do so. If this is assumed to be a legitimate way for others to play the game then the best strategy is to so structure your e-business dealings that it would not be in their best interests to do such things.

A little trick I learned from a shrewd old Jewish milliner was to give people a chance to cheat early in a relationship. If they cheated her when she gave them the opportunity to do so, she would consider it a small premium to pay for a little insight into their character. It paid her to find out early in a relationship because it might save her from being at a greater risk of loss later, when dealings might be more substantial. It didn't stop her doing business with the cheaters though, she just dealt with them differently.

The question of trust in e-business is a calculated risk based on the perceived relative values of the immediate gain of the cheat balanced against the loss of potential gains they might have by not cheating.

In the particular case of the collaborators involved in this book, the gains and losses of the 50 people have to be individually assessed on the basis of whether it will be more profitable for them to leave the group and run by themselves with any emergent opportunity, or whether it will be more profitable for them to develop an emerging opportunity within the group.

This is another reason why ideas are not appropriate at an early stage in creating an e-business; people can steal or copy ideas, especially if the ideas are any good. Better for ideas to emerge after valuable relationships have been established; then the cost of running off with an idea has to be balanced against the cost of losing the relationship. Ideas are cheap and plentiful, but relationships cost time and effort to establish.

The thought that you can work without ideas and without trust or loyalty will seem utterly bizarre to most people. The trick is to realize that the e-business environment is about connectiveness and dynamic systems. Products, services and businesses are not isolated separate entities. They are all part of a whole where each part is dependent upon many other parts.

The individual, the isolationist, is at an extreme disadvantage because in any dynamic system the whole is worth much more than the sum of the parts. In a relatively simple world, people can offer a product or service which is complete in itself. They can be self-contained and self-sufficient. In a highly complex, interconnected environment such as the internet, business or personal contributions are mostly only a very small component of a much larger and often incomprehensible higher order of natural organization.

The benefits of being included within a system of many others are likely to be far greater than striking out alone. This knowledge provides a good reason for collaborators to remain with a group rather than cutting and running. Ideas are plentiful, but links into a system of people are much harder to acquire.

It also gives a clue as to what we should start looking for in an e-business opportunity. We should be searching to find or create a system to join. As a foundation, this would be far more valuable than simply a novel idea.

what are we looking for?

In 1999, Bill Gates gave an in-depth interview for the first time to a UK television station. For many people in the UK computer industry, this broadcast was eagerly awaited. Here was the most successful exploiter of computer technology in the world, setting out his views. What gems of wisdom would be forthcoming? What vital clues might he reveal that would point to a new direction forward?

The day following the broadcast there were discussions on most of the UK e-mail discussion forums that I belonged to, analyzing what he had said in the interview. The general consensus was that he'd disclosed no useful information at all. The whole interview had seemed to most people to be banal and completely lacking in any useful information or knowledge.

I was totally amazed by this reaction because it had seemed to me that Bill Gates had summed up, in a nutshell, his entire strategy for success. It was so simple, so obvious, that most people had missed the significance. They had been looking for something clever, something that only a super brain could have thought of. In fact, it wasn't anything like this at all: it was just plain common sense.

Bill Gates had explained to the interviewer that Microsoft had created an environment. Then, in trying to make full use of that environment, they had designed tools for themselves. Other people wanting to explore and exploit this same environment would also have use of these tools. These people became customers.

The important clue this revealed was that Bill Gates saw his success in terms of pioneering and finding out for himself what could be achieved rather than trying to work out what other people wanted. It was a reasonable assumption that the tools he found necessary to develop for himself would also be needed by others.

This, then, is another pointer to a way of discovering an e-business opportunity. We simply explore an environment. The tools or methods we need to create along the way may lead to a revenue-generating situation. As Bill Gates discovered, it is inefficient for people to reinvent the wheel; if somebody has already discovered some time-saving method or application, others will be willing to pay a small price to acquire that same advantage.

As a metaphor, we might think of America in the seventeenth and eighteenth centuries. Settlers arriving from Europe would have found a land of potentially unlimited opportunity. But their first problem would have been where to travel in order to find the best place to settle. They would have needed maps, guides, transportation, tools and provisions. The earliest pioneers, the explorers, would have been in the best position to know what was wanted and to be able to provide these services, thus they would have been able to profit as a result of their pioneering experiences.

The first settlers arriving in America wouldn't have been sensible to have set off alone. They would have travelled with many others. In this way, they could get help from each other with any problems that came along. They would each have needed a variety of services and these could only come from within a community.

When the settlers found an appropriate place to settle, they would have needed to settle as a community, each taking up a necessary niche to cater for a particular aspect of the community's needs. In this way it can be visualized that it is the community that is the key to everyone's success and everyone contributes to and feeds off its strength. Yet, at the same time, everyone can be independent and free to act on their own initiative.

The internet is much like the unexplored Americas. We need maps, guides and tools. We will have great difficulty in going alone so we need to look for travelling companions who can provide assistance or speciality help as it is needed. In short, everyone needs to be part of a collaborative community. Thus, this should be the first consideration when starting to look for an e-business opportunity.

the self-centred virtual community
Communities are usually thought of as being based on trust and loyalties. But these are not relevant in an e-business environment because it has to be assumed that everyone will be looking out only for themselves and will help others only if it is in their interest to do so.

What kind of community can be created on this basis? To solve this problem we have to tear up our idea of what a community is in the world of bricks and mortar and create a more practical version for the world of e-business.

The conventional idea of a community is that it provides an environment where people are tied together through a common set of rules and protocols. These rules and protocols override personal idiosyncrasies and there is great pressure on all individuals to obey implicit or explicit common codes of conduct. This is illustrated in Figure 4.1.

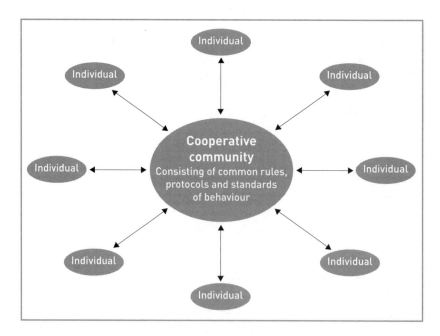

FIG 4.1 Conventional communities are based on implicit or explicit common rules and understanding

A conventional community in the world of bricks and mortar would see the individual as being subservient to the community as a whole. Individuals would have to observe common protocols and rules of behaviour and would not be expected to seek special privilege or advantage over anyone else. This also holds true in most e-mail discussion forums.

Outside of the e-mail discussion forums, individuals on the internet are free to create their own virtual groups by establishing relationships with a number of other people. This is much like the strategy of an entrepreneur cultivating a number of key contacts, a salesperson building a list of important clients or a contractor with a list of subcontractors.

This is a very different type of group from the conventional idea of a community because the individual who creates the group is effectively at the focal point of the group of contacts he or she establishes. Yet, in the environment of the internet this kind of group has to be treated as part of the community because of the massive connectivity.

It has to be appreciated here that the person who creates a group of personal contacts isn't the leader of that group any more than a salesperson is the leader of the clients on his or her list of clients. The person who creates the group simply provides a personal concentration of communication, a local hot spot, in a vast network of interactivity.

It is probable that when someone forms such a group around themselves every person in their group of contacts has also formed a group. This would allow for everyone in a network to be both at the centre of their own group and also at the periphery of many others. In diagrammatic form, a system of interconnected self-centred groups would look like Figure 4.2. In this figure, everyone is at the centre of a local group of eight contacts, yet, at the same time, they are also on the periphery of eight groups where other people are the focal point.

An example of a hot spot of communication is the collaborative group assembled together in the virtual café for the purpose of this book. To the author, these are 50 people focused on his project, but to each of the people taking part in the café discussions, this is just one of many different communication activities they will be party to.

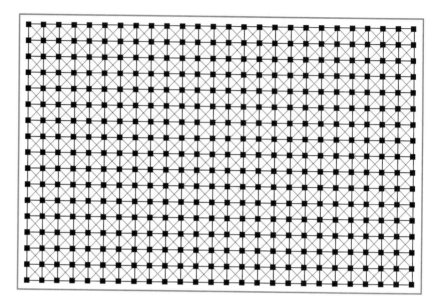

FIG 4.2 People can simultaneously be at the centre of focus of one group, yet, through the same contacts, be on the periphery of other groups where other people are the centre of focus

The bond that holds these individual centred groups together is usually information exchange. By sharing knowledge and information, individuals can form strong bonds with many others, especially where they can provide vital or strategic information to the people they have bonded with. In return, the individuals will have on hand accessibility to the knowledge of their virtual group of contacts and will be able to rely on them to cover some of their own knowledge gaps or skill weaknesses.

The advantage of the internet environment is that contact is not limited to one-to-one conversations. Groups of personal contacts can be gathered together for discussions. The nearest simile to this situation, in the world of bricks and mortar, is dinner parties, where groups of friends or business colleagues are invited along for an evening to exchange information, views and opinions.

The virtual café is the online equivalent of a dinner party. Special guests are invited along for a short period of discussion. Interesting guests are invited back, boring guests are not invited again. In this way, everyone running their own virtual cafés will gradually improve the quality of their own dinner parties.

The advantage of running such discussions in the environment of the internet is that many of them can be run simultaneously. Also, it is possible to be at more than one discussion at the same time. Imagine being able to hold different dinner parties in every room of your house and, at the same time, be present at them all.

Imagine each of your guests also being at home having dinner parties of their own with you as one of their guests, while at the same time having a discussion with your group at your dinner party. This can happen in the environment of the internet. Is it any wonder that it takes some people such a long time to wrap their heads around the possibilities available on the internet?

NOTE More detailed explanations of groups and cafés are contained in the second book in this trilogy, *The Ultimate Game of Strategy*.

becoming a super individual

By creating a group of useful contacts around themselves, individuals will effectively become more knowledgeable, capable and aware. Through the exchange of information and through collaborative associations, they can enhance personal abilities, perhaps to the point where they become super individuals, able to vastly increase their natural capabilities. This is illustrated in Figure 4.3.

By building up a virtual community of contacts with whom they are exchanging useful information and knowledge, an individual can effectively become a super individual because he or she can draw on the knowledge and skill sets of this personally created community. The bonding is through the mutual exchange of information, knowledge and help.

In the world of bricks and mortar, there are practical limitations to the number of contacts that can be maintained and the extent of information that can be readily accessed and exchanged. In the world of the internet, the ease and low cost of maintaining contact with many others allow a wide variety of information and knowledge sources to be established. Figure 4.4 illustrates the make-up of a typical super individual who makes

" IMAGINE BEING ABLE TO HOLD DIFFERENT DINNER PARTIES IN EVERY ROOM OF YOUR HOUSE AND, AT THE SAME TIME, BE PRESENT AT THEM ALL "

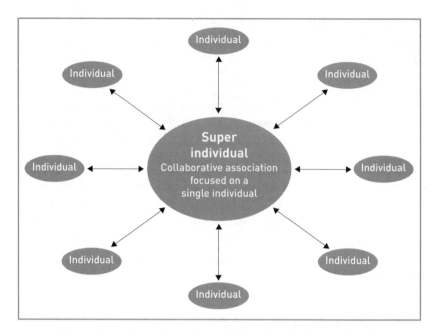

FIG 4.3 Through creating a group of personal associations where there are information exchanges and implicit understandings of mutual collaboration, an individual can effectively become a super individual

full use of the internet. His or her personal power and capability are greatly enhanced through a number of different channels.

Individuals taking full advantage of the internet to enhance their knowledge and capabilities will effectively gain power and influence. In the world of bricks and mortar such a strategy would be treated with suspicion because it may be viewed in the context of some kind of pecking order – where everyone, even close colleagues, could be regarded as potential rivals or competitors.

In groups centred on individuals, such pecking orders do not exist. The bonding isn't about fitting into a niche in a hierarchy, it is about exchanging value. This also explains why loyalty and trust are not necessary in such groups: people bond and collaborate with each other because of the value they can give to each other.

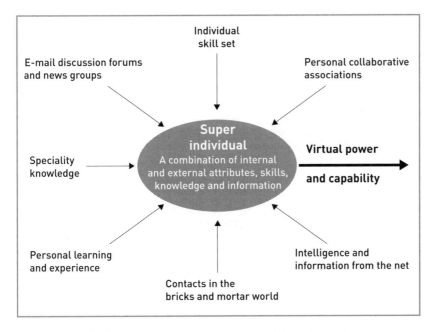

FIG 4.4 An individual can become a super individual through opening up a wide range of information sources which enhance his or her own abilities and knowledge

If it is assumed that everyone acts in their own best interests, people will endeavour to acquire the most knowledgeable and capable people to be amongst their group of personal contacts. This will put the super individuals, who are making effective strategic use of the internet, at a distinct advantage as they will be potentially more valuable as associates. The consequence will be that those who are most efficient at turning themselves into super individuals will be attracted to each other, as is illustrated in Figure 4.5.

In hierarchical organizations, obtaining advantage by creating such a group of close associates is often treated with suspicion and even jealousy. Efforts are often made to compromise these associations or break them up.

In the environment of the internet, rather than being resentful of others forming personal associations that enhance their knowledge and

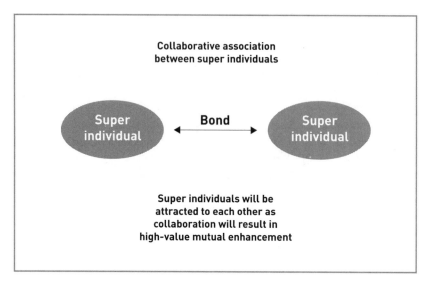

FIG 4.5 Super individuals will be attracted to form bonds with each other if they are each seeking to create a personal community of valuable contacts

capabilities, it is strategically more sensible to encourage everyone to do this. This is because rivalry is less of an issue in the massively connected world of the internet; it is more important that you have powerful and knowledgeable friends and associates.

For this reason, people who create cafés and strategic associations try to encourage all of their contacts to do the same. The more connected they become, the more valuable will be the association.

creating relationships on the internet

If we take the view that the most important first step in creating an e-business is to establish a number of strategic relationships to compensate for our limited ability to know all that is needed to be known, we must devise a suitable strategy. In other words, we need to know how we can form strategic bonds with people.

In the world of bricks and mortar, a group of personal friends and contacts is often regarded as a prized possession and jealously guarded.

Similarly, many people will not reveal their sources of information. Information is regarded as valuable; people will hoard it and are reluctant to share it with any but their closest associates whom they can trust not to take advantage of them.

In hierarchical organizations, many people build power bases for themselves by deliberately restricting the amount of information they give out and will conceal their contacts. Businesses are built around having carefully guarded mailing lists of potential customers.

In the world of the internet, such attitudes are misplaced because information and contacts are forms of currency – used to fund relationships and provide the oil that keeps dynamic systems moving efficiently. This benevolent attitude towards information is common to all industries and business environments that are subject to constant and unpredictable change. People have a need to be constantly informed of new developments, changes and trends. The entertainment and fashion industries are typical. These worlds are well known for their parties and social functions which facilitate the exchange of contacts and the rapid dissemination of information.

The problem with these environments is that information and contacts are plentiful, cheap and too often unreliable. This means that the currency used to build relationships, information and contacts, has very little value unless it comes from a credible and authoritative source. The trick, then, is to be seen as being credible.

Imagine yourself in a bar at a race track. You wander around, listening to conversations going on around you. It is quite likely that you'll hear several people discussing the likely outcome of the next race and there will be all kinds of different predictions as to which horse will win.

What value would you place on each of these opinions? A tipster approaches you and for a small sum of money offers to name the winner. Do you pay him to find out? Then you notice a group of people standing at the bar whom you know to be a group of trainers and jockeys. What strategy could you employ to get into conversation with them?

This scenario is a good metaphor for the situation you find on the internet. There are countless numbers of people with ideas and information, but because of the inherent unpredictability, the information tends to be contradictory and cancels out. The most reliable sources (even though they may not be accurate) would be the people who are professionally involved in the activity, but it is not easy to get into their company.

Returning to the bar at the race track, you would want to take advice and be influenced by the group of trainers and jockeys because their information would have greater credibility. But how could you gain their respect and confidence? What could you do that would get you into their company (apart from the crass tactic of offering to buy them all a drink)?

Now imagine that you are a manager of a restaurant, and one day you recognize one of the customers as being one of the group of jockeys and trainers you saw standing at the bar at the race track. You could introduce yourself and give him some advice on the food in the restaurant and then make sure he gets special service. The next time you go to the race track and see the group of jockeys and trainers standing at the bar, it is highly probable that you will be invited to join the group.

The trick now is to abstract the essence of this scenario and apply it to the internet. Let's do this by isolating the main features:

1 A group is identified as having specialist knowledge which you consider to be valuable to yourself.

2 At least one of the group must be able to discover that you have a speciality that is of interest to them.

3 It needs only for you to make contact with one person to be privy to the conversation of the whole group.

The key is that somebody must be able to discover that you have some knowledge or a speciality that interests them. But how do you manage to do this on the internet? How can people know about you, your fields of interest and speciality knowledge? The only way to do this in the environment of the internet is to create a personal website — and then find a way of getting it 'discovered' by the right kind of people.

establishing an identity on the web

Let's start with a green frog. This is your web identity. It is not very efficient as a web identity so you have to think about how you can change that green frog to give you an effective web presence.

The first step is to turn the green frog into a computer. Next is to connect this computer to the internet. Seems perfectly straightforward, after all there are three hundred million others who are connected, so it must be quite easy. Right?

Here is where you encounter your first knowledge gap. You'll need to ask somebody how you get connected. They give you some algorithmic instructions which involve getting a modem and making arrangements with a company who will give you more algorithmic instructions to set up your computer so that you are connected.

Most likely, you won't have the faintest idea as to what is going on. It all seems so complicated that you'd rather not know. You are just relieved and amazed at some point when you discover you are connected and you can send and receive e-mails and visit websites. Pretty soon you are so overwhelmed with the huge variety of information you are exposed to that you forget all about that initial step you took in becoming connected.

As a casual user of the internet it may not concern you very much how you are connected. You have a direct connection to another computer (your ISP) linked directly or indirectly to the whole of the network. It works fine, so there is no need to go into details as to how it all happens. However, as a professional user, someone who is going to use the internet as part of their professional business life, it may be prudent to take the trouble to look more closely at what is happening.

For starters, the initial connection you made was probably opportunistic – a decision made in ignorance. Was it the best choice you could have made? How easily can you change if you realize there is a better choice elsewhere? What if you wanted to change? Your e-mail address is likely to be valid only while you are using your current ISP.

In a world of constant change, flexibility is vital. If your ISP goes down or becomes slow because it is trying to handle too much traffic, you are handicapped. What insurance have you got that your ISP won't suddenly go out of business? If you change your ISP you lose your e-mail address and will have to notify everyone you know. You'll have to resubscribe to e-mail discussion forums, change the details on many websites that recognize you through your e-mail address. If only you'd known a little more when you connected to the internet, you could have saved yourself all these potential problems.

By appreciating that you have knowledge gaps, you can take precautions. In the first place you can think of your first connection as simply a temporary expedient to get on to the internet to be able to get enough information to connect more efficiently.

There are thousands of websites that will give you information, but it is likely to be thoroughly confusing. The best way is to find some e-mail discussion forums to join and ask questions. Strike up online acquaintance-ship with knowledgeable people and ask their opinions. It is essential that you ask several people because everyone has knowledge gaps and you'd have no way of knowing whether you were getting the right advice unless you could make comparisons.

In my own case, I was very slow at understanding what the internet was really about. I had a vague mental model as to how it all worked and this had served me faithfully for years. But as I contemplated the possibilities of being involved in an e-business situation, I became aware of many limitations.

It was a chance e-mail discussion I had with a contact in Canada that first opened my eyes. This contact, Yvan Caron, was investigating the commercial possibilities of P2P (person to person) file transference. He sent me an e-mail enthusing excitedly about the business opportunities it opened up. His e-mail contained so many terms I was unfamiliar with that I couldn't understand what he was talking about.

I confessed my ignorance and he went to a great deal of trouble to explain how the transference was organized. I didn't follow all the technicalities, but it was enough to change totally my conception of how the internet worked. It provided me with a new insight and at the same time made me acutely aware that for years I'd been using the internet without really understanding how it worked.

As I understood from Yvan Caron's e-mails, the internet isn't about computers talking to each other, it is about applications talking to each other. This may be obvious, but it is such simple changes in emphasis that can lead to greater understanding. As he explained, application programs send each other messages and listen out for messages being sent to them.

The problem, however, was that although Yvan's explanation had given me a valuable new insight, it had totally destroyed the mental image I had built up over the years. I now had to start from scratch to create a new model.

I was reluctant to start going into much technical detail because it is so easy to get sucked into weeks of hard study. I wanted to stay away from the detail and work with broad concepts; this might not make me technically competent, but at least I might be able to see through the fog.

In trying to form a new mental model of how the internet works, I discovered many different kinds of knowledge gaps. Try as I might, I couldn't get a complete picture into my head. Fortunately, I belonged to a very techy e-mail discussion forum (**www.evolt.org**) where many internet gurus and website designers hang out. To this forum, I sent the following post:

I'm trying to figure out a neat mental model to explain how the internet works without having to involve any technical detail. I thought I had a good idea as to what goes on under the hood until I tried to write down a simple explanation. The more I try, the more knowledge gaps I discover.

Starting from the beginning, I make a connection to my ISP. I guess some application does this by making a telephone connection and in computer speak identifies itself and presents an appropriate password. The ISP then allocates my computer a temporary IP (internet protocol) address.

Presumably, the ISP then listens out for any messages for this temporary address and passes them straight on to me. If I send out messages, where do they go? Does the ISP computer simply pass them on, adding my temporary IP address? If it passes them on, where does it pass them on to? How do they get to a destination I want them to go to: 1) when I send someone an e-mail; 2) when I specify a link with my browser?

Once I'm connected, does my ISP computer keep listening to my connection to see if I am sending any messages? How does my ISP computer detect the messages that are being sent to me? Are these messages being routed directly to it or is it just listening to all messages on the internet and selecting those that apply to its own clients?

It's a very hazy picture I have. Every time I think I'm beginning to understand, I get stumped with another knowledge gap.

I'd be grateful for a little light...

There were three responses. The first was from Anthony Baratta, President of KeyBoard Jockeys, who described how the initial contact was a shout to your ISP to give you an identity (a temporary IP address). Your application then sends this identity in a short message to a universal database that is constantly recording who is currently on the web and where they are (the database can tell where you are by the route the message takes through different computers to reach it).

NOTE The map is in fact duplicated on many computers around the internet. These computers are in constant communication with each other, exchanging updated information at least every 30 seconds. Each collects information about computers in their own locality: to know which are currently connected, their identity and where they are located. This information is then passed on to all the other computers holding a 'map', so within a few minutes of logging on, every computer in the world knows how to find you.

A mystery had been cleared up. I had always wondered how messages found their way around the internet. The answer was so elegantly simple: you create an identity when you log on and this identity is placed on a map that resides in a computer that every other computer has access to. If an application wants to send a message to somebody, it just routes it through the computer that has the map.

The second response was from one of the people in the virtual café, Scott Dexter, from California. He is also one of the more active members of evolt.org and is involved in the construction and content of the **www.evolt.org** website. He explained the internet in terms of a metaphor of the café, explaining how messages get passed from one computer to another as they pass from the sender to the receiver.

He explained how messages get sent with a lot of extra information (in a header), which is read by all the computers that handle the messages.

This information includes the name of the sender, the time it was sent and the name of the intended recipient. It is this information that enables computers to know if a message is for them, or, if not, to know where to pass the message on so that it gets nearer to the intended recipient.

The third response came from Miraz Jordan, who runs internet education courses in New Zealand. Besides directing me to his own lecture notes on the web, he pointed me to a very authoritative website (**www. livinginternet.com**) that explained the internet in a reasonably non-technical manner. Although it contained a great number of pages of detailed information, by spending a whole day on this site I found most of my knowledge gaps closing and I was at last able to construct a new mental model of how I understood the internet to work.

a mental model of the internet
The most important change in the way I started to view the internet was that I ceased to imagine it like some form of telephone network where computers connected to each other in order to communicate. I'd always viewed the internet as a complex arrangement of wires and switching mechanisms. I was shocked to find it wasn't like this at all. In its place I now had a 'name space', where the names were like islands in a vast ocean of water with no connection between them other than the currents in the water.

For these islands to communicate, they had to break all their messages up into bits, put each bit in a bottle and throw the bottles into the ocean to let the currents take them to their destination. This was the key breakthrough. It wasn't about making connections with other computers: the moment a message or any part of a message is sent it becomes stateless, the sender loses all contact with it and there is no contact at all with the intended recipient or any of the computers through which the messages are passed.

Once it dawns upon you that all data packets and messages are stateless – quite isolated and independent of sender and receiver while they are in transit – you can look at the environment of the internet in a completely different way. Not only are the data packets and messages stateless, so are the senders and receivers.

> " FOR THESE ISLANDS TO COMMUNICATE, THEY HAD TO BREAK ALL THEIR MESSAGES UP INTO BITS, PUT EACH BIT IN A BOTTLE AND THROW THE BOTTLES INTO THE OCEAN "

THE WAY THESE STATELESS MESSAGES get passed around from computer to computer on their way to their destinations is both ingenious and remarkably simple. To limit the effect of a breakdown the messages are all sent as small data packets (about 1,000 characters long, i.e. 1 kilobyte). All the data packets are sent to a main highway (the backbone of the internet). This consists of a number of heavy-duty computers — known as routers — that pass all internet messages between them.

They each carry continuously updated maps of the internet that tell them the location of every computer currently online. This allows them to work out the best way to send the packets to reach their destination. However, they don't just send a packet the physically shortest route; they try to send it in the shortest time, which might mean routing it around heavily congested parts of the internet.

Each data packet, passing through a router, contains a record of its travels through the network together with the times at which it reached each computer it passes through. This allows routers to work out all the current transmission speeds throughout the entire network and calculate the probable fastest routes to pass the packets on towards their destinations. Routers pass these data packets to each other until they reach the locality of the destination computer. Then it is passed into a local network to be passed on to the computer the packet is addressed to. This destination computer will wait until all the packets of a particular message arrive and then put them all together to re-create the original message as it was sent by the sender.

Routers are constantly communicating with each other, updating each other about maps and transmission speeds, working as a kind of team to ensure that all packets of data get to their destination in the shortest time possible. They correspond with each other every 3–30 seconds and if a communication goes over the 30-second limit the receiving router assumes the late sender is out of action and tells all the other routers to route messages around it.

A sender can pop up anywhere on the internet to send a message. It doesn't matter where they are physically located. Similarly with receivers: they can change their position in this name space at any time and still receive messages that are addressed to them. This can give rise to a phenomenon that is impossible to create in the world of bricks and mortar, a virtual entity.

virtual entities

A virtual entity is an entity that has no fixed form or shape. It is created out of components that are connected only by the imagination. Such things are impossible in the physical world. Imagine creating a perfect partner for yourself, choosing all the best features and body parts from a host of film and television personalities and putting them all together to create the perfect person. Imagine being able to give this virtual partner the personality of the nicest person you know and the intelligence of the cleverest.

5

MORE IMPORTANT THAN THE BUSINESS IDEA

a new place to explore After reading Chapter 4, one of the readers in the café commented:

I don't know why Peter wasted so much time and space explaining his 'mental model of the internet'. We don't need to know all these details in order to use the internet effectively. When I ring my sister in India from Canada, I don't need to know how the analogue sound is modulated and transmitted over wire, how amplifiers are used along the way to boost the signal, etc. All I care about is conversing with my sister!

Peter said, 'The internet isn't about computers talking to each other, it is about applications talking to each other'. Actually it is about people talking to each other! The applications are the tools that make our communication, collaboration, or whatever, possible. Just like the phone-wire, I don't need to know how the applications work unless I am developing them for profit.

This was swiftly answered by another reader, Mary Rickman-Taylor from The Arizona Institute of Business and Technology, who countered:

I don't agree that the time and space spent on the 'mental model of the internet' was wasted...

... it is helpful for understanding and useful to be clear that the messages are pretty well cut up like the *Star Trek* transporter machine and then literally reassembled at the other end, and that it takes programs (applications) to do this to keep everything straight.

I do agree that the internet is about people talking to each other and it is true that I don't need to know how the applications work to use the system – but knowing how the system works allows me to be an informed participant, whether as a user, as a consumer, or as a citizen – it allows me to participate in the process, and allows me to avoid being gouged or hustled by charlatans or overly greedy folk, or hoodwinked by the likes of...

...I see this exercise as an opportunity to think 'outside of the box' for all of us, and do some real speculation as to what sort of e-business might be created.

These two contrasting viewpoints illustrate the inherent problems associated with knowledge gaps. Certainly we can work without all the detail that goes on behind the scenes. We have to do this most of the time – after all, why bother to learn non-essential detail when there is so much else to know and to learn? But with lack of knowledge there is a risk of becoming trapped inside stereotyped metaphors. Only by exploring the details are we able to see beyond the obvious.

The problem is, of course, that there are so many areas to understand and explore that everyone is forced to ignore the details of most of them. But this is why it is so important to become involved in different groups and discussion forums, because although each individual might be limited to exploring only a few areas in detail, many people between them can explore many more.

Using the metaphor of the caves again, we can think of many people exploring an underground system of caves together. Each might be in a different cave looking for a hidden passage into a new cave system. When one person discovers an opening in their area, they can call to the others – taking everyone along with them to explore the new area that has opened up. In this way a group of people can act like a unified organism, which has the ability to explore many different areas at the same time. This is the principle behind the virtual café.

For years, I saw the effort to spend time learning how the internet really functioned as an unnecessary waste of my time. It was only a chance event, the communication with Yvan Caron, that drew my attention to the detail. Yet it had a profound effect on my thinking and allowed me to see beyond the stereotyped view I'd always had and into a new cave of wonder and unexplored opportunity.

Having a knowledge of what happens inside the box – even though it may be perfunctory – has opened up a new environment outside of the box to explore.

starting to explore

Having a totally new conceptual model of how the internet works, I wanted to experiment. Using the green frog approach, I started from scratch: deciding to create an identity for myself. Checking around, I discovered that the cost of registering a domain name varied wildly: from $35 per annum down to free.

Checking this out, I noticed that the full retail price of registering a domain name was $35 with one of the principal registering services, but for a few hundred dollars I could become a subordinate registrar myself and register names for other people at a cost to me of only 20 per cent of the full market price.

Click! A little light bulb went off in my head. Here was a product that could be sold which had a 400 per cent mark-up. It then began to make sense as to why there were so many different prices on offer. There were thousands of people who had paid to become subordinate registrars and could make money through registering domain names for other people and charging them for this service at a profit on what they had to pay themselves.

I soon discovered that this was a highly competitive marketplace, with all kinds of tricks involved. People were registering domain names for others very cheaply, even for free, as an inducement to getting their business to provide them with web space, site design or ISP services. Some of these secondary registrars were providing domain names for clients but registering in their own names, forcing the client to deal exclusively through them, or pay a high fee for name transfer if the client wanted to dispense with their services.

Even more ingenious, some ISPs were giving away free name domain name registration and then providing an auction service for clients to auction the name off. To my chagrin, I found my own name <petersmall. co.uk> had been registered by one of these services as a domain name only a few weeks previously. Perhaps someone is registering the names of all authors in the hope that some of them will want to buy these domain names from them at an auction at some time in the future?

It then occurred to me that having a domain name <petersmall. something> might be useful to add to the end of my e-mails, to let recipients know something about me. By checking with one of the sites that tell you if a given domain name is available, I discovered that the address <petersmall.net> was still available. The question then became one of deciding which registrar to use to register the name.

After making a few inquiries and visiting a number of websites I began to formulate a few essential requirements. The domain name would be my permanent IP address, but it didn't have to be attached to any particular computer. I could choose which computer it referred to and change that computer whenever I wished simply by informing the registrar and the administrators of the computers involved in the transfer.

The thought then occurred to me that, if I could move this domain name around, effectively I would have a kind of phantom identity that could be located on any computer in the world. And, wherever this identity was located, any messages directed to this identity could be redirected to wherever I chose.

I then chose a web-hosting service that had a web administrator I could actually talk to. He advised me that I could simply 'park' my domain name on his server and any messages would be directed to wherever I instructed him to redirect them. This service, including the registration of the domain name in my own name, would cost me no more than £10 ($15) a year.

At the time I already had a local ISP, from whom I was receiving my e-mails, and a website located in another country (USA). I then directed the administrator of the website where I'd parked my <petersmall.net> domain name to redirect any e-mails addressed to <anyname@petersmall .net> to my regular e-mail address <peter@genps.demon.co.uk>, and redirect any web reference to http://www.petersmall.net to my established website at http://www.avatarnets.com.

It may seem a pointless exercise, but it completely changed the way I started to think about my presence on the web. I could have many different personalities all directing messages to where I wanted them to go. I could have several 'front doors' to my website. It wasn't long before I was thinking in terms of a nebulous system of locations and entry points, allowing all kinds of complex presences to be created on the web.

This revelation, combined with the previous revelation that messages were stateless, started to excite my imagination. I could have a stateless existence that could take on an infinite number of configurations. I could exist in many forms and in many places at the same time. I was not committed to or restricted by any particular ISP, hosting service, name or location. The possibilities were endless.

The main advantage that came to mind was that this provided a perfect vehicle for coping with change and uncertainty. By spreading my identity over a number of locations I wouldn't be tied to any particular one. The different parts of my identity could be duplicated on different servers in many different places in the world, which would give me total independence to switch and change around at will.

Simply by changing a few links I could reconfigure my identity to choose the servers that were the most useful or efficient. I could collaborate with different people through different parts of this system of identity. This is what I had been looking for, a flexible interface to the internet that could easily cope with change and uncertainty.

The words of Bill Gates came flooding back to me. Hadn't he discovered a new and novel environment? Hadn't he learned how to use that environment and had built appropriate tools to take full advantage of it? Hadn't those tools been useful to others, who were prepared to pay to gain this same advantage? The possibilities that e-business opportunities might emerge from this new way of looking at the web then took on a practical reality.

creating a source of wealth creation

The best way to make money is to find, or create, a non-zero-sum game: a wealth-creating situation where all the players (collaborators) can gain by sharing the wealth created. Such situations invariably arise out of discovering new ways to improve efficiency. Here we have just such a situation.

A flexible web presence can lead to improvements in efficiency because this is a way to cope with change and uncertainty. Adding to this advantage, a flexible web presence can also provide a framework for collaboration that will facilitate a system capable of adaptation and evolution. Wouldn't this be beneficial to everyone involved?

Bill Gates' strategy had been to begin by constructing tools that would be useful to him and his collaborators. Couldn't a flexible web presence be considered a tool? Couldn't a framework of collaboration also be considered a tool? Figure 5.1 illustrates how a website can be thought of as a tool by combining these features.

Returning to the green frog approach, I'd already determined that the first step beyond the green frog was to establish an identity on the web. This I'd done by creating a domain name and IP address, but a name and IP address aren't of any use unless they can be used for a purpose. I needed to give this identity a purpose. Once given a purpose, the website has to be provided with the ability to fulfil that purpose effectively.

The problem is that a website has the capability of being a highly complex identity. It isn't enough that it should act as a brochure or a catalogue. It isn't even enough that it should act as a retail outlet. A website needs to be an interactive part of a dynamic community – which is likely to be constantly changing and evolving.

This suggests that the web identity should be such that it plugs into a

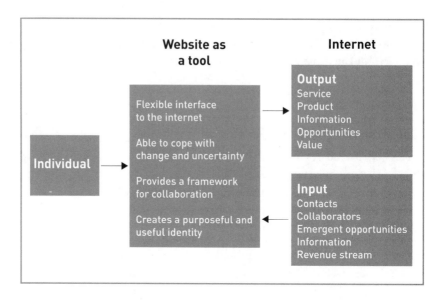

FIG 5.1 A website can be thought of as a tool that provides an efficient interface to the internet

dynamic system of communication and collaboration, which provides intelligence and direction. It should be designed to be adaptable and receptive to new and emergent opportunities. It is only by creating such complexity within a website identity that the full benefits of e-business can be realized.

This is an important initial need – common to anyone wanting to make strategic use of the web for e-business – establishing a sophisticated identity on the web that not only has purpose, but will also optimize opportunities for collaboration and be able to adapt continuously to change.

Paradoxically, this starting place might be a good area to begin looking for an e-business opportunity. Everyone has to make a start somewhere and there are no obvious guidelines. By creating a suitable tool to deal with uncertain beginnings, you would be pioneering a pathway. Others might want to follow along this same pathway and be prepared to pay for the tools that have been created.

The first question that comes to mind is: what kind of identity to establish? The generic answer is that the identity should be such as to be able to take part in a profitable enterprise. The temptation then is to leap forward immediately into thinking about what kind of profitable enterprise that should be. However, this thinking would be pointless, if all you had was a domain name. How would people get to know about your enterprise? If the enterprise is based on a good idea, how would you compete with others who might either copy that idea or improve on it?

Rather than think about the idea and the enterprise, the first priority must be to give the internet identity substance and power. Only then will it be sensible to think about the specific details of the enterprise because only then will you be in a more effective position to implement any business dealings or put ideas into effect.

To get this strategy into perspective, you might compare a website to a retail store. With this metaphor, it is easy to realize that a store (a website) is not going to be located in a busy high street when it is created. A website, on its own, is more like a store built in the middle of the Sahara desert. Clearly, whatever ideas you have for such a store are going to be totally useless until you get that store moved into an area where customers can know about it.

First thoughts might turn to advertising and marketing. The experiences of the early dot coms are adequate proof that this is not a cost-effective way to acquire a customer base. Besides being a very expensive way to attract customers, there is very little incentive for customers to stay loyal if they can find something more attractive just a mouse click away.

Certainly an expensive marketing campaign might attract customers, but the cost has to be recouped. If the result is successful, it is only too easy for a competitor to look at what you are doing, make a few improvements and then offer the same service or product at a reduced price (or better service) because they haven't the liability incurred in the cost of the marketing. All too often, an e-business advertising and marketing campaign has attracted competition rather than customers.

Money and effort are better spent moving the store out of the desert and into a busy high street. In the world of the internet this involves becoming a part of a network of communication and activity – in the parlance of the web, this will mean creating or joining a portal or a vortal.

a system of portals and vortals
There are many different ways and buzzwords used to describe portals or vortals. However, whatever they are called, or whichever way they might be described, tney all mean the same thing: a point of attraction for a particular interest group.

Portals and vortals are common in the everyday world of bricks and mortar. Shopping malls are prime examples of portals. People shop at shopping malls because there is a large variety of goods on offer and the duplication of traders ensures sufficient competition to produce excellence and bring prices down to reasonable levels. In large towns and cities, particular areas become specialized in certain types of commodities or services. These are vortals: each area providing a depth of service in a specialized niche.

Sometimes, these centres of attraction will attract complementary trades or business, where they act symbiotically. This is evidenced by the number of different businesses and services that will congregate at tourist or entertainment centres.

Vortals and portals are a naturally occurring phenomenon. People prefer to go to places where there is choice and competition. And, because people go there, it is attractive for traders to be there. There is a mutual attraction for traders and customers to be at the same place. This same phenomenon occurs on the web.

A useful metaphor to use for this situation is the attraction force of gravity. The more atoms in a body (the greater its mass), the more it will attract other atoms and bodies. An atom on its own, or even a small body, does not have the pulling power of a larger body. In a similar way, an e-business on its own, or even part of a small local group, will not be able to attract clients or customers anywhere near as easily as a large group of e-businesses that have integrated together in a common portal or vortal.

This is why advertising and marketing schemes often fail for start-up companies which try to establish a business in isolation. They cannot compete against the natural attractiveness of the larger conglomerations. They would be far better off spending their money on achieving excellence and becoming part of a portal or vortal where the combined pulling power has no need for advertising or marketing.

Web-based portals and vortals are not always as tangible as they are in the world of bricks and mortar. Sometimes a company will set up a website specifically to act as a portal or a vortal, but more often a portal or vortal comes in the guise of a search engine, guide or directory. Thousands of websites are setting up as self-proclaimed experts in all manner of niche areas of special interest or technology. These point to other sites and other sites point to them. In this way, they form naturally occurring portals and vortals that direct and influence thinking and actions.

As more and more search engines, guides and directories come on stream, it has produced the phenomena of search engines that incorporate other search engines, guides that are guides to other guides and directories that are directories of other directories. Even experts are pointing to other experts in efforts to become the experts of experts.

In one sense, this can be seen as ever-increasing competition as many information sources compete with each other to be the ultimate authority. But on a different level, this can be viewed as the natural tendency of a dynamic system to self-organize. Any dynamic system which includes competition for survival and success amongst its component elements will self-organize in this way. It will proceed relentlessly towards a state of greater and greater organization and efficiency. This is evident in all biological systems, where the same thing happens spontaneously, over and over again, without the appearance of any organizing intelligence.

To be involved in the world of e-business brings you into this type of self-organizing environment, which is driven by constant competitive pressure. It may seem to be created by humans, but this tendency of a system – to promote the efficient while driving out the inefficient – is beyond the level of human control: it is simply an inherent characteristic of all dynamic systems. To be successful in any e-business venture, it is necessary to be acutely aware of this situation and to design any business ventures not only to cope with but to take advantage of the system's natural dynamics.

It is for this reason that we have to approach the creation of any e-business by first working out how we are going to fit into a system of vortals or portals; only then can we move on to the details of how to take part.

the links are not in control

All web-based portals and vortals, in their own way, attract people who seek knowledge, guidance, entertainment, products or services. They direct people; sometimes giving advice, sometimes pointing to advantages or price differences. They may also carry advertisements in the form of banners that can transport people off on an impulsive whim. Advertising can also be embedded into the copy of text in the form of links that take the reader to a particular place of interest. Seen in this way, portals and vortals can be seen as systems of links that direct people around a system of interaction and trade.

With this view, it is easy to think that the sites providing the links are in control of the system, but it is a fallacy. The sites that control the system are those that provide real substance and value – but this is not immediately obvious. Figure 5.2 shows the various ways in which customers might be routed to a website.

Figure 5.2 indicates that the most efficient routing of customers to a website is through providing good value and good service. As obvious as this might seem, it is largely ignored at start-up because it relies on the website having already been created and a business already running. It is this question of the starting process that throws many people because it is a chicken and egg situation. You can get people to come to the site if others recommend it, but how do you get those initial people to visit the site in the first place?

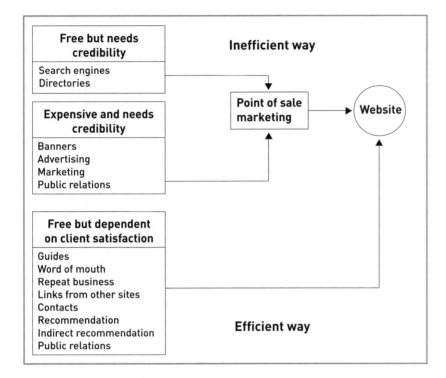

FIG 5.2 There are a number of ways in which people are routed to websites. The most efficient are those that are a consequence of the website providing real value

Most people new to e-business will attach great importance to search engines, directories, advertising, marketing and banner ads. They will want to use on-site marketing ploys, flashy appearances, entertaining displays and novelty. However, a little careful thought will soon tell you that such methods are actually counter-productive. On the internet, people do not want to be convinced to become customers: they will arrive with the hope of being customers and expect efficient service, not a sales patter. Selling is treated with suspicion and puts customers off.

There is no substitute for providing real value, efficiency and reliability. If a site provides these there is no need to advertise or hard sell because the internet is a communication environment and word quickly spreads. This is particularly true in a portal or vortal environment because of the proximity of competition and the ease with which comparisons can be made.

In a world where search engines, guides and advisers are vying with each other for authority, credibility and recognition, a good site will not have to make itself known to them. A superior search engine or authoritative guide will find it for themselves. Remember, they are all seeking to be authoritative sources and they will not want to be seen missing out on an important site within their area of speciality.

At the time I finished writing the last chapter, I had to go to New York to speak at the BOT2000 seminar. Most of the speakers were involved in one way or another with gathering information from and about websites. Every one of these speakers was far more concerned with the quality of the information they were gathering than the volume. Simply trying to catalogue all information indiscriminately, regardless of its value, was seen as an unintelligent approach for search engines and directories to take.

At the end of the seminar, all the speakers were asked in turn to give their view as to the future for search engines, bots and intelligent agents. The consensus seemed to be that future development would be in the direction of increasing specialization and more accurate ways of seeking out quality, value and excellence.

One of the speakers described an intelligent agent that his company was developing that would be used to check out current prices and availability of specific consumer products being offered on the internet. It didn't wait for companies to submit the details of their websites; the agent acted as a spider, constantly crawling around the web, searching millions of web pages a day and looking for key words.

This activity produced an unedited list of references, but then these findings were sorted and classified to produce short lists whose final inclusion in the search engine's recommendations was decided by humans. In this way, a portal of quality was being created that preferentially selected only the best and the most efficient traders in the various categories. It is in light of such intelligent portal- and vortal-creating systems that any e-business has to be designed.

It is obviously an advantage to be within the route map of a suitable portal or vortal because this is where the traffic will be. But what has to be appreciated is that these portals and vortals are highly competitive environments. It's no good setting up business in one of them with simply a good idea. All the other traders will only say, 'Good idea, thank you very much', and use or improve on that idea themselves. The stark reality is that you must be in a position to maintain a competitive position with any business idea you come up with.

This shifts the emphasis away from the idea itself and onto the problem of being able to put the idea into effect in a highly competitive environment. To be able to do this, it is necessary to be able to make full and optimum use of communication technology. In effect, this means there is a need to create a super identity on the web in the same way that it is necessary to create a super individual in the environment of the internet.

To create such a super identity, the green frog will have to acquire superior knowledge in the ways of the internet and the technologies involved in website creation. It is at this stage that the eyes of most bricks and mortar business people begin to glaze over. They are faced with an incomprehensible confusion of technology.

Rather than plunge into this seething mass of unfamiliar techniques and concepts, most brick and mortar businesses will hand over this responsibility to somebody else, someone they think might be able to understand this highly technical world better than them. Unfortunately, they usually have no way of knowing who are the experts and who are the charlatans. This leaves them vulnerable to a huge wastage of investment capital and the establishment of inferior trading positions. This is the first problem an e-business strategist has to solve.

in the land of knowledge gaps

Creating any kind of business usually begins by recognizing an opportunity, but how do you spot them? As a one-time professional poker player, I learned to look out for anomalies, elements of play that strike you as being unusual or out of character: something that you wouldn't expect somebody to be doing. Such anomalies alert you to both dangers and possible opportunities.

A similar technique can be used for spotting business opportunities, especially in the environment of e-business. Anomalies occur when players in the e-business game who should know better appear to be acting foolishly or inefficiently. Such anomalies expose knowledge gaps, or a service or product that is not available.

In an effort to keep up with the latest developments on the web, I subscribe to several different kinds of technical e-mail discussion forums. There I discovered some interesting anomalies.

The first anomaly was that most of the programmers and graphic designers working on websites had only a cursory interest in the core businesses of the sites they were designing for. They were primarily concerned with the problems and solutions revolving around their own particular speciality niche of expertise.

The second anomaly was the contempt with which most of these technical specialists regarded the people who employed their services. A commonly held view is that the majority of people directing major e-business projects are totally incompetent.

To try to understand why this attitude should prevail, I sent in the following post to a couple of e-mail discussion forums where many expert website designers hang out:

Reading through some of the posts in this forum and others, I get the distinct impression that many people involved in authorizing the work that web designers do are far from competent.

I'm aware that many small businesses haven't the faintest idea what the web is about and how it might benefit them. They simply pay someone to create a website so as to see what it might do for their business. How common is this attitude? Do many of these experimental efforts succeed? Are there any really savvy businesses which know how to make efficient use of the web and use web designers' time effectively and efficiently?

There are many agencies and consultants who claim to know what they are doing and engage the services of freelancers on their client's behalf. What proportion of these are competent? Are there many for whom freelancers have much respect as far as being capable of creating viable e-business solutions is concerned? Is the same sort of situation prevalent with in-house design teams?

BTW I'm not expecting everyone to be competent. That isn't the point I'm making. It just seems, from what I'm hearing everywhere, that the complete solution providers (as opposed to the technical specialists) involve an extremely high proportion of people who don't really know what they are doing. Unlike most other business areas, the incompetent seem to be in the majority. However, I'm not stating this as a fact, I'm just looking for confirmation as to whether this proposition is true or false (with maybe an anecdote or two thrown in).

There were no posts contradicting this proposition, but many supported it, some providing examples and anecdotes. Here is a selection of the responses:

Marcus Bointon wrote:

Many companies really don't have much of a clue, even some very big ones. I waste a good proportion of my time educating my clients about what it is they're asking me to do! I'd say that this occasionally hits around the 75% mark. You really have to do this otherwise they'll complain that you didn't do what they wanted, but only because they didn't know what they wanted! It's usually in your interests to keep things as simple as humanly possible.

Damian Thomas wrote:

I had a client very recently; apart from knowing nothing about the internet or websites, he didn't know the first thing about e-mail or its uses, and quietly asked, and I quote, 'Can you see my website from your place?' !!

I replied, Of course, but it can also be viewed worldwide'. He was amazed, responding, 'phew! s**t! I didn't know that, wow, bla, flipping eck, etc.'

So I agree with the comments made earlier, at least half my clients want a website thinking it is just the thing to do. Imagine his surprise when I explained that anyone could send him an e-mail directly from his website :–00hh

Garrett Coakley wrote:

Sometimes they haven't even thought about it that much. They want one because everyone else has one. Remember the IBM advert from last year with the two guys in the boardroom?

Guy 1: [reading a paper] We have to be on the web.

Guy 2: Why?

Guy 1: [looks back at the paper] ...(comedy pause)... It doesn't say.

I deal with a lot of small companies which have been toying with the idea of having a site built. Most of them dip their toe in the water by having a small (4–5 pages) brochure site. The one thing they have in common is that they don't understand how it all works. They expect their profits to suddenly shoot skywards. They expect their company to instantly gain a coolness factor. They can't understand why their staff haven't metamorphosed into sexy, hip 30-somethings.

Deciding to create an online presence involves a lot of work on their part. They have to look at themselves and decide what exactly it is they are offering. What is the user going to get out of visiting their site? How can they best use the medium? Can they streamline their support process? Going to publish an e-mail address? Better be damn sure the customer gets a reply within 48 hours, etc. etc.

How common is this attitude?

Do many of these experimental efforts succeed?

Hmmm, if they have no fixed idea in the first place, how would you measure success? Profits? Name awareness? Unfortunately, the attitude is far too common.

I think it should be our job as web developers to educate our clients as to the possibilities of the medium. If you're just going in, taking their money and building what they ask you to, then I'd like to have a word. It's up to us to educate them on browsers, platforms and technologies.

I'm not talking about degree level here, just enough to get them over the initial language barrier. Once you've got that, they start to investigate for themselves, start to understand what the web is capable of (and why they can't have that image three pixels to the left).

Offer to show them cool things, things that are useful, spend a bit of time with them, give a bit of after-care service. Hell, one of my clients is now using Mozilla M18 as their default browser after I showed them it (they had asked what this 'open source thing' was all about).

They're also much more likely to come back to you with more work. And do you know what? The next time they come back, they're a little wiser, a lot more trusting, and eager to learn more.

Dave Gray wrote:

Oh my god, don't get me started. Incompetence runs rampant all the way up the food chain.

Martin Burns wrote:

The more clueless ones I see tend to have the latest everything (Flash5, WinME, IE5.5 on fast connections) and look at you funny if you don't automatically offer to do the site in Flash.

Buzzword city!

Peter Van Dijck wrote:

Buzzword density reaches intolerable levels:

▶ They will say things like: 'Yes we make very interactive sites' without being prompted to do so.

▶ Ask them what testing they do, they'll say: 'We test for the browsers' or something (clued-in ones will have a real testing program: stress testing, compatibility, usability).

▶ Ask them why if they propose a certain feature.

Aardvark wrote:

Think about the environments...

▶ software development shop...

Would they even know how to hire a creative guy? What to look for? What web skills to ask for? Would they do the web stuff, or let the creative guy do it? And then, how do you get a creative guy to stick around when he could make more elsewhere and work in an environment that promotes creativity as opposed to a more rigid SDM? If the creative guy is bad enough, he'll have nowhere else to go...

▶ ad agency...

Would they even know how to hire a tech? What to look for? What programming skills to ask for? Would they do the web stuff, or let the tech guy do it? And then, how do you get a tech guy to stick around when he could make more elsewhere and work in an environment that promotes an efficient SDM as opposed to a more touchy-feely creative process? If the tech guy is bad enough, he'll have nowhere else to go...

Alan Herrell – the head lemur – wrote:

Peter, your suspicions are correct: 'complete solution provider' is an oxymoron.

Sales will tell you anything to get you to sign. Marketing will require sales to do anything to sign. The buzzword weinie will fill you with buzzwords to get you to sign. They like to do meetings, lunch and golf.

I have yet to find a 'complete solution provider' that performs due diligence in terms of: what the client wants to do; who the competition is; what the market size is; if the product/service requires all the toys they wanna sell. If a website is the proper venue for the product and service. (I believe that everyone can benefit from a website, but I am also not blind to the fact that some marketing efforts are better conducted in your face.)

I get cruised by these folks on an annoyingly regular basis. Their e-mails start: 'Saw your site! We are a complete solution provider and would like to offer/work with you.' Their phone calls start: 'Saw your site! We are a complete solution provider and would like to offer/work with you.'

On interrogation, the mailer/caller is working from a script, has no idea what website they are supposed to be talking about, and when asked why did you call/mail me since you are a 'complete solution provider', the answer is the dreaded pregnant pause...

Ruth Arnold wrote:

The way I look at it, an educated client is a better client. So much of our time as website developers is spent telling customers why splash screens are a bad idea, why Java is slow and sometimes just plain sucky and why their site has to be designed to fit other people's screen resolutions and not just their own. Allowing them to find this stuff out for themselves via mine or other people's websites can be an empowering experience. They often have a light bulb moment. This can make my job a lot more rewarding.

There are no shortcuts to educating folk other than automating the process as much as possible and letting them know it's not brain-surgery, it's just something new.

I'm sure the same applies to agency staff, but they don't have any incentive to learn the stuff that I tell my customers, and nor do they have time to I expect. It's all bottom-line stuff in their industry. I don't know what the answer is... maybe starting an agency staffed with designers and developers. But let's face it, developers and designers don't exactly make great sales people and are hardly likely to enjoy spending all day, every day on the phone ;-)

Complementing these anecdotes was a conversation I'd had with the owner of a successful ISP. He'd told me he'd just taken over a web design company that had got into financial difficulties.

I asked why the company had failed and he explained that in their early days they'd been spectacularly successful, expanding rapidly to meet the demand from all the local businesses that wanted to get onto the web.

'The problem,' he explained, 'was that most of these clients weren't really sure what the web could do for them and, after paying out not inconsiderable sums for website designs, found they received no benefit whatsoever and lost interest. This happened so often that the web design company found they were continually having to seek new clients to maintain the level of their business activity. As they exhausted new business opportunities in their own locality, the difficulty and costs of finding new clients increased to the point where the overheads exceeded revenues.'

Applying this scenario universally, it isn't hard to see that most of the blossoming e-business activity is being funded with risk capital. Businesses are hearing so many stories about the vast potential of the internet that they decide to spend some money just to get into the game to see what it is about. A vast proportion of the e-business activity is driven simply by 'me-too-ism', with the blind leading the blind.

Even when a web developer does know what they are doing, it isn't always possible for them to get their message across. One competent web solution provider I know told of a large amount of time she'd spent preparing a proposal for a retail chain of 70 small specialist stores.

> A VAST PROPORTION OF THE E-BUSINESS ACTIVITY IS DRIVEN SIMPLY BY 'ME-TOO-ISM', WITH THE BLIND LEADING THE BLIND

Together with the marketing manager of this company, she'd laid out a plan whereby each store could have its own version of a website where the local manager could provide content and interest specifically for the customers in their own locality. The running costs were negligible and she had quoted a very small fee for setting up this operation because she wanted to have this as a case study for her portfolio.

When the design was finalized, it was presented to the chairman of the company for his acceptance. He took a quick look at the prototype and the price he was being asked to pay and declared, 'No. I'm not going to go for this. My office manager's schoolboy son knows how to build websites, I'll get him to do it.'

emergent opportunities

Such stories abound in the world of e-business. Time and again, examples arise of businesses being unable to take advantage of the internet because of knowledge gaps, misunderstandings and false expectations. Billions of dollars are being thrown away on e-business projects that fail to reach fruition. Expectations and hopes are constantly being dashed. Investment monies are being poured down the drain.

The tragedy is that it needn't be this way. The internet and the web can bring real benefits, increased efficiencies and substantial business expansion, if only business leaders knew how to use the internet to their advantage.

But doesn't this situation provide a plethora of possible opportunities for any e-business ventures that can solve the problems of businesses being able to use the internet efficiently?

6

EXPLORING THE WEIRD

looking beyond what exists already It is easy to see how confusing and incomprehensible the environment of the internet can be for newcomers to the world of e-business, but it is not generally appreciated how even people experienced in communication technology can be equally confused and overwhelmed by the magnitude and lack of stability of the knowledge base. There is too much to know and everything is constantly changing. This viewpoint has been endorsed over and over again in the many different areas of e-business that I've explored.

An even bigger problem is that most people approach the e-business environment with the idea that they should adapt this technology to what they know already. They hate the idea that this is a new environment where they have to forget the past and start from scratch. They seldom accept that this represents a totally new experience where they have to look for opportunities which currently don't exist. This is probably why so many young people succeed in this environment: they are not handicapped with attitudes and conceptual frameworks that they have inherited from the pre-Information Age.

At the start of writing this trilogy, even though I'd been involved in the industry for many years, I certainly didn't understand or even know about all the complexities involved in e-business technology. However, I did have enough sense to realize I didn't know everything and, more importantly, that I couldn't even hope to be able to learn it all. This left me with the choice of selecting a narrow area of speciality where I could have complete and authoritative knowledge of specifics, or working at a higher level of system organization where I'd need a firm grasp of the general.

My preference was to look at the general rather than the particular. After all, this had been my preference over many years as an entrepreneur. However, I'd spent the previous few years in the world of the specialists – specializing in multimedia programming – and I knew that most of the more successful businesses coming out of the information environment were based on exploiting and developing niche areas of technology.

This state of affairs represented a paradox because although niche technical specialists might have to use strategies to become successful in their chosen areas, they were fundamentally tacticians whose activities are ordered up by strategists working at a higher level of organization – the business level. In this way, these technical niche specialists are at the same level of system organization as store keepers who supply picks and shovels to gold-miners: reliant on the exploration and initiatives of others.

For this system of dependency to be maintained, there have to be profitable outcomes for at least some of the explorers and initiators, otherwise the whole system breaks down. This is the area I personally find most interesting – at the business level: finding the gold, not providing the picks and shovels.

To work at the business level, it is necessary to use conceptual models rather than hard facts. However, the problem with e-business is that the field is so new and so changeable that no generally accepted conceptual models have yet emerged. Conventional conceptual models used for businesses in the pre-internet, industrial world don't seem to apply in the environment of mass connectivity.

For me, this meant starting from basics: using the fundamental building blocks of business and applying them in new ways: firstly, in *The Entrepreneurial Web*, creating an abstract framework to think about e-business; secondly, in *The Ultimate Game of Strategy*, to create conceptual tools.

Many readers of the chapters in these two books were impatient with this approach because it wasn't dealing with what they were really interested in, which was to be able to get started straight away to create practical, real-life, e-business ventures. They saw my approach as too theoretical and scholarly, with little relevance to what was happening in the real and practical world of e-business.

They did seem to have a good point at the time because those first two books were written at the time of the dot-com bubble, when many people were making fortunes without bothering to take into account any of the more esoteric aspects of the new communication environment. People were just plunging in, with traditional, Industrial Age concepts, and making lots of money.

However, the bursting of the dot-com bubble justified the time I'd spent considering the more theoretical implications of the new information environment. Those who had plunged in during those early days – trading on other people's ignorance and misconceptions – were stopped dead in their tracks and left wondering where to go next. On the other hand, I was armed with many useful conceptual tools that allowed me to look beyond the day-to-day activity towards a more pragmatic future of the e-business environment.

Perhaps the most significant effect this theorizing had on my thinking was to see e-businesses quite differently from the way businesses had been viewed in the past. Instead of seeing e-businesses in terms of struct-ured forms, fixed physical locations, managed organization and definable assets, I began to see e-businesses as more nebulous entities: as functions within a rapidly changing, universal dynamic system.

From this perspective, it becomes apparent that the most likely route to creating any successful e-business wouldn't be about adapting the new

> I BEGAN TO SEE E-BUSINESSES AS MORE NEBULOUS ENTITIES: AS FUNCTIONS WITHIN A RAPIDLY CHANGING, UNIVERSAL DYNAMIC SYSTEM

technology to established business solutions, but using the communication environment to produce solutions that have no parallel in the everyday world of bricks and mortar. This means using the imagination not to explore the businesses that are already in existence today, but to look for opportunities that might emerge from the more bizarre and unusual properties of the internet environment.

This chapter is about seeing e-business in this light. We are not going to look at conventional business practices and investigate how we can put them on the web, we are going to explore the unusual and the weird, looking for a breakthrough that might lead us to discover a completely new approach to solving problems.

Instead of looking to these old-world business solutions for inspiration we are going to use a green frog approach and start from scratch, seeing e-business as a function of indefinite form in a system space. It is only by looking at e-businesses in this abstract way that it will be possible to create a viable e-business that is likely to survive and prosper in such a fast-changing, competitive world.

visualizing activity within a space

The idea of a system space is not easy to visualize. It is even more difficult to visualize a function within a system space, especially when it is a dynamic system that is constantly evolving. To understand this way of thinking, you might consider a game of football. Normally, it would be considered as a game played between two opposing teams on a football pitch.

A different way to look at this is to think of the pitch as a space that contains football players: a football space. The football would travel around in this space, passing from one player to another. Patterns of play would be observed that involve cooperative movements of players in the football space, which influence the movement of the ball in one direction or another. Players move around in this space, changing their positions and relationships to each other. The coach can alter the patterns of play in this football space by substituting players, or by changing the relationships between the players.

Imagine now that on this football pitch (in this football space) four games are being played simultaneously. There would be eight teams of players and four footballs in the same football space. Imagine the confusion that might be caused; it would be chaos.

Now, imagine you are a coach for one of these teams; wouldn't it make sense to talk to one or more of the other coaches to get your respective teams to cooperate and help each other rather than get in each other's way? With such arrangements being made, it wouldn't be long before other similar arrangements were being made between other coaches. Teams would form strategic alliances and structure their play so as to maximize their ability to assist each other in winning their respective games.

In this situation, it wouldn't be appropriate to think in terms of teams playing on a football pitch; it would be preferable to change the conceptual model and think of players in a playing space that could realize all kinds of innovative patterns of play. It is just this kind of paradigm shift that is needed when transferring from traditional bricks and mortar business thinking to e-business thinking.

an individual within an information space

In Chapter 4, we saw how the metamorphosis of an individual into a super individual is brought about by an individual building up an appropriate group of close contacts and establishing links into various communities – becoming the centre of a network of on-demand information sources.

This can be viewed as an individual being a node in a vast system of information transfer – a point in an information space. This is illustrated in Figure 6.1. (Note: this is identical to Figure 4.2, but we are looking at it with an emphasis on the characteristics of the space rather than the individuals.)

In *The Ultimate Game of Strategy*, it was explained how individuals could enhance the efficiency by which they could acquire information by using the internet to reach out across the information space to acquire

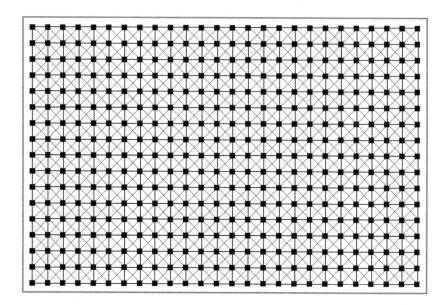

FIG 6.1 Individuals in an information space, where information flows around the space through individual nodes communicating with surrounding contact nodes

information that was not available from their immediate physical surroundings. This is illustrated in Figure 6.2.

This second book in the trilogy also described how the ease and speed of communicating with many contacts in so many different areas can easily lead to an information overload. It described how it would be essential to be able to limit the quantity and control the quality of the available information.

To maximize the efficiency of obtaining information over a wide area, it was proposed that relationships with contacts should be set up so that information is exchanged only on a 'need to know' basis and that contacts should be carefully chosen and selected for their appropriateness to current situations in hand.

It was proposed that the most effective way of doing this would be to limit the number of contacts, and arrange that these contacts are changed at frequent intervals according to how useful they are in current

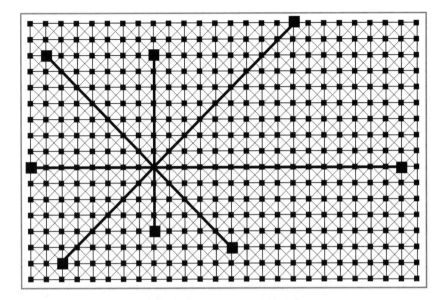

FIG 6.2 An individual can greatly enhance his or her knowledge by using the internet to reach across the information space to gather information from anywhere on the planet

situations. This would see the diagram illustrated in Figure 6.2 as a snapshot at a particular moment in time of an individual's contacts in information space – when the contacts shown would be appropriate to a given situation at that particular moment in time.

As soon as this particular individual's situation changed, it would be strategically more efficient for the individual to form different links with other contacts in different parts of information space. Seen in this way, information space would be seen as a constantly changing dynamic environment where the communication links between individuals are constantly changing as they each respond to the current demands of their local situations. Figure 6.3 illustrates the way in which some contacts might be replaced by others in the information space as a project or situation goes into a different stage.

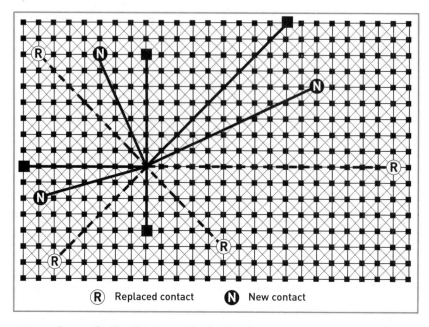

R Replaced contact   N New contact

FIG 6.3 As a project or situation changes direction, some contacts are dropped to be replaced by others in the information space

Such changes in contacts would be a necessary continuous activity for all individuals in the internet information space, as everyone pursues different goals in the face of changing technology and fast-reacting competition. In the far slower and more predictable world of bricks and mortar, the changing and casting off of contacts would be seen as neither practical nor ethical, but in the mass connectivity of the world of e-business, establishing, dropping and re-establishing contact with people is so obviously sensible that it is regarded as normal behaviour.

the virtual café

The practical advantages of being able to change and replace contacts rapidly in the information space of the internet has been adequately covered in the first two books in this trilogy. In *The Entrepreneurial Web*, this was seen in terms of an abstract concept known as Hilbert's space. In *The Ultimate Game of Strategy*, a conceptual tool was described – the virtual café (also described in Chapter 1 of this book) – that can be employed to use information space more efficiently.

The virtual café is a method by which people can optimize a strategy of creating and maintaining a constantly varying contact base. The population of an individual's café of contacts is constantly reviewed and reconfigured at frequent intervals in order for the total information available to an individual to evolve continuously according to their current aims and interests.

Using the metaphor of a café, it is possible to supercharge the relationship of an individual with their contacts by arranging for the contacts to socialize virtually with each other and so cross-fertilize ideas. This involves bringing specific groups of contacts together in mini e-mail discussion forums of short duration, the metaphor being that these are the equivalent of short discussions at a table in a café where selected contacts are invited (or paid) to take part.

It is easy to see how an individual working with an evolving virtual café of contacts and at the same time belonging to a number of e-mail forums can access a wide variety of information and ideas on demand. It is this ability of an individual to use information space intelligently that can transform the individual into a super individual.

The trick now is to employ this same intelligent use of information space to create a superior web presence.

web presence as a system

A virtual café, centred on an individual, can be thought of as a system of interacting components (people) that change and reconfigure as the system (café) responds to the needs of that central individual. Such a system cannot be planned, it has to be grown in order for it to adapt and evolve.

In trying to use a similar approach to building a website identity, the question becomes, 'Where do you start?' The answer has to be 'With a green frog'. The solution has to emerge without preconceptions and free of any stereotyped ideas.

In the last chapter, the green frog approach got as far as creating a web name. But when it came to going on from there – to give the name and address a purpose and functions – there appeared to be a confusion of technology. By asking around, to see how other people were faring in their efforts to create web identities, the way seemed fraught with pitfalls and knowledge gaps.

It would seem that many owners of websites, their advisers and technicians do not really understand what they are doing. They are following each other's lead in a blind attempt to get involved in what they conceive as a potentially beneficial business environment. They follow the latest trends and fashion: from novelty to content, from content to eyeballs and click-throughs. It is like a treasure hunt where the clues are in the form of the latest buzzwords.

Vast sums have been spent on sites that attract mainly other website designers who are eagerly searching each other's sites looking for new ideas. The mystery isn't that some people are getting it wrong: it is that most people are getting it wrong. It seems incredible that so many websites are bleeding the core businesses dry while contributing very little, if anything, to the bottom line.

At the time of writing this chapter, an internet statistics report was published by Pegasus Research International (http://www.pegasusresearch.net), which had analyzed the current burn rate (rate at which companies are spending their capital base) of 339 prominent internet companies. Out of those 339, 80 per cent were found to have a negative cash flow and between them they were burning up cash at the rate of nearly $2 billion every three months. Analysis of the cash flow projections of these companies showed that at least a third of them would probably run out of cash within a year.

The alarming reality is that this was not an analysis of the progress of amateur hopefuls and hastily formed start-up companies: it was a report on most of the leading internet companies of the day. These companies were large and had passed through the traditional avenues of funding where there were safeguards and gateways that were designed to filter out all but the most promising prospects. The inference is that each of these companies must have received their funding after careful screening, after submitting detailed business plans and providing convincing evidence of strong, sound and capable management.

This report then is clear evidence that there is no reliable screening process available. People do not know what elements make up a successful internet company. All the report shows is that the current method of assessment – a seemingly sound business plan, accompanied by strong management – is not only fallible, but has a very high chance of failure.

Given this high failure rate of companies using the conventional and traditional benchmarks for predicting success, we need to find another way: a way that avoids the possibility of cash burn-out before reaching viability. This will almost certainly involve using a strategy that spreads risk and will have to include the ability to change direction rapidly at any time and be able to eliminate quickly any parts of the business that are haemorrhaging cash.

In the first book of this trilogy, *The Entrepreneurial Web*, it was suggested that the best approach to e-business would be to create a system consisting of many small components that interacted with each other. This approach is modelled on OOPS (object-oriented programming systems) used to design highly complex software programs.

It was further suggested that instead of being concerned with the detailed technology of individual system components, attention should be paid only to their functions and the human designers of the components. In this way, a system could be controlled and engineered through interaction with people rather than the underlying technology. Then, all that any system architect would need to be concerned with would be the observable functioning of the components and the messages that are needed to be sent to them to get them to perform.

This makes sense because it would allow fundamental business considerations to become dominant and prevent decision making becoming clouded over with technological issues. Components could be judged only on the basis of whether or not they functioned efficiently. If they do: fine. If not: out of the door next case.

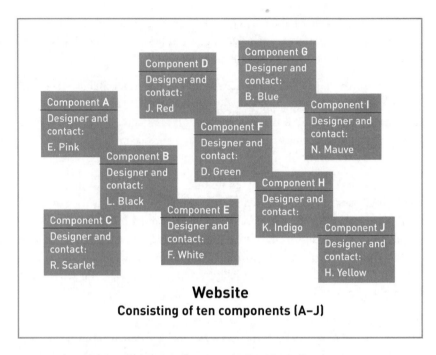

Website
Consisting of ten components (A–J)

FIG 6.4 A complex website – a web presence – can be built up a component at a time, with each component being designed by a different designer

Such a strategy, when applied to the design of a web presence, would see a website and all its functions being broken up into many separate components, with each component being under the responsibility of a specific, named and identified designer (see Figure 6.4).

Viewed in this way, the design of a website can be seen as a process of communication between people rather than a matter of high technology. This will allow the café concept to be used, to arrange the addition of components suitably appropriate for the evolving system. Figure 6.5 illustrates this arrangement with the auteur (the architect of the web presence for the core business) shown as the café owner, dealing with the principal designers of a ten-component web presence system.

By using the virtual café as a conceptual device for organizing e-mails, an auteur, as a system architect, can localize discussions concerning the

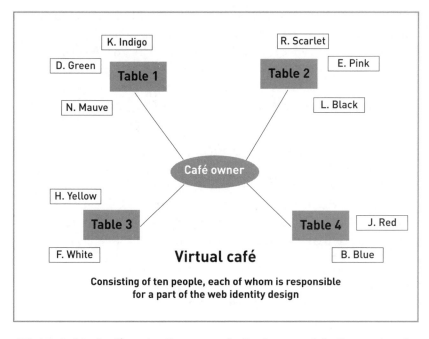

FIG 6.5 A virtual café used as the communication framework for the running of a system to provide a web presence that adapts and evolves

overall requirements of the web presence. Individual components and their functions can be discussed with their designers and the auteur can bring designers together when necessary (at virtual table discussions), to discuss interactions and messaging between components.

Such discussions have no need to be very technical. Technical aspects (and more importantly, technical terms and vocabulary) are best confined to the separate worlds of the component designers. The auteur, or architect of a web presence, will have enough concerns and matters to attend to without needing to learn the technicalities of several totally foreign worlds. All they need is to have their web presence capable of performing certain functions efficiently. The details of how this might be done should be the concern only of the technical designers of the components, not of the auteur or architect of the full system.

NOTE This idea of an organizing level not being concerned with the internal workings of any component at a lower level of the system is one of the principal tenets of object-oriented design. Interaction is confined strictly to message passing, which triggers appropriate functional responses to the messages.

System components can easily be added or removed, simply by changing communication links to bypass or replace them. Similarly, component designers can be included or excluded by including or removing them from the café. The café can also be used to communicate in all kinds of ways with various advisers, consultants and other useful contacts. These can also be brought in and taken out of the café as needs arise or results dictate.

In this way, a web presence can easily be manipulated and tweaked, so that it adapts and evolves quickly enough to cope with fast-changing technology, customer preferences and competitive initiatives. Simply by adding or replacing components, or changing the population of the café, an auteur will have full control of the system – ensuring that it performs efficiently to fulfil the fundamental requirements of the core business.

A complete system – a core business, a collaborative group with a common identity or a single individual – interfacing with a web audience through a website is outlined in Figure 6.6.

the magic of a virtual world

Without any knowledge of the way in which the internet works, it might be assumed that all the components that make up a web presence would have to be based around a single server: namely, the computer that hosts the domain name of the core business. However, the statelessness of the internet data packets means that it doesn't matter where the components of a web presence are located on the web. Each separate component can be on a different computer and these computers can be spread all over the planet and each use different servers. It is only the client that needs to view them all in the same place.

NOTE Websites are just a number of computer files on the server side, with absolutely no connection between them. Connections are only provided by a browser on the client side when it reads the instructions embedded in the files that are downloaded onto a client machine.

It has to be remembered that websites (and total web presences) are assembled as a complete whole by a viewer's browser on the client side. It is only in a client's RAM space that complete websites exist in their viewable forms.

Providing the correct hypertext links are in place, it doesn't matter where the components reside. As far as the audience is concerned these files are

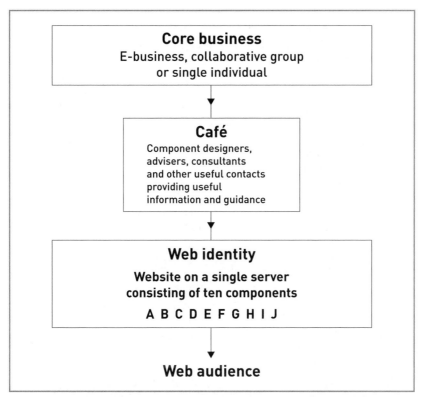

FIG 6.6 The total system consisting of a core business with an interface to a web audience. The interface is a web identity that is made up from components that are organized from within the environment of a virtual café

viewed as a single seamless web presence. Any geographic separations are transparent and the viewer isn't even aware they exist. Such an arrangement is illustrated in Figure 6.7.

How odd this must seem to the mindset of a business executive from the bricks and mortar world of the last century. A web presence that is spread over a number of different computers that might be anywhere in the world? It would seem an incredulous state of affairs; a perverse use of the medium, introducing unnecessary complication where all kinds of things could go wrong. There would seem to be no way to control the system: it would appear to be a manager's nightmare.

NOTE Although in theory it doesn't make any difference where any component of a web presence is located, routing and traffic congestion can greatly affect the arrival times at a client location. This is a design consideration that would have to be taken into account by a component designer to make sure the server chosen to host a component has adequate bandwidth, suitable load balancing facilities and a direct connection to the internet backbone.

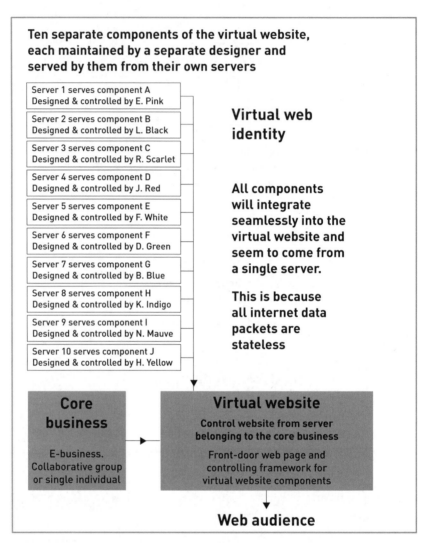

Ten separate components of the virtual website, each maintained by a separate designer and served by them from their own servers

Server 1 serves component A
Designed & controlled by E. Pink

Server 2 serves component B
Designed & controlled by L. Black

Server 3 serves component C
Designed & controlled by R. Scarlet

Server 4 serves component D
Designed & controlled by J. Red

Server 5 serves component E
Designed & controlled by F. White

Server 6 serves component F
Designed & controlled by D. Green

Server 7 serves component G
Designed & controlled by B. Blue

Server 8 serves component H
Designed & controlled by K. Indigo

Server 9 serves component I
Designed & controlled by N. Mauve

Server 10 serves component J
Designed & controlled by H. Yellow

Virtual web identity

All components will integrate seamlessly into the virtual website and seem to come from a single server.

This is because all internet data packets are stateless

Core business

E-business.
Collaborative group
or single individual

Virtual website

Control website from server
belonging to the core business

Front-door web page and
controlling framework for
virtual website components

Web audience

FIG 6.7 A website can consist of many components, each located on different computers in different parts of the world. As far as the audience sees them, they are all part of a single web presence as if they were located on a single server

MANAGERS
HAVE NO PLACE IN
OBJECT-ORIENTED
SYSTEMS

It may well be a manager's nightmare, but managers have no place in object-oriented systems. It is through all the components being separated out that the necessary framework to allow the system to be easily controllable, more adaptable and capable of complex evolutionary growth is provided. Components are not managed, they are simply judged on their performance. If they do their job they stay in, if they don't they are thrown out and replaced.

There is simply no time for a system architect to get involved with anything that goes wrong with a component. The similarity is with the servicing of a modern television set when it develops a fault. The service engineer doesn't spend hours working through all the circuitry to find the problem; it is far more efficient just to locate the fault to a single module and then replace that whole module. In this way, television service engineers don't have to know anything at all about electronic engineering: all they need to know is how to associate any problem with a particular module of the system.

modules can have a life of their own

It is easy to visualize how a television set can consist of different plug-in modules and how the modules can easily be replaced when something goes wrong. It is not too much of a step further to imagine each module being made by a different supplier – and all brought together for a final assembly.

Take this one stage further. Imagine a new company inventing an improved version of one of a television set's modules. This improved module could replace the inferior module – improving the overall performance of the television set. If this kept happening over and over again, with new and improved modules being developed, the performance of the television set would continuously improve with every module change.

It could be that an improvement in a module would be made by the company already supplying that module. At other times a new company might come along, with an innovative design, and so become the new supplier of that module – replacing the previous supplier.

Imagine now a situation where the technology was constantly changing and there were continuous opportunities for modules to be improved. Imagine keen competition between several television set manufacturers.

Wouldn't this create a pressure for more and more improvements in modular designs as each manufacturer strives to get ahead of the others?

Into this scenario, imagine a progressive company developing a new kind of module that could significantly enhance the picture quality of television sets. Wouldn't all the television set manufacturing companies have to include that module in their design? Wouldn't this make the module supplier independent of the television set manufacturers: able to set up a specialist niche?

Imagine this happening over all aspects of a television set, with various module design companies coming up with all kinds of different innovations and improved designs. Would the television set manufacturer need to get involved in any of the detail that went on inside any of the modules? Couldn't the manufacturers save themselves the cost of employing designers and engineers and the costs of all the development and testing? Would they need to get involved with the design at all?

Surely, the core product producers would end up as managers of a system of modules that was evolving autonomously? Their function would be to test the modules and gauge customer reactions. Instead of being designers involved in the technology of television manufacture, the television set manufacturers would become customer relations experts, providing the feedback that influences the way in which the system of modules evolves.

It doesn't happen this way with televisions because there aren't many television set manufacturers and the technology is changing relatively slowly. But what if there were as many television set manufacturers as there are websites? What if the technology involved in television sets changed as much as the technology changed on the web? Wouldn't this breed hosts of module design companies who would be in keen competition with each other to produce new and improved modules?

The trick now is to see a virtual web presence in this same way. It too can consist of modules made by different developers. These web presence modules can be improved or replaced by a multitude of different developers and in this way allow web presence systems to evolve and adapt quickly to a fast-changing, competitive environment. It is this situation we are in now and it is a fertile landscape in which to create viable e-businesses either as system designers or as component developers.

a bottom-up approach to design
Looking at Figures 6.4 and 6.7, they would seem to be illustrating a complete web presence solution that has been broken up into different sections to create the components. This process is known as decomposition and is associated with *top-down approaches* to object-oriented design.

The idea of a top-down design approach is that you carefully plan out what you want to achieve and the way you are going to go about getting the desired results. Costs and time-scales are entered into this plan to produce a model that is then used to monitor and control the progress of the construction. By splitting the project up into different components – object-oriented design (OOD) – different parts can be given to different specialist teams so that they can work simultaneously on the same large project without getting in each other's way or conflicting with each other's designs.

This top-down approach to object-oriented design is used by most large companies and major contractors because it facilitates efficient organization and control as well as meeting the requirements of most traditional funding or investment bodies.

Most people's idea of object-oriented design doesn't extend beyond this top-down approach, with its decomposition of a master plan into components. Unfortunately, a top-down approach is totally unsuited to the volatile environment of the internet because rapidly evolving technology and fast competitive reactions often cause master plans to be out of date even before they are finalized and approved.

The only realistic way to work in such a volatile environment as e-business is to use object-oriented design techniques with a *bottom-up approach*. With this approach there is no master plan; solutions are grown, one component at a time. Each component is integrated sequentially into an expanding whole: added separately to a dynamic design that is constantly adapting and evolving.

> RAPIDLY EVOLVING TECHNOLOGY AND FAST COMPETITIVE REACTIONS OFTEN CAUSE MASTER PLANS TO BE OUT OF DATE EVEN BEFORE THEY ARE FINALIZED AND APPROVED

To the business mindset of the Industrial Age, such an approach is unthinkable because without a master plan such a system would seem to be disorganized and liable to spin out of control. Yet, in the volatile and unpredictable environment of e-business, the reverse is true. It is the master plan that is liable to become unstable rapidly and the gradually evolving system that is most easily controllable.

This state of affairs throws many conventional businesses into total disarray. This is typified by the following post that was sent in by one of the readers in the virtual café after reading the last chapter:

I am head of marketing for a fast-growing young company that trains business people in the management, marketing and strategy issues of the internet.

I've just finished reading Chapter 5 of *Web Presence*. It's fascinating for me, as it is moving so close to problems and issues I come across every day. Previously, my attempts to interest my work colleagues in the ideas contained in *The Entrepreneurial Web* – which I was very excited by – were hampered by the perception that you were engaging with problems at a very conceptual level, and the company prides itself on providing help and advice of a very practical 'real-work' kind.

My own limited experience of managing an e-business project – when I was put in charge of project managing a piece of development on our own website – has shown me how completely on-the-money your views are about the efficacy of managed teams and forward planning. The team kept asking me for my vision of what the finished site overhaul would look like, and I kept refusing to provide it.

I told them that any vision we had now would be completely out of date in three weeks' time, and that instead we were going to evolve the site from where it was at that point towards something we would all feel was a site we wanted to use.

When I started talking about green frogs they looked at me as if I were mad. However, despite serious doubts being cast on my sanity, I succeeded through this method in opening our membership area and getting the site – which contains some 1,000 pages – more or less completely up to date for the first time in a year.

My successor in the hot seat has adopted a more traditional approach. He currently faces familiar problems of overruns, loss of key members of his team and the consequent non-appearance of deliverables within the original time-frame.

This post illustrates a dilemma common to many people at the cutting edge of e-business solutions. Their professional position forces them to hold conventional views, but their personal experiences tell them that these ways aren't working. It's a catch-22 situation: if you propose or advise a strategy that is unacceptable you lose credibility – yet, if you propose or advise on a strategy that is acceptable you know it won't work.

The only way around this impasse is to go back to basics: go through the steps of conventional decision-making processes to see where they might be going wrong. Isolating e-business problems in this way might not only find solutions but also lead to discovering unexpected e-business opportunities.

> **IF YOU PROPOSE OR ADVISE A STRATEGY THAT IS UNACCEPTABLE YOU LOSE CREDIBILITY – YET, IF YOU PROPOSE OR ADVISE ON A STRATEGY THAT IS ACCEPTABLE YOU KNOW IT WON'T WORK**

object-oriented, e-business solutions using FSPs

A phenomenon that has emerged in the Information Age is the FSP (function service provider). This is effectively a virtual employee, who performs a speciality function for a company based on some speciality knowledge or expertise in a particular software application. Although these FSPs will be owned and run by people outside the company, they will perform in much the same way as a regular employee working in house: fulfilling particular essential roles. The difference is that they will be responsible for purchasing, running and maintaining any software or hardware they use.

These FSPs are evolving out of ASPs (applications service providers) to provide a variety of niche service functions. The services are usually provided on the basis of low rental, short time commitment SLAs (service level agreements). This enables auteurs and entrepreneurs to construct low-cost, highly complex businesses – simply by piecing together the ready-made modules in the same way that a child might build a structure with Lego-set components. This is illustrated in Figure 6.8.

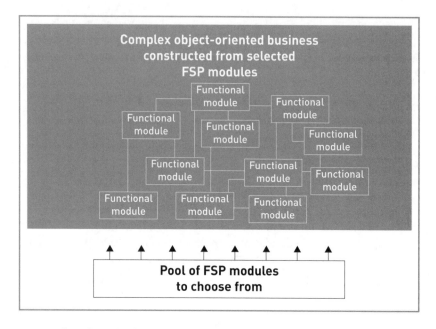

FIG 6.8 Complex e-businesses can be constructed from ready-made FSP modules

As FSP services are provided on a one-to-many basis, the monthly rental costs charged to individual clients will be far less than clients could provide the same service for themselves in house. Also, the fact that the SLAs allow short-term commitments means that modules can be changed very quickly and at virtually no capital cost.

low-cost flexibility

Industrial Age business strategists also build businesses in a modular way, but they are very different from the modular structures possible in the Information Age. Modular functionality will be added by treating the new modules as projects and appointing managed teams to develop the functions.

The conventional Industrial Age sequence of events would be:

1   plan the construction of the function;

2 submit those plans to a funding authority and, if the funding is agreed:

3 appoint a team and a team leader;

4 build and test the new modular extension to the business.

In the environment of the Information Age, there is seldom a need to custom-build a modular function. Almost invariably, somewhere on the internet, there will be somebody providing a suitable service to carry out any particular function needed. Therefore, Information Age strategists will not have to plan a design, spend capital to build the function or take time to test it – they will simply select a ready functioning service and start using it straight away.

If Industrial Age strategists find a functional module unsuitable, or becoming redundant, they will have to write off the capital investment. For Information Age specialists there will be no capital investment to write off – they simply cancel the renting of any functional service if it proves unsuitable or becomes redundant.

The cost of continually adapting a business to a fast-changing competitive environment might require many sequences of modular replacements. For the Industrial Age strategist this will involve innumerable delays and capital costs. For the Information Age strategist, adapting the business to change is simply a matter of exchanging functional services – instantaneous changes, involving no capital costs.

Renting functional services, instead of custom-designing them, also changes the nature of the funding requirements for business expansions. With Industrial Age strategies, large sums of capital have to be allocated to allow a company to expand. But with an Information Age strategy, expansion is arranged simply by increasing the total amount of the outgoing service agreement rentals to cover the rentals for any new modules needed for the expansion.

The ability to expand and contract a business easily and cheaply is vital in the e-business environment. New technological developments, competitive initiatives, and rapidly changing trends and fashions can leave a business high and dry almost overnight. A business needs to be able to survive these periods without extensive financial loss or having to suffer debilitating cash haemorrhaging with the burn rate eroding the capital base.

This marks the difference between Industrial Age and Information Age businesses: one is designed for stability in a stable environment, the other is designed for adaptability and survival in a chaotic and unpredictable environment.

AN AUTEUR'S THINKING PROCESS

AT THIS MID-POINT IN THE BOOK, I realized time was running short if I was to create a business before the book was published. Also, the readers of the chapters in the virtual café were getting impatient because I hadn't told them what kind of business I was going to set up.

The fact was that, at this stage of the book, I had no idea as to what the business was likely to be. All I had was a number of potentially useful contacts and a range of conceptual models that were waiting for the right opportunity to come along. Not surprisingly, it looked for all the world as if the previous chapters were nothing more than the fanciful speculations of an academic dreamer.

However, as has been pointed out in previous chapters, ideas and opportunities are of little value unless they can be acted on. This needs an infrastructure in place *before*, not after, the decision to create a business is made. Creating this infrastructure may take months, even years, but once in place, opportunities can be seized upon and put into action immediately.

In almost all books dealing with the creation of a business, this period of building a suitable infrastructure is never fully covered. Probably, the reason for this is that it is a very nebulous area that is highly dependent on the nature of the business and the personality of the auteur.

These next two chapters, 7 and 8, are an attempt to throw some light on this enigmatic, infrastructure-building process – which is so necessary before an auteur can be in a position to take positive action.

Be warned though, the thinking processes described are personal to the author and are specifically applicable to dealing with the highly volatile environment of e-business. Also, it must be taken into account that this is the rationalization of a thinking process, which may be somewhat different from the actual thinking process itself. However, the reader may gain some little insight into the mysterious circumstances from which many businesses emerge.

7

BOUNDARIES OF THE
SOLUTION SPACE

reverse engineering a thought process This chapter was
particularly difficult to write because I wanted to describe a rational
approach to creating an e-business from scratch, while, at the same time,
actively trying to create an e-business myself (to use as a real-life example
and a proof of concept). The problem was that the way I was describing
how it should be done wasn't the way I was actually going about it.

What I then had to do was to reverse engineer the thinking processes I'd
been using to create an e-business, to see why it differed from what I'd
written. To my surprise, I discovered I'd slipped into a top-down approach
when describing what had to be done, yet, in real life, I'd been using a
bottom-up approach.

The difference hinged on the way I'd described a solution space. In describing what it is and how it can be used, I'd made the mistake of treating
the solution space as a static environment that contains a number of
different possible solutions that are selected from.

This is a conventional, top-down approach that first creates possible
solutions and then uses some form of decision theory to select between

them. In other words, I was seeing the solutions space as a place to hold a number of possible business ideas, which can be selectively tried out.

By reverse engineering my thinking process, I realized that I wasn't starting off by creating a list of possible e-business solutions. What I was actually doing was to treat the solution space as a dynamic environment where components are thrown together and business solutions allowed to manifest by themselves out of the mix – my solution space was a dynamic space from which e-business solutions evolve spontaneously.

However, understanding what I was doing was one thing; being able to describe it, quite another. I was completely stumped for a simple way to describe how a dynamic solution space works. Then, out of the blue, from one of the tables in the virtual café, came a perfect example of a dynamic solution space being used to create paths on a university campus.

an unplanned, emergent solution

In the café discussions following the last chapter, there were various speculations on various types of strategy that wouldn't need a plan. At one table, an interesting anecdote was told by Yvan Caron, who described how some 50 years previously an architect had submitted plans for the design of a college campus that didn't include any pathways between the buildings.

When this omission was pointed out, the architect told the client that he'd purposely left out the pathways because the students would find their own best routes between the buildings. When these routes became visible, as worn tracks through the grass, he could pave them over.

Another at the table, Joe Repta, responded:

The campus of Yvan's anecdote was in fact Michigan State University, where I spent my undergrad days. I've always remembered that story as having an important message.

We see this effect in many different places today, dirt paths that cut through planted grass in places where sidewalks don't take people where they want to go. Most successful web services have grown in a similar way, as have most computer application programs: all beginning from some minimal seed concept, minimally (and cheaply) implemented and developing according to user wishlists.

I suggest that one way to grow a set of contacts and attract relevant strengths is a cheap, quick and dirty implementation of what seems like a good idea.

This anecdote, of the paths that evolved without any plan or deliberate design, captures perfectly the essence of a bottom-up strategy using a dynamic solution space. An unstructured landscape is presented and then allowed to take its own shape. But Joe Repta put his finger on the stumbling block of this approach when he suggested starting out with 'what seems a good idea'.

This highlights the real problem: it is easy to get a system to self-organize, but from what base do you get the system started? What should be the initial 'good idea' that triggers a dynamic system into self-organizing? In other words, what components and framework of ideas have to be present to enable a business to self-organize by means of a bottom-up process?

Normally, the framework and components for a business are provided by the business plan, but the catch-22 is that we can't create a business plan because, just like the pathways between the campus buildings, we can't be sure what the best plan will turn out to be.

What is needed, therefore, is the equivalent of the untrodden grass between the campus buildings: a virgin space from which a solution can emerge. We need a framework that will allow the initial ideas for a business to manifest spontaneously, similar to the way in which paths manifest on the campus grass – a solution space that will birth optimal e-business ideas.

a static, top-down solution space
A top-down solution space is simply a mental construct with which to visualize a rich search area when searching for a solution when a goal has been specified. It is a static space to hold the most likely solutions.

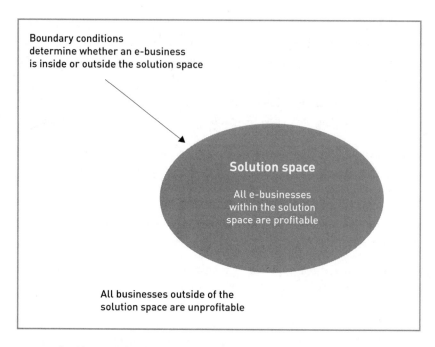

Boundary conditions
determine whether an e-business
is inside or outside the solution space

Solution space

All e-businesses
within the solution
space are profitable

All businesses outside of the
solution space are unprofitable

FIG 7.1 In this example of a top-down solution space, the single boundary condition is that the businesses should all be profitable. Therefore all businesses within the solution space contain profitable solutions

Figure 7.1 illustrates a typical top-down solution space that relies on using historical information to find a profitable e-business solution. The boundary conditions are such that only profitable e-businesses are included in the solution space as, by definition, these must have solved the problem of becoming profitable.

Such a top-down solution space, as illustrated by Figure 7.1, is used by Industrial Age business strategists to find business solutions for success. They isolate successful companies in an area of business they are interested in, put them into the solution space and then examine them closely to look for pointers to successful ideas, strategies or tactics.

However, this is a top-down approach, where the solutions within the solution space have been tried and proven. E-business is too new and too volatile to be able to use this kind of solution space; it needs a solution

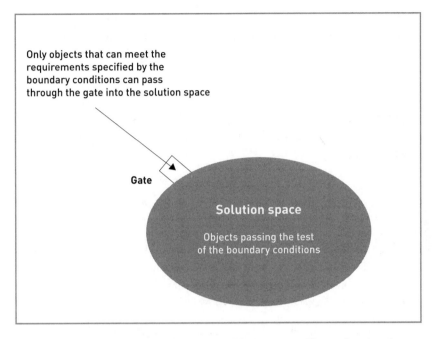

FIG 7.2 The generic form of the top-down solution space, illustrating that the boundary conditions act like a gate to let certain objects in and keep other objects out

space that contains promising ideas, solutions that perhaps nobody has tried before. The difficulty, though, is to know what is and what is not a promising idea.

What boundary conditions would need to be imposed to create a solution space that included only good ideas and excluded all the bad ideas? If we could arrange such a space, it would allow us to concentrate our efforts more efficiently and not waste our time on dead-end ventures.

To do this, a more generic version of the solution space will be needed. This is illustrated in Figure 7.2, where the boundary conditions are shown as creating a gateway into the space. The objects that satisfy the boundary conditions are allowed to go through the gateway into the space and those that don't are kept out.

What is needed with this top-down approach is a way to separate good ideas from bad ideas. But this assumes that it is possible to work out what the critical criteria for success are. We don't know this.

In the volatile world of e-business, nobody can know what these criteria should be. This is self-evident, because if it were possible to work out the boundary conditions for separating good ideas from bad ideas everyone would be able to become rich and venture capital companies wouldn't make mistakes.

a dynamic, bottom-up solution space

In the last chapter, it was proposed that rather than starting out with an initial idea, it might be better to begin by building a core strength and a number of useful contacts. In this way business ideas can be preferentially selected to match the capabilities of the business (as opposed to creating a business to match any business ideas).

This strategy can be described in terms of a dynamic solution space, where the solution space is the catchment area for all ideas that can be managed by the system of assets, skill sets and potential collaborative associations that together constitute the capabilities of an individual or a business. This is illustrated in Figure 7.3.

The solution space is thus defined as a selection of business ideas that can adequately be handled by the core strengths that have been developed by the business (the core strengths being enhanced through having a number of trusted contacts who can be called on to advise, assist or form collaborative alliances).

To appreciate the dynamics of this model, think of the ideas in the solution space as being observed under a magnifying glass. Adding extra assets, skill sets or useful contacts to a business will have the effect of moving the magnifying glass over to another group of ideas which are more appropriately suited. This is illustrated in Figure 7.4.

In this way, it can be seen that business ideas are a dynamic consequence of the structure and components of the business. This is quite different

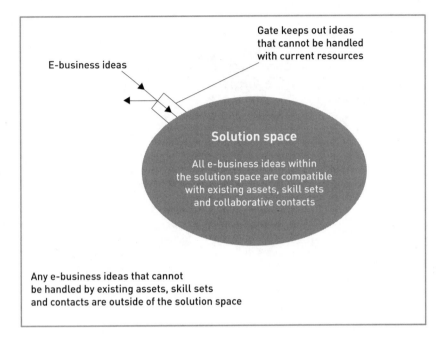

FIG 7.3 A dynamic, bottom-up solution space that includes only those ideas that are compatible with existing assets, skill sets and contacts

from a top-down approach, where once an idea is decided on it becomes the basis for reshaping the business to accommodate the idea.

This strategy, of creating the core strengths before coming up with an idea, is not intuitive. When Wendi Murray, an entrepreneur from Australia, read the last chapter in the virtual café she responded:

In Chapter 5 Peter wrote:

'A business idea has the best chance of being brought to fruition if it is born into the right environment (where a suitable infrastructure and the necessary contacts are in place). Surely, then, it would make sense to wait until these conditions are in existence before firming up or going ahead with any specific e-business idea?'

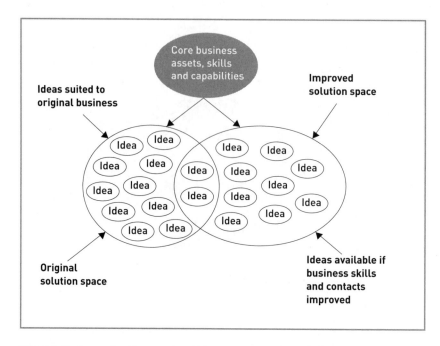

FIG 7.4 By improving the assets, skills or contacts, the solution space will effectively move to include a different set of business ideas that can be accommodated

Although I agree with this, it implies that the 'right environment' is known and so the 'suitable infrastructure' *can* be in place. Surely a pre-existing environment and infrastructure will limit the kinds of ideas to be considered, so again, a top-down weeding-out of environment/infrastructure ideas is needed?

This illustrates where a conceptual difficulty can occur because it is natural to assume that a 'right environment' or a 'suitable infrastructure' is planned for a particular purpose. But the whole point of a bottom-up approach is that the future is not anticipated so it cannot be planned for or taken into account.

The environment and the infrastructure are created without any specific business idea in mind. They are created in the same way that people get themselves educated: there is no specific application in mind, just the accumulation of various contacts, knowledge and experiences that create a favourable position to be in to be able to take an opportunity when it arises.

If you ask students what job they are going to get when they finish their education they are unlikely to be able to give a definite answer. They are just building up a favourable position for themselves, so as to be more easily accepted by a company when a suitable job opportunity arises. This is exactly the same strategy that is needed for the volatile environment of the web: build an asset base; a skill set; a personal (or local) knowledge base; a set of useful contacts – and then search for a suitable opportunity that is suited to this mix.

This strategy will create a filter, which will rule out many possible options, but doesn't the choice of education do exactly the same thing? Doesn't a particular choice of education or set of experiences act as a filter to direct you towards a limited selection of options? Doesn't an increased education, or a richer set of work experiences, open the door to better opportunities? Looked at in this way, it makes a lot of sense to spend time building up a strong position first before looking for ideas.

The concept is clearer if you consider the business strategy of a typical niche specialist who might decide to concentrate on a particular small area of speciality. The specialist will need to build up this expertise before taking on any substantial assignments. The area of expertise chosen will limit the type of assignments that can be taken. Their solution space might then be defined as consisting of all the businesses that would have need of the speciality service they are capable of handling. This scenario is illustrated in Figure 7.5.

services and consultancies
Figure 7.5 describes a limited area of business known as the service industry (this would also include all manner of consultancies and advisory services). The prime focus of these service businesses would be to:

1 establish an expertise in a chosen area of speciality;

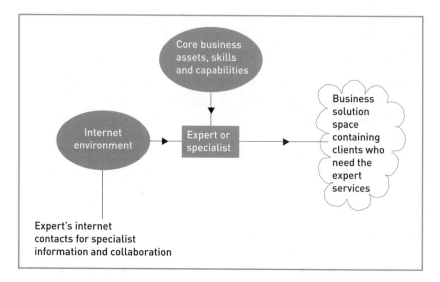

FIG 7.5 A typical special service company whose business solutions could be described as a space containing all the clients who would have need of their services. Improve the expertise or ability to collaborate and the content of this solution space will improve

2 maintain this expertise in the face of competition and continuous technological change;

3 build a reputation for competence, reliability and value;

4 make sure there is sufficient continuity of work to maintain the workforce.

It might seem that such businesses would not be subject to undue risk because the work projects and goals would be specified by a client and the contracts would be such that these service providers would get paid whatever the success or otherwise of the client's business venture.

In the Industrial Age, this might have been the state of affairs, but in the rapidly changing world of the Information Age, any business based on a service is basically unstable for the following reasons:

1 It is a gamble as to whether or not the area of expertise chosen for a service business remains fashionable for any reasonable length of time.

2   Maintaining expertise in the light of continuous technological change
    is time consuming and expensive and can eat away at profitability.

3   Unrealistic expectations and a lack of technical knowledge by clients
    can easily cause clients to be lost and reputations ruined.

4   Fast-changing technological trends can quickly cause skill sets to
    become redundant. Staff who do have currently fashionable skill sets
    tend to be highly mobile because of high demand for their expertise.
    These factors make it extremely difficult for companies with skilled
    employees to maintain a constant level of reliability and competence,
    resulting in reputations having short shelf-lives.

5   Because of a lack of technical knowledge it is extremely difficult for a
    client to know whether or not they are getting good value for a
    highly technical service. This makes it very difficult for truly superior
    service companies to compete against inferior services that put special
    emphasis on sales and marketing. This does not put them out of
    business but often sees them at the poorly paid bottom of a food
    chain (see note below).

Such instability does not suit either investors or large companies so the
bulk of this service work is done through individual freelancers, small
companies or associations. They can be more flexible, able to change
direction easily. They can build and develop their knowledge and
expertise in specific niche areas, gradually establish a reputation and a
portfolio of regular clients. This is usually sufficient to ensure a reasonably good income: enough to reward them amply for their efforts.

who hires the services?
There are millions of people working in
the service industries. By definition, they are all earning money by
helping others to make money, so their earnings are dependent on the
needs, ideas and initiatives of others. These others might be described as:

1   other service industry individuals or companies which need specialist
    niche services to augment their own range of services;

THE TECHNOLOGICAL FOOD CHAIN

Most technical specialists are not sales people and resent having to use their valuable time visiting and talking to clients who seldom appreciate the depth of their technical knowledge. Sales people on the other hand have no time to spend learning the technicalities because they spend most of their time looking after clients and chasing around looking for new business.

This situation creates symbiotic relationships and hierarchies of dependencies – known as the food chain – which although essential is often resented, as is illustrated by the post to a table in the café by Stephen Roberts:

... everyone who works in the new-media industry in London knows that there exists a food chain. A big client goes to its PR department with a requirement for a website. They contact an advertising agency which will brief a specialist web agency. Often this large agency will then subcontract to one of the small website companies around town. Below this chain is a huge raft of bottom-feeding freelancers, picked up on an *ad hoc* job-by-job basis.

I assure you this is true and sometimes the chain is even longer. It's a sort of evil version of what we were talking about and it's honestly not a fulfilling way of working (I've often been told to lie to a client as to where I was calling from with a project-related inquiry).

2   managers in companies who are outsourcing services;

3   entrepreneurs who are creating speculative business enterprises.

In the Industrial Age economy, entrepreneurial contributions were confined mostly to the early phases of the life cycle of a business. As soon as a business became established, it would be restructured and formalized to ensure the activities of the business would be carried out efficiently, reliably and consistently. This transition normally involved replacing the entrepreneurial functions with managerial functions. The call for services was then switched from being under the control of entrepreneurs to being under the control of managers. This situation is illustrated in Figure 7.6.

In the e-business environment of the Information Age, there are constant technological changes and developments. This continually opens up new opportunities for competitive initiatives. In such an environment, it is not reasonable to expect a business to reach a state of stable maturity where the running of a business can be handed over to trained managers.

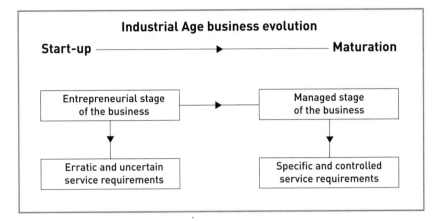

FIG 7.6 Industrial Age business usually matured from an entrepreneurial stage to a managed stage. This changed the nature of the service requirements

Instead, a business has to be organized to be highly adaptive to cope with unpredictable change. This situation is illustrated in Figure 7.7.

The need for a business to become flexible and adaptive requires that a business becomes predominantly concerned with change and uncertainty.

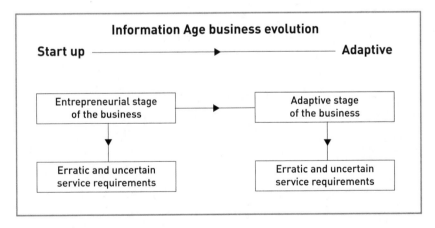

FIG 7.7 In the volatile environment of e-business, there is continuous change. This prevents businesses settling down to a stable state of maturity. Instead, they have to become adaptive

This will need entrepreneurial rather than management thinking, making it impossible to replace entrepreneurial functions with managerial functions.

Managers and entrepreneurs have to have completely different mindsets; these are not compatible. Managers will try to eliminate change as much as possible, while entrepreneurs relish change and use it to gain advantage. This difference in attitudes will greatly affect the way each will make use of services:

▶ Managers will be looking for methods, procedures and controls, to provide stability and consistency. Entrepreneurs will see these as handicapping the ability of the business to adapt and respond to new situations.

▶ Managers will want to formalize all arrangements with services. They'll want specifications and binding contracts with long-term commitments. Entrepreneurs on the other hand will prefer very loose arrangements with built-in flexibility and no long-term commitments.

▶ Managers will prefer to keep service arrangements to a minimum, bringing as much work in-house as possible where they can exercise more control. Entrepreneurs will prefer to use as many outsourced services as possible, so that the core business has a minimum of overheads and does not get locked into redundant or out-of-date methods or technology.

It is this difference, between the strategy of a manager and the strategy of an entrepreneur, that epitomizes the difference between Industrial Age and Information Age businesses. This will be critical when it comes to devising a suitable e-business strategy.

8

THE BACKGROUND TO CREATING AN E-BUSINESS

the uncertainty of an entrepreneurial strategy

By sending each chapter of this book out to readers in the virtual café as soon as it is written, I get feedback as to how different people are reacting to the content. At this stage of the book, these opinions and reactions are varying immensely.

Because the stated aim of the book is to create an e-business during the writing, a few are getting impatient because they are expecting me to come up with some great idea where everyone in the café will be involved. Some are even waiting to be given detailed instructions as to what to do next. But it doesn't work that way. Ideas and plans emerge. They are not the starting point in the birth of an e-business.

In a conventional, Industrial Age business environment, businesses can start with ideas and plans because it is possible to make predictions and work with known quantities. Generally speaking, needed assets and services can be bought, hired or loaned because they have a known value. This allows profit sharing by means of employment or work contracts, where the principals take the risks and the hired services or labour can be allocated a fixed amount for their contribution regardless of the success or otherwise of the business outcome.

Businesses associated with risk or uncertain outcomes are usually set up in ways that offset some of the risks to the principals or the investors. Stock options, sales incentives, profit sharing or bonus schemes are introduced. Direct employment is replaced by agencies or affiliate arrangements that pay for results on a commission basis. As a general rule, the higher the risks, the more appropriate it becomes to replace fixed costs by variable costs that are dependent on actual profits earned.

This is what makes e-businesses so different from Industrial Age businesses. There are so many uncertainties and unknowns, so much unpredictability that there has to be an extremely high proportion of variable costs and a minimum of fixed costs. It is the skill of the auteur or entrepreneur to set up a business in this way.

Planning only works if somebody is willing to finance the plan, because it involves instructing people what to do. This is why e-business is not about organization and control because it doesn't make sense to finance labour in situations where outcomes are unpredictable. With e-business environments so volatile, the game is about the spreading and sharing of risk, rather than the spreading and sharing of profit.

> **E-BUSINESS IS NOT ABOUT ORGANIZATION AND CONTROL BECAUSE IT DOESN'T MAKE SENSE TO FINANCE LABOUR IN SITUATIONS WHERE OUTCOMES ARE UNPREDICTABLE**

Even when a strategy is concerned with sharing risks, this sharing does not mean gratuitously giving people shares just for taking part. Shares would be offered and taken up only by the people whose contributions would be deemed essential to the success of the business.

At the start of a business, there is nothing tangible to share; all there might be is some vague expectation of a profitable outcome. If everybody had the same expectation and everyone could put in the same effort and each be equally valuable to the business, then a sharing agreement might be possible.

In a high-risk, unpredictable situation, the reality is far from this. Everyone would have a different personal assessment as to the risks and possible outcomes. As a consequence, each would contribute with different commitments and enthusiasm. As the direction and progress of the enterprise are likely to be unpredictable, there is no way of knowing what the value of any single person's future contribution might be. This makes it extremely difficult for auteurs or entrepreneurs to make deals and arrangements because there is no tangible foundation on which to base share-type agreements.

The alternative to agreed sharing is to form alliances, or collaborative associations that are based on dependencies. These are arrangements where people cannot proceed in a venture without certain vital assets or capabilities that they do not possess themselves. The strategy of the entrepreneur is then a matter of searching for these dependencies and melding them together into some kind of interactive dynamic system, where the dependencies are the glue that holds it all together.

The way this is done cannot be formularized. There can be no rules or guidelines; the exact nature of the system that emerges would be dependent on what components are available and the combinations that turn out to be compatible. However, as the object of this book is to explain all the stages of creating an e-business from scratch, I have to make an attempt to describe this enigmatic process.

There are three different ways I could approach the writing of this birthing stage of a business:

1   as the description of a strategy I intend to use;

2   as the description of a strategy I have used and found successful;

3   as a strategy I'm currently using as I write this chapter.

I am using the third of these approaches and rationalizing the thinking processes as I go along.

the business situation at the start of this chapter

With no specific business idea, no business plan, no management structure and no finance, the situation might seem utterly hopeless. Yet that is exactly the position I find myself in at the start of writing this chapter.

However, I have three important assets:

1 a web presence: my personal website that explains who I am, what I have done and what I am doing;

2 a virtual café, which contains a number of valuable contacts;

3 a conceptual toolbox: a collection of mental models based on past experiences.

With only these three assets, I have to achieve the stated aim of the book, which is to create an e-business before the book is completed.

In fact the situation isn't as hopeless as it might appear to be. The apparent handicap of having no fixed business plan, no management structure and no funding is a distinct advantage at this stage. Freed from the constraints that would normally be imposed on a conventionally funded business, I am able to use a low-cost, low-burn-rate, freewheeling strategy that allows me to change course and direction at will, switching between opportunities and prospects as events unfold. I have total freedom to use my own discretion and have to account to nobody.

Such freedom is not available to funded businesses or businesses that have sold some of their equity in the stock market. They have to maintain a reasonable appearance of order and stability – which burns up capital even when the company is not trading. They have to rationalize their strategies, formalizing them into written plans so that decisions can be explained and justified.

Imagine telling a funding body that you are not sure whether the business is going to be creating a database for medical treatments, developing an internet course for schoolchildren, designing and selling intelligent agent software, providing website construction services, building a system of ASPs, forming a virtual social club, opening a penny bazaar, organizing the servicing of aircraft, or perhaps something else altogether. They would be tearing their hair out and insisting on bringing in new management. Yet this is the exact situation I find myself in at the start of writing this chapter. These are the opportunities at hand.

How can such a situation make sense? This chapter is an attempt to provide a rational explanation.

copying the master strategist

As was explained in the first book of this trilogy, *The Entrepreneurial Web*, an auteur, or an entrepreneur, might appear to be acting in an irrational manner, but underlying the apparent randomness and disorder there is usually some kind of abstract model that forms the basis for a rational strategy. These abstract models are not always easily explainable. They are usually generic, seldom relating to any specific business situation.

The advantage of working with these abstract models is that they can be applied to any situation. This is why entrepreneurs are often successful in many different kinds of businesses. They might see openings and opportunities in unfamiliar fields, which have not been recognized by people who have been working in the fields for a long time.

The abstract models I use are based on the mechanisms that have been devised to explain biological evolution. This may seem utterly bizarre, but in terms of strategies that deal with uncertainty and competition, Mother Nature is the master strategist of all time. Her strategies for creating viable products and system solutions have proved consistently successful over billions of years. Why look for something different when such a provenly successful model is readily available?

> " MOTHER NATURE IS THE MASTER STRATEGIST OF ALL TIME "

Mother Nature's evolutionary strategy doesn't have any initial ideas or preconceptions. There are no plans or management structures, no rules or protocols. Connectiveness and associations are through chance and necessity. The main goal is to survive and prosper in the face of intense competition, but isn't this the fundamental goal of all e-businesses?

The key to Mother Nature's success is her strategy's ability to reverse the second law of thermal dynamics. This is the fundamental law of physics, which states that all systems progress relentlessly towards a state of increased entropy. In simple terms, this law is saying that all ordered systems have a tendency to become progressively less ordered and more disorganized.

Mother Nature's way of reversing this law is to create self-regulating systems that employ feedback to eliminate ruthlessly all elements that degrade the system and, at the same time, promote the elements that enhance it. It is a blind approach – relying on chance and opportunity – guided only by feedback from results.

It is just such a strategy that will be employed here. The engine to drive this process will be the virtual café.

many ways to use the café

The breakthrough in appreciating the full potential of the virtual café comes from the realization that the café can be used in many different ways and for many different purposes. As a conceptual tool it is a polymorph: it can be reconceptualized to suit any number of different situations.

In *The Ultimate Game of Strategy*, it was explained how the concept of the virtual café can be used to organize and control a conventional Industrial Age business environment. Executives can use the concept to visualize the various people within their sphere of responsibility as sitting at various tables in a café and, through the asynchronous nature of e-mail communications, appear to be sitting at each table at the same time.

In effect, this would be like the executive spending all the time in various different meetings with everyone in the company but not having to be physically present at any particular time or place. In this way the café can be used to create a virtual world, where time can be distorted in ways that would put any science fiction novel to shame.

Also described in *The Ultimate Game of Strategy* was a way in which the virtual café can be used to inspire and guide the writing of books. This saw the author sitting at many different tables in a café where different groups of readers were commenting on the chapters as they were written.

As mentioned in Chapter 4, the café can also be treated as a conceptual framework, to organize personal interactions with various contacts, peer groups, people with complementary knowledge or skill sets. Communications can be structured and organized in the café to be optimally efficient for the purpose of enhancing personal capabilities and effectiveness.

Most people's first reaction to the virtual café is to think of it in terms of its bricks and mortar counterpart, where it fulfils the purpose of a social meeting place. This would see the café as generating business opportunities through rational discussion, mutual agreement and cooperation between the people in the café. But the way the café is used involves moving people from table to table, and removing them from the café altogether if they aren't contributing to the discussions.

Such behaviour would be frowned on in a real-world café, but in a virtual world it becomes acceptable because the café is not the same as its bricks and mortar counterpart; it is in fact an abstract framework for organizing personal internet communications efficiently. Certainly the café can be usefully employed to simulate a conventional café with conventional social protocols, but there are more subtle and powerful ways in which the café can be used.

creating an adaptive café of contacts

A virtual café is simply a list of currently active personal contacts. It will contain people who have become established as confidants, friends, cooperators and collaborators; people who provide reliable information, specialist help or services. It will contain useful contacts who know other useful contacts in many different areas of knowledge and experience. It will contain people who can provide funding, legal help or accountancy services. Most importantly, it will contain people with problems – problems where the solutions might lead to the discovery of profitable business opportunities.

In effect, the virtual café is a personal interface to the world at large, a collection of people who would be likely to assist the café owner to survive and prosper in a competitive world of high technology and massive connectivity. Such a virtual café is illustrated in Figure 8.1.

Creating a café full of personal contacts has been fully covered in the previous two books in this trilogy. Suffice to say here that the café will contain only people with whom the café owner has built up some kind of

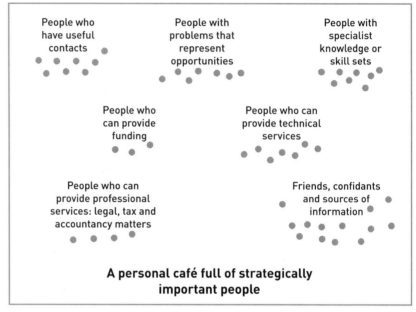

People who have useful contacts

People with problems that represent opportunities

People with specialist knowledge or skill sets

People who can provide funding

People who can provide technical services

People who can provide professional services: legal, tax and accountancy matters

Friends, confidants and sources of information

A personal café full of strategically important people

FIG 8.1 The café as a personal interface to the world

special relationship. As such relationships have to be established over a series of many exchanges that engender mutual trust and credibility, these cafés can take quite some considerable time to build, even in the environment of the internet.

In theory, it is possible to create personal cafés of any size. But from a practical and strategic viewpoint it is preferable to limit them to a particular maximum number of contacts. From a practical standpoint, it is only possible to maintain continuous and constant personal communication with a finite number of people (in my own café, this limit is set at 50).

By deliberately and specifically limiting the number of contacts in a personal café, the café can then become an immensely powerful tool because it will facilitate the adoption of Mother Nature's strategy of evolutionary improvement and adaptation.

Consider for a moment the consequence of having a strict limit to the number of people in a personal café of contacts. With a strict limit, it

❝ FROM A PRACTICAL STANDPOINT, IT IS ONLY POSSIBLE TO MAINTAIN CONTINUOUS AND CONSTANT PERSONAL COMMUNICATION WITH A FINITE NUMBER OF PEOPLE ❞

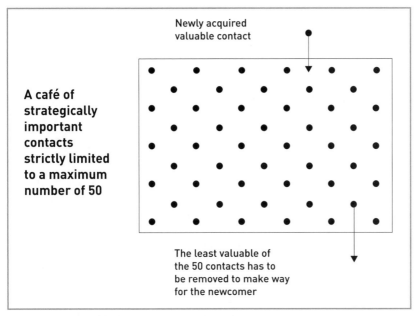

Newly acquired
valuable contact

A café of
strategically
important
contacts
strictly limited
to a maximum
number of 50

The least valuable of
the 50 contacts has to
be removed to make way
for the newcomer

FIG 8.2 By having a strictly limited number of contacts, new contacts will push out the least valuable. If this is an ongoing process, the quality of the contacts in the café will constantly improve and continuously adapt the café to changing conditions

becomes mandatory that any newly acquired contact must replace somebody else in the café before they can be included – shown graphically in Figure 8.2.

As the people pushed out will be the contacts judged to have the least value (in a current situational sense rather than in absolute terms), the café becomes progressively more useful and valuable to the café owner. Not only will the quality of the contacts improve, they will also change to suit the changing current needs and interests of the café owner – effectively, adapting the café to the changing conditions to which the café owner is exposed.

This suggests that café owners should not confine their communication activity exclusively to the people inside their cafés. They must allocate a fair proportion of their time to speculative associations in the wider world – looking for fresh contacts. The more effectively they can do this, the faster their cafés will be able to evolve and adapt to changing technology and competitive initiatives.

using several cafés for different purposes
As the contacts included in a café owner's café will be there as a result of painstakingly establishing a relationship with each of them, it may seem to be a poor strategy that can dispense with contacts in such a cavalier fashion whenever a more favourable person comes along. But in fact, they are not dispensed with at all, they are simply moved to another of the café owner's cafés – one that covers a different category of relationship.

Remembering that a virtual café is just a conceptual device for mentally organizing personal communications, there is no reason why a person shouldn't have more than one café. Just as people can have one set of friends for social reasons, another set for a hobby or sporting interest and yet another for business purposes, so a person can have more than one café to separate various categories of communication. This is illustrated in Figure 8.3.

The advantage of working in a virtual world is that you don't have to pigeonhole contacts into any single area of activity. Any contact can be assigned to more than one area of interest. In this café metaphor this would mean a café owner could assign a contact to more than one café. In each café, this could be extended even further: to assign a contact to sit at more than one table.

A bricks and mortar world example, of an individual contact who might be placed in more than one category, is when a business colleague is also a social friend or a member of a local sports club. In the different environment there might be totally different relationships. For example, the boss at work may be a player in the local football team where an employee is the team captain. In the two physically and conceptually different settings, there would be a reversal of roles – but this is likely to seem quite natural and acceptable to both parties.

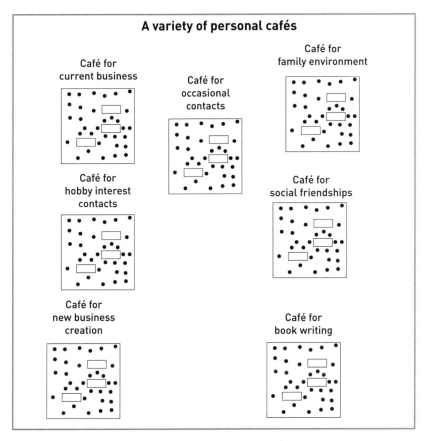

FIG 8.3 A person can have several types of virtual café running concurrently, each used to organize communications in a different field of interest

In the environment of the internet, there are no physical distinctions between different communication environments. This can greatly confuse and interfere with personal internet relationships, especially where a contact relationship is on several different levels. The simple expedient of dividing contacts into separate conceptual areas – where a single contact can be assigned to more than one area – can greatly improve the efficiency of communication.

Using the concept of cafés to divide personal contacts into different categories is typically characteristic of an object-oriented strategy. In each

> **❝** IN THE ENVIRONMENT OF THE INTERNET, THERE ARE NO PHYSICAL DISTINCTIONS BETWEEN DIFFERENT COMMUNICATION ENVIRONMENTS **❞**

café there is a different focus and there is no intermixing of the separate café domains. In fact, this principle is not particularly novel because the human brain thinks like this anyway. We can instinctively divide our various interests and contacts into various logical groupings and keep them apart.

Unfortunately though, the human brain hasn't evolved to deal with the large number of situations and contacts that become available to everyone in the communication environment of the internet. This is why we need to have computer assistance and conceptual metaphors like the café to help us overcome the complexity that can rapidly escalate.

By using a computer to aid mental processing, many different contacts and activities can be arranged in discreet groupings on a screen. This is far more convenient than trying to keep all the relationships and the relative activities in your head and trying to juggle them around in different combinations that have to be remembered – especially where any particular contact or activity might appear in more than one grouping.

With this idea in mind, we can now look at a special kind of conceptual café: the kind used to probe and explore the possibilities of creating an e-business from a sea of opportunities.

using a café to explore opportunities
A café used to explore new business opportunities in a solution space is conceptually different from a café that might be used to write books, accumulate contacts or run an established business. However, the interactions in such a café are not easy to explain because so much of the activity is dynamic and in the mind.

Any easily understandable description has to be based around particular incidents or moments in time. This doesn't quite do justice to the fast-changing complexity of the many different interactions that occur in the conceptual space of a virtual café – where so many thoughts, ideas, approaches, dialogues and actions are continuously being explored and, more often than not, abandoned at an early stage.

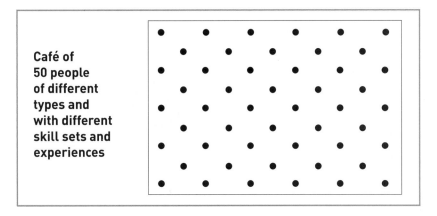

FIG 8.4 Café represented as a space containing 50 dots

Perhaps it is more easily described by way of an animated diagram. Such a diagram emerged out of a correspondence I had with Dr Thomas Thum, from Munich, Germany. Dr Thum has an engineering consultancy business that helps companies in the chemical and food processing industries to design and optimize manufacturing and logical processes. His work involves mathematical modelling and the design of simulation software.

In an effort to understand the virtual café, Dr Thum wrote a Java applet that provided an animated demonstration as to how he visualized the café working. His first demo is on his website at: http://www.thomas-thum.de/evolutionary_strategy_1.htm.

The essence of this animated simulation is shown in Figures 8.4 and 8.5, where the screen opens to a space containing 50 dots to represent people in the café.

Upon clicking a start button, the dots (people) move towards a project, with the animation causing the dots to move randomly around in the vicinity of the project to signify the people in the café working on the project together. This is illustrated in Figure 8.5.

When I saw Dr Thum's simulation, I pointed out that the café wasn't intended to work this way. Only a few people in the café would be involved in any project because they would have been specifically chosen

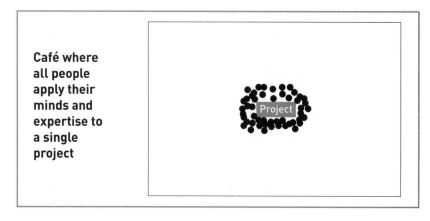

Café where all people apply their minds and expertise to a single project

FIG 8.5 Animation simulates all people in the café becoming involved in a single project

because their particular experiences or skill sets matched the requirements for the project's fulfilment.

Dr Thum then reprogrammed the simulation (as shown in Figure 8.6) to illustrate how just a few of the people in the café would become involved in any particular project. The simulation was arranged such that repeated

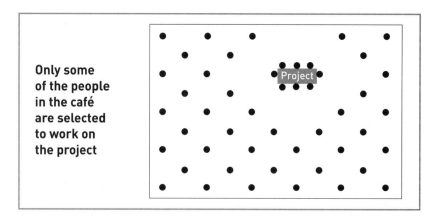

Only some of the people in the café are selected to work on the project

FIG 8.6 Simulation showing that just a few of the people in the café would be involved in a project. These would be those whose skills set and knowledge were most appropriate

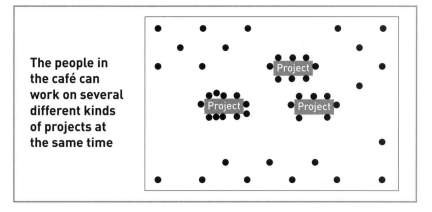

The people in the café can work on several different kinds of projects at the same time

FIG 8.7 Illustrating how the café might be involved with several projects simultaneously, with the people in the café dividing up to work on different projects according to their capabilities and interests

clicking on the 'New Project' button would introduce new projects at different places on the screen where different groups of people in the café would be attracted towards them.

When I saw this modification to the animation, I realized that the animation would more accurately reflect the dynamics of the café if it showed several different projects being worked on at the same time – with each project attracting a different group of people according to their individual suitability and personal interests.

Dr Thum duly modified the animation, as illustrated in Figure 8.7, to show different projects appearing in the café space, which would attract different people in the café.

After seeing Dr Thum's new modification to the animation, I realized it still wasn't quite reflecting the way in which I was currently using the café. Perhaps it might work this way after I had identified and decided on a few projects to definitely go for, but at this point I was still only investigating opportunities. The activity in the café was mostly in my mind.

Trying to set down on paper how I was using the café to associate different people with different opportunities as they came along, I tried to analyze the mental processes I was using. I visualized how I'd think about who might be interested in working on an opportunity; who would have the necessary skill sets; who might have appropriate and relevant experience or knowledge. I'd look for knowledge gaps, needed skills, snags and pitfalls. I'd think about the possibilities of creating a profitable revenue stream, possibilities of funding, about the competition and possible alternatives.

There is nothing very precise or formal about this mental processing of opportunities. They are just quick assessments made to eliminate rapidly those opportunities that would obviously be non-viable or too difficult to handle. I'd be looking for a match between a possible way to take advantage of the opportunity and the capabilities available in the café.

Very few of the many possible opportunities that occur pass this initial mental assessment, but if one does, I identify who in the café might be needed to play a key part in bringing about a solution. I'd probably sound out one or two of them first; then, if they agreed on the potential of the opportunity, I'd get them into a discussion around a virtual table to explore the possibility of creating a business that could take advantage of that particular opportunity.

Seen in isolation, these opportunities and discussions can be rationally explained, but they are not in isolation: many come along together. The activity is mainly instantaneous reactions to ideas and opportunities that seem to come along at random, most of which are quickly postponed or abandoned as flaws or snags are revealed. The more promising ideas or opportunities are investigated and developed further, giving them a longer life with different people involved in different aspects of the opportunities.

Dr Thum then redesigned the simulation to show opportunities coming in and out of existence for varying lengths of time. At each appearance of an opportunity, some of the dots would move towards it. The dots didn't always stay with an opportunity; they might only stay for a short time before moving on to another opportunity, maybe being replaced by other dots.

In this way, Dr Thum simulated the café as a dynamic hive of activity as opportunities come and go and dots flit between them like a swarm of

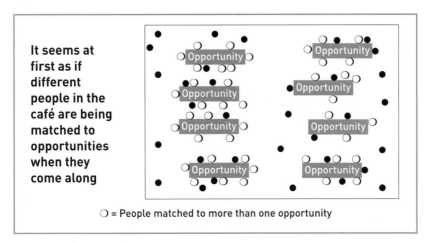

It seems at first as if different people in the café are being matched to opportunities when they come along

○ = People matched to more than one opportunity

FIG 8.8 Illustrating the activity within a virtual café as opportunities appear at random. People are shown as being attracted to different opportunities, but in actuality, much of this action only goes on inside the café owner's head as he or she visualizes who might be suitable collaborators for any particular opportunity

flies. A static illustration of this animation is shown in Figure 8.8, but it does small justice to the real activity that takes place – which goes on mostly in my head and opportunities seldom surviving long enough to involve actual interactive collaboration in the café.

After this further development of the animated simulation of the café, I still felt something was seriously wrong with this model. Something was missing because it still wasn't fully representative of the thinking and the actions I was currently taking in my efforts to create an e-business. What I was doing was involving far less change and mental activity than the model was suggesting. Paradoxically, there was much more stability and simplicity in the café I was using, yet it was producing more complexity.

At the beginning of the chapter, I mentioned all the various e-business possibilities I was currently considering. These included: creating a database for medical treatments, developing an internet course for schoolchildren, designing and selling intelligent agent software, providing website construction services, building a system of ASPs, forming a virtual social club, opening a penny bazaar, organizing the servicing of aircraft … and

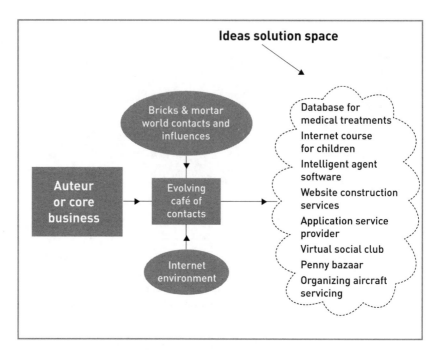

FIG 8.9 The ideas currently being considered at the start of this chapter which will be processed by means of the virtual café

many others besides. The situation can be represented as shown in Figure 8.9.

Did I really have all these highly complex business possibilities under consideration at the same time? Each in their own right would require the whole of my thinking time, yet I was seriously considering them all. How was I managing to do this and how was it represented in the animated simulation of the virtual café?

It then struck me that it wasn't detailed plans I was contemplating at all. I was considering a relatively small number of conceptual components. These components, in different combinations and applied in different ways, were yielding a large variety of possible scenarios, each of which appeared to be highly complex.

Then I had a thought: reconfiguring a number of basic components?

Wasn't this the way Mother Nature created her stupendous array of different life forms? They aren't each individually designed. They are formed out of different combinations of discrete components. At the most basic level these components are genes, viruses and bacteria. These combine and interact in a variety of ways to produce every life form on the planet. The human form contains something like 30,000 genes. They are not unique to humans; identical genes can be found in all kinds of different animals, even in plants and other kinds of living organisms.

At a level of organization higher than the genetic level, there are combinations of genes that stay together to provide similar functions or structures in the physiology of a number of different species. These combinations of genes act as more complex components – which Mother Nature is using in different mixes to make all her insects, animals and plants.

From Mother Nature's point of view, she had evolved not complete life forms but many different components that can be mixed and combined in a multitude of ways. To her, the components are the more stable elements; the life forms are merely transitional arrangements that have little permanence or long-term stability.

This throws a totally new light on the way to create e-businesses. The main concern isn't about looking for smart ideas or problems to solve: the primary objective is to build up a powerful set of components that can be applied to ideas and problems. The components are the main focus. The ideas, problems and opportunities are simply transient possible arrangements for the components at hand.

From this perspective, components must be created before any business ideas can be contemplated because they will determine what kind of e-business opportunity can be seized. To the world at large, this concern with components will seem like dancing around the fire, but, in reality, it is the gathering together of a suitably large pool of genetic material.

> COMPONENTS MUST BE CREATED BEFORE ANY BUSINESS IDEAS CAN BE CONTEMPLATED

This realization also throws a completely different light on the café as it is being used to consider possible opportunities for an e-business. It isn't about a collection of individuals, who have to be instructed what to do. Neither is it about bringing people together to join in a general brainstorm

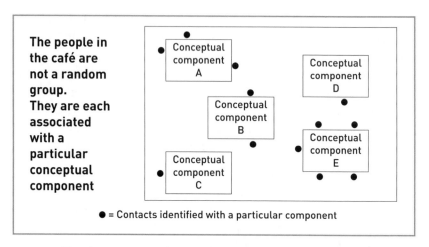

The people in the café are not a random group.
They are each associated with a particular conceptual component

Conceptual component A

Conceptual component D

Conceptual component B

Conceptual component E

Conceptual component C

● = Contacts identified with a particular component

FIG 8.10 The people in the café are not there as isolated individuals with particular skills and knowledge. They have been selected because they are associated with the implementation of a particular conceptual component

to work out solutions to problems. It is about a collection of functions and services being provided by the people in the café. These provide conceptual building blocks, concepts from which e-business solutions can be created.

This different way of viewing a virtual café – when it is being used to search for a suitable e-business opportunity – is illustrated in Figure 8.10.

This makes the café environment fundamentally different from most conventional business situations; the people in the café aren't there to be of service specifically to the auteur. They're there because they provide some essential function in a conceptual component – a component that might be needed in a dynamic system emerging as a response to an opportunity.

The people in the café wouldn't have to know how any particular system worked, or even have to be concerned with its overall purpose. Their inclusion in any newly created system would involve doing little more than they would normally do – which is doing whatever it is they are good at doing.

Combining concepts and the people associated with them as components allows a system builder to work above the level of technological detail. Although each component might be complex in itself, it can be treated much like a child might treat a component of a Lego set – the pieces can be fitted together to make a construction without having to be concerned about their composition or manufacture.

In this way, a system builder will be free to concentrate on the overall behaviour of a system, mixing and matching components to quickly construct an e-business solution to any opportunity that presents itself. This is illustrated in Figure 8.11, where the letters A, B, C, D, E, F, G represent seven conceptual components that are combined in different ways to provide a variety of solutions to a number of different opportunities.

what makes a conceptual component?

One of the first hurdles to overcome in using the concept of object-oriented design is understanding what constitutes an object. The difficulty arises because of its vagueness: it can literally be anything at all. Even more confusing,

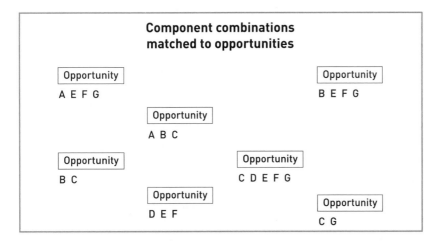

FIG 8.11 In the mind of the entrepreneur, it is the matching of conceptual components to an opportunity that is the main concern

an object can consist of other objects, which blurs the idea of an object even further. However, this vagueness is the strength of objects. They can consist of people, software programs, concepts, processing procedures or any combination of these and all kinds of other things.

A conceptual component is an object. It can be a database. More usefully, it can be a person with a database who will provide a database service and do all the necessary work associated with its functioning. In this way the component will provide a function where the user does not have to learn how to use it or have to maintain it.

A component can be a programmer or a website designer, but more usefully, it can be a generic website design that covers a site owner's needs and comes with somebody who will set it up and handle all the running and future developments of the website.

A conceptual component might be a knowledge of bandwidth and load balancing for websites. It might be a suite of programs that can be used to optimize the functioning of a website. More usefully, such a component will come as an inexpensive service that someone can provide.

Similarly with a software product. A component can be a programmer who'll create a custom-made design. But far better if the component is an off-the-shelf design that can easily be customized by a service that will be continuously responsible for its efficient performance.

It is such components that will be in the cafés of Information Age auteurs and entrepreneurs who are looking for opportunities to create e-businesses in the post-dot-com world. These components will involve no capital outlays or costs until they are profitably used. They are known as function service providers and are a reincarnation of the old concept of application service providers. We shall be dealing with these FSPs in more detail in a later chapter.

Vital to this object-oriented scenario are intangible conceptual components. These are the little mental models that have been abstracted from past experiences. The previous two books in this trilogy were full of these little mental models, mostly consisting of metaphors, similes and anecdotes. These intangible components can be combined in various ways to create a plethora of different organizing frameworks for the more tangible components to fit into.

In subsequent chapters we shall be examining how conceptual components and frameworks combine to explore and take advantage of opportunities, but before going there, it is vitally important to understand some of the more subtle aspects of bottom-up design.

the subtlety of bottom-up design

A great problem I had in writing this chapter was in being able to explain the difference between top-down and bottom-up approaches when applied to finding and taking advantage of opportunities.

I made several attempts, but the descriptions of a bottom-up approach seemed to come out as just a different way of describing a top-down approach. For example, an opportunity opens up to create a solution to a problem. The components in the café are examined to see if some mix or combination can provide a solution. Isn't this a classic top-down approach, where the requirements of a solution are determined before the components are assembled?

A bottom-up approach is about not even knowing what the problem is, let alone knowing the solution. Yet the idea that you have a solution space full of possible solutions does suggest that you have to start with ideas and opportunities first. Either I was fooling myself about using a bottom-up approach, or some crucial element was missing from my explanation.

This same thought troubled Tillman Pearce, the medical director of an oncology business unit for a large pharmaceutical company in France. Writing to a table of readers in the virtual café, he provided an interesting parallel in the medical world:

I have been going over Chapters 5 and 6 trying to decide what I think before communicating with the group. I am having difficulties putting things together.

Part of the problem I think we all are having is going back and forth between bottom-up and top-down thinking. A good figure to use in visualizing this is Figure 7.4. The bottom-up approach is to look at the business assets, skills, and capabilities, and 'wait' for the *Star Trek*-type concretization to manifest itself as the right idea. On the other hand, we are all thinking of a good idea to apply our resources to, but then we are applying a top-down approach.

As I am a physician, I relate this to the process of approaching a patient with an uncertain diagnosis. A good physician switches back and forth between two different modes: he has studied physiology and the pathology of disease and comes to the bedside with these concepts, or boxes, in which he tries to place the patient's signs and symptoms.

This conceptual approach is obviously necessary as a pattern detection device. On the other hand, it can also blind you to the less than obvious since you risk seeing only what you want to see in order to satisfy the pre-established concepts you brought into the patient's room – this top-down approach works 90% of the time, but obviously depends on how learned is the physician.

A gifted clinician knows how to suspend his judgement and allow his percepts – sight, smell, touch, sound – to simply observe what is before him. This phenomenological activity of letting things appear as they are is a technique for breaking out of the ruts which your learned concepts place you in – you proceed in this case from the particular (raw sensory inputs, navigation markers) to the general (a diagnosis), i.e. bottom-up.

This technique is particularly useful in resolving a difficult diagnosis. However, what usually happens is that all signs and symptoms lead to a seemingly obvious but incorrect diagnosis, yet a single isolated finding, which doesn't fit the general picture, can lead to discovering a seemingly less likely but more accurate diagnosis. Others discount the anomalies and thus miss the point.

It is just such a similar situation that occurs for café owners. Opportunities and ideas are very much like diagnoses: they are possible end solutions. To start with these would necessitate working backwards from them. It would suggest configuring the components in the café to test each possible opportunity or idea to see which of them would provide the best fit for the components in a café owner's café. This is a top-down approach, when what is really needed is a bottom-up approach.

The two different approaches to clinical diagnosis as described by Tillman Pearce illustrate perfectly the subtle difference between a top-down and a bottom-up approach. In the top-down approach, an experienced physician knows of a number of possible solutions to the problem of what is wrong with the patient. The symptoms are then used to see which of these solutions provide the best fit to explain what is wrong with the patient.

This can be compared to a café owner having many ideas and opportunities and then choosing the idea or opportunity that most closely matches the skills and knowledge available in the café. The café owner's choices are limited to those that are known.

Tillman Pearce's second physician, on the other hand, doesn't have any preconceived ideas as to what the solution might be. This allows for the possibility that the solution might be outside of all the solutions that he or she is currently aware of. By looking at all the symptoms and concentrating on what symptoms cannot be accounted for, the clinician will be able to look outside of the limited range of the probable to the much wider world of the improbable where a breakthrough solution might be found.

Looking for solutions outside of the probable? Isn't this the way Sherlock Holmes solved his mysteries, and didn't the creator of Sherlock Holmes, Arthur Conan Doyle, base this character on an eminent Scottish physician, Dr Joseph Bell, who was Conan Doyle's professor when he was studying to become a doctor?

Writing in the final decade of the nineteenth century, Dr Bell commented on Conan Doyle's work and the techniques of detection that had been ascribed to Sherlock Holmes. He wrote:

Dr Conan Doyle has made a well-deserved success for his detective stories, and made the name of his hero [Sherlock Holmes] beloved by the boys of this country by the marvellous cleverness of his method. He shows how easy it is, if only you can observe, to find out a great deal as to the works and ways of your innocent and unconscious friends, and, by an extension of the same method, to baffle the criminal and lay bare the manner of his crime.

Dr Bell then carried on to explain that the secret of the detections is not simply the observation of detail, but the ability to relate it to some specialist knowledge. He wrote:

The great broad characteristics which at a glance can be recognised as indicative of heart disease or consumption, chronic drunkenness or long-continued loss of blood, are the common property of the veriest tyro in medicine, while to masters of their art there are myriads of signs eloquent and instructive, but which need the educated eye to detect.

A fair-sized and valuable book has lately been written on the one symptom, the pulse; to any one but a trained physician it seems as much an absurdity as is Sherlock Holmes' immortal treatise on the one hundred and fourteen varieties of tobacco ash. Trained as he has been to notice and appreciate minute detail, Dr Doyle saw how he could interest his intelligent readers by taking them into his confidence, and showing his mode of working.

He created a shrewd, quick-sighted, inquisitive man, half doctor, half virtuoso, with plenty of spare time, a retentive memory, and perhaps with the best gift of all the power of unloading the mind of all the burden of trying to remember unnecessary details. Holmes tells Watson: 'A man should keep his little brain-attic stocked with all the furniture that he is likely to use, as the rest he can put away in the lumber-room of his library, where he can get it if he wants it.'

NOTE A full version of Dr Bell's commentary can be found on the web at: http://calibercomics.com/SHERLOCK/sherlock_holmes_Dr.%20Bell.htm

Mapping this technique across to a café owner who has a solution space: the solution space is not first filled with ideas and opportunities (to see which would be the best fit for the skills and knowledge represented by the people in the café). The café owner would start with the components in the café, playing around with various configurations, and then search for ideas and opportunities that would be a suitable match. The ideas and opportunities identified in this way would then be placed into the solution space – for further investigation.

In other words, the café owner shouldn't be organizing and configuring the people and components in the café to provide solutions to known problems: the café owner would be starting with the components and looking to find a suitable problem that might be solved by means of this unique mix. The system of components is fixed; it is the ideas and opportunities that have to be changed.

Perhaps this situation is best seen in the way Mother Nature employs this strategy. Mother Nature's equivalent of a café full of people and concepts is an ecosystem. When new life forms are introduced into this ecosystem, it is the life forms that have to be compatible with the environment. Mother Nature doesn't reconfigure the environment to cater specifically for new life forms.

This interaction of the life form with the environment may result in them both changing as each adapts to the other, but the starting point is with the ecosystem – and the kind of life forms that it can sustain.

why should people collaborate with a café owner?

Viewing the activity of a café from the café owner's perspective, it is easy to forget that any collaborative associations would be dependent on all parties involved needing to be able to see a substantial personal gain for themselves. After all, everyone in a café will have many alternative opportunities and options outside of the café environment; any that arise inside a café owner's café will have to compete with those.

This may seem obvious, but what is not so obvious is that a situation seen as a good opportunity by the café owner may not seem such a good opportunity to other people in the café whose collaboration is needed by the café owner for the opportunity to be taken advantage of. To put it bluntly: Why should the people in the café want to collaborate with the café owner? What benefits are on offer that would be preferable to alternative offers of collaboration they might have from elsewhere?

An answer to this question might be that the café owner has a good idea that the others want to be part of. However, this is a top-down approach because it necessitates starting with a good idea. The café owner then has to convince the others that it is a good idea and, because invariably there will be unknowns and uncertainties, the reality of the good idea will be on very shaky ground. Almost certainly, it would not be convincing enough for any of the people in the café to give their full and whole-hearted commitment.

Certainly if the café owner obtained funding and ensured that everyone could share in that funding there would be many willing collaborators. But again this would be a top-down approach because to obtain the funding in the first place the café owner would have to have had a good idea and a convincing plan that persuaded the funding body to provide the funding. The skill of an entrepreneur is in resolving just this kind of problem.

The clue to resolving such situations is the duality of the café concept. To a café owner, all the contacts are in his or her café. But to all the people in the café, the opportunity appears in their café, with the café owner being just another person in their café. This duality is illustrated in Figure 8.12.

This duality effect means that once an opportunity is revealed, it appears as an opportunity in all the personal cafés of everyone who is a party to that opportunity. Nobody can thus lay claim exclusively to the ownership of an opportunity once it is revealed.

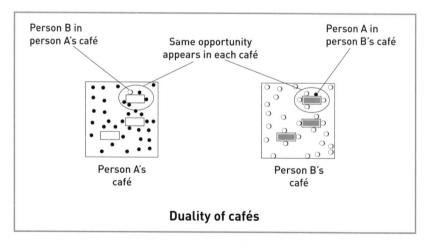

Duality of cafés

FIG 8.12 An opportunity identified in one café will automatically become present in the cafés of anyone else who is party to it

At first thoughts, this state of affairs might suggest it would be unwise for anyone to reveal an opportunity they had discovered. However, the whole point of having cafés is to arrange collaboration with people who can provide needed assets or resources that a café owner is missing. This makes it imperative to reveal an opportunity, to have any chance of securing a collaborative association that will enable an opportunity to be taken.

The appropriate strategy therefore is for anyone who discovers an opportunity to reveal it to those whose assets and resources are complementary to their own and at the same time declare their own assets and resources that would be valuable in taking advantage of the opportunity. Each then (in their own conceptual cafés) might recognize the others as ideal collaborators.

This of course raises the question of trust, but as explained in the second book in this trilogy, trust in the context of Information Age strategies isn't about loyalty and honesty, it is about trusting people to act sensibly in their own best interests.

If you present an opportunity to someone and they run off to do it without you, it simply means you are playing with a weak hand and deserve to lose. Your position wasn't strong enough to justify yourself as a key collaborator to them. You cannot blame them if they think they can take up the opportunity better without you, any more than you can blame a poker player for winning a pot with four aces against your four kings. You are just unlucky in that the hand you presented just didn't hold the right cards to win the game.

Sensible entrepreneurs will anticipate this situation and will not waste time or effort in presenting opportunities to others when they aren't holding a key position that would be essential for the success of a venture. This is where the concept of the super individual comes into play. Although you might not have all the necessary assets, resources and skills yourself, you might have a suitable collection of contacts who do. This puts you in a position of being a key collaborator who would be vital to the success of a venture.

Of course, you might still get someone who will cut you out just to get a larger share of the pot, but that would be because they will be playing a zero-sum game. You are better off without them and losing to them straight away would be a benefit. After all, opportunities come along very much more frequently than sensible players whom you can rely on to know how to play the game.

AN OPPORTUNITY EMERGES

DURING THE COURSE OF WRITING the last two chapters, an e-business opportunity did emerge. It was totally unexpected, arriving out of the blue from an area of activity that had never entered my mind before.

A post from one of the readers in the virtual café mentioned the anomaly that there were no websites providing a definitive reference to all the various treatments that were available for cancer. It wasn't the thought that this might be an opportunity to create such a site that interested me: it was the surprise that it hadn't been done already.

About a third of people in the developed world are afflicted with cancer at some time in their lives. It is the second most common cause of death. Wasn't it odd, with so much money poured into all kinds of different e-business ventures, that somebody hadn't come up with a site that could provide millions of anxious patients with the kind of information they so desperately need in order to alleviate their condition?

It is just such anomalies that are often the start of a successful business venture and I put my mind to discovering the reasons why such websites weren't in existence. I could then try to come up with a possible solution.

Realizing that many people must have had the idea to help cancer patients find suitable treatments, it could be reliably assumed that a solution could not be found through any conventional approach. So, calling on the strategy used by Sherlock Holmes, I looked for a solution in the realm of the unconventional.

Such an unconventional strategy I had in mind already, through my work in writing the book *Magical A-Life Avatars*. In this work, I'd taken the view that the internet was an environment best investigated from the client side. In essence, this means that instead of thinking about creating websites that broadcast out to audiences, you think in terms of people using a personal application to help them use the internet for their own particular individual purposes.

In the context of cancer treatment, this would involve forgetting about any idea of creating a website to provide information, but creating a situation where patients could be given the power to get the information they need for themselves. The next three chapters describe the essence of this approach.

When reading this part of the book, don't take too much notice of the mechanics of the solution. Just think about how the solution is simply the creation of an efficient means for people to make the right contacts via the internet.

9

A FORMATTED PEOPLE SPACE

welcome to the world of the entrepreneur The last chapter illustrated how subtle the differences can be between top-down and bottom-up strategies. It revealed a fuzzy separation between ideas and opportunities. It presented conceptual components as enigmatic entities without definition or tangible form.

Not surprisingly, several of the readers of the last chapter, who'd had no experience of being entrepreneurs, were left feeling bemused and frustrated. They'd been looking to be led directly into creating an e-business. Instead, they felt they'd been getting a kaleidoscope of inconsequential theory, a smoke screen, that was obscuring the real purpose of any e-business: to make money.

Reading the various posts at some of the tables in the virtual café, it was quite clear that some of the readers were still looking for algorithms: step-by-step guides as to how to set up a money-making business. They wanted to be given roles, shown what to do. It didn't occur to them that the world of the entrepreneur isn't that simple; if it were, everyone would be an entrepreneur.

To an entrepreneur, such vagueness is par for the course because creating businesses isn't about following known paths and clear directions, it is about peering into a world of uncertainty and creating order where none exists. It is about adapting experiences from the past to deal with the present; it is about mixing and matching concepts, people and skill sets to produce systems of interaction.

To illustrate the essence of entrepreneurial activity, and to show how chance and opportunity replace ideas and planning, I'll explain how years of training as an electronic systems engineer, together with an intensive study of marketing and investment strategy, led to me sorting out piles of used clothing in rag merchants' yards.

From there, we'll see how the lessons learned in the smelly rag yards of England can be applied to the high-tech world of electronic communications – proving that entrepreneurship in e-business is really about concepts, not technology.

rags to riches

In the first book in this trilogy, *The Entrepreneurial Web*, I described how I made a radical change of lifestyle, going from the formal and structured environment of banking and stockbroking to join the hippies in a hippie fashion market that had just opened in Kensington High Street in West London.

Hippies and fashion may not seem a logical combination, but the hippies in Kensington soon found out that there were plenty of people willing to pay to buy into their lifestyle. Wannabe hippies were prepared to buy the kind of clothes the hippies were wearing to be able to emulate them – even if only at weekends. As most of the hippies were making their own clothes, or finding them in used clothes shops, it didn't take much extra effort to make or find a few more that could be sold to the many who wanted to copy them.

As soon as the emulators started wearing the clothes that were being worn by the hippies, the hippies started to wear different clothes so they could look different from the wannabes. As soon as the emulators saw the hippies wearing new clothes, they wanted them as well. Pretty soon, a whole industry came into existence, with hippies working out new and exotic ways to dress and this creativity feeding a continuous demand for their wares.

Recognize the pattern? Isn't this very similar to the strategy that Bill Gates had described as being the formula for success used by Microsoft? Hadn't they found themselves in an environment, pioneered new products in that environment and sold all their learned know-how and techniques to those following on behind?

I'd joined in this trading environment in the then fashionable area of 'old clothes' (later to be called 'antiquarian clothes' when some of the garments became so sought after they cost considerably more than new clothes). I'd partnered with a girl on a stall in Kensington market selling 1920s and 1930s garments that we'd search for in the many used clothes shops and flea markets that were dotted around London.

One day, as we were driving around looking for used clothes shops, my partner spotted the characteristic look of a 1920s velvet dress poking out of a lorry load of old rags that were on their way to a rag yard. The lorry was parked outside a workman's café and we decided to go in to find the driver of the lorry.

To my surprise, the lorry driver turned out to be an ex-boyfriend of my sister, a person I'd known since school days. Over a cup of coffee in the café, he explained that he was now in the rag business and had a large warehouse in Fulham sorting through tons of old clothes every week. He then invited us to go back with him to his warehouse to see if there were any more 1920s or 1930s dresses lying around.

When we arrived at his warehouse, we found it contained a gigantic mound of assorted used garments (known as rags). This was feeding a conveyor belt. Along the conveyor belt were several sorters who were sorting through these rags to divide them into various categories. Although they'd sort out a few usables that could be sold to traders in the flea markets and the second-hand shops, they were mainly concentrating on sorting the rags by the type of material they were made from: woollens, cottons, synthetics, fur, leather, etc.

My friend explained that he bought in mixed rags at a certain price per ton. When sorted into the various categories, each category sold to specialist processors at a much higher price than the price he was paying for the unsorted mixed rags. Effectively, the act of sorting the rags was increasing their value. It was a very simple formula and he was finding the business highly profitable.

The astute reader will likely spot the parallel with information on the web. The information equivalent of the pile of unsorted rags at one end of the rag merchant's warehouse is the vast assortment of information available on the web. Added value can be created by a sorting process that turns an unsorted conglomeration into sorted categories that are immediately usable.

This simple formula is the key to the success of all media products: newspapers, magazines, books, directories, search engines, etc. A value is created because the information they contain has been selected, sorted and categorized. This is why websites that provide just content are not profitable in their own right because that content doesn't acquire value until it has been passed onto somebody who can make profitable use of it. In isolation, all information on the web is the equivalent of just another rag on the unsorted pile of rags in a rag merchant's warehouse.

The value of the sorting process really hit home when the rag merchant invited us to look through his unsorted rags to see if we could see any more 1920s or 1930s dresses. My partner and I spent an hour sifting through piles of smelly garments and came across only three items of interest.

The rag merchant waved me away when I offered to pay for them and told us we could come along at any time and take what we wanted. As generous as his offer was, the thought of spending much more time sifting through mounds of smelly clothes didn't fill me and my partner full of excitement. I suggested to the merchant that perhaps his sorters could pull out these garments for us while they were doing their sorting.

The merchant gave us a condescending smile and explained that he'd love to help us, but if his sorters were looking out for these 1920s and 1930s clothes they would lose their rhythm and slow up his whole operation.

It made perfect sense, but having just spent the past year writing about investment strategy, I had a little model in my head that fitted this scenario. Investment value was based on a continuous regular revenue stream. Once a revenue stream could be defined, the value of a business could be determined.

The 1920s and 1930s clothing garments would appear at random in the unsorted pile. Over time, and averaged out, this would create a continuous revenue stream as far as my partner and I were concerned. However, to the rag merchant, pulling out these garments represented a cost in terms of loss of efficiency. The problem then became one of finding a way to turn this loss into a profit for the rag merchant.

I thought about my partner and me sorting randomly through the mound of rags for an hour and finding three items. The rag merchant had four sorters and they were working 40 hours a week. A quick calculation told me that if they could uncover items at the same rate as my partner and I, there was every chance that they could uncover 240 items a week. This would be quite a considerable sum of money in sales. The capitalized value of such a regular income could greatly increase the value of both my and the rag merchant's business.

I then asked the rag merchant to do a trial run for a week to get his sorters to pull out the kind of clothes I was looking for. I offered him a compensation for the decrease in efficiency and he agreed (probably just to humour an old friend).

As a compromise, it was decided that the sorters wouldn't inspect every garment carefully, but just throw to one side any item that roughly fitted the characteristics of 1920s and 1930s clothing. This would select for the type of fabric, the length, patterns and various other criteria that could quickly be associated with the styles and fashions of that era.

After a week, I returned to the rag merchant's warehouse and found that the sorters had put aside quite a sizeable pile. With my partner, I went through this pile and found a quarter of them to be sellable items. A quick estimate of the price I could sell them for gave me a ballpark figure as to what this revenue stream was worth to me.

I then estimated how much the rag merchant would be paying his sorters every week. I compared this with the value of the revenue stream I would be getting if the sorters put aside all these garments regularly. I then realized that I could probably afford to pay all the sorters' wages out of the profit I'd be making on the sale of the dresses they'd be putting aside for me.

I then divided the estimated weekly wage bill by the number of sellable items the sorters had pulled out over the week. This gave me a price per item that I could offer to pay to the rag merchant. This delighted the rag merchant when he realized that by simply adding an additional sorting category he could eliminate one of his major outgoings: the weekly wage bill.

Parallels can be drawn here with many situations on the internet. If information is compared to a valuable garment lying in piles of unsorted used garments, the value isn't in offering the information; the real value emerges only when this random information is selectively extracted from a background of noise: selected to specifically target a particular type of need.

> THE REAL VALUE EMERGES ONLY WHEN RANDOM INFORMATION IS SELECTIVELY EXTRACTED FROM A BACKGROUND OF NOISE: SELECTED TO SPECIFICALLY TARGET A PARTICULAR TYPE OF NEED

Looking at web-based businesses today, it is evident that the pure content providers and the general cataloguing and indexing operations are struggling to be viable. On the other hand, the businesses targeting the particular information needs of small niches are consistently successful and profitable.

The model of the rag merchant also illustrates another important characteristic of a successful business: the ability to extract several revenue streams from the same processing activity. This allows bottom-up strategies to come into play where a single revenue stream by itself may appear insubstantial, but facilitates the creation of many others. This, as we shall see in the next chapter, can be applied very effectively to produce not only revenue streams but sources of funding.

The reader might note that this particular example is unique to my own experience. It is my equivalent of Sherlock Holmes' treatise on the one hundred and fourteen varieties of tobacco ash. The abstractions from my unique experiences in the rag yards can be regarded as some of the conceptual components that appear in my personal solution space.

Everyone has or can create their own equivalent of these personally unique conceptual contributions to the models they build. These can then be used to help turn opportunities into profitable solutions. Not only can these 'Sherlock Holmes' treatise on the one hundred and fourteen varieties of tobacco ash' equivalents be used personally, the astute entrepreneur will look out for them in others – so as to be able to include them in their own repertoire of conceptual components.

scaling by duplication

After the arrangement with my Fulham rag merchant had been working satisfactorily for a few months, I began to realize that most of the rags were coming from the merchant's local West London area. I then asked my friend about other areas and he gave me the addresses of other rag merchants who covered different areas.

With the Fulham arrangement as a working example, it wasn't difficult to convince other rag merchants to try out the deal. It wasn't long before I had supplies from several rag-sorting warehouses all over the London area. Pretty soon, I was getting in more stock than I could sell, so I opened another sales outlet. The success of this sales expansion then brought into mind the possibility of covering the whole country.

Within a year, I'd made arrangements with practically every major rag merchant in England: effectively filtering most of the 1920s and 1930s garments that were discarded in the country every week, down to my warehouse in London. This massive and regular supply enabled me to open a large store in the then fashionable Carnaby Street and also to wholesale garments to other stores all over Europe.

A chance observation, an unlikely coincidence, a few conceptual models and a substantial business had been created out of apparently nothing. This is the essence of entrepreneurial activity.

> " A CHANCE OBSERVATION, AN UNLIKELY COINCIDENCE, A FEW CONCEPTUAL MODELS AND A SUBSTANTIAL BUSINESS HAD BEEN CREATED OUT OF APPARENTLY NOTHING "

the concept of space

The business of selling old clothes appears to have no relationship at all with the modern high-tech world of electronic communications until the organization is abstracted away from the actual business. What we then find is a large space (the area of England) covered with collection points where the weekly produce of a commodity in the local area is brought together and sorted.

At each collection point, people sift through the local produce to pull out items according to certain broad criteria. A human expert then undertakes a further examination of a particular category and makes a more precise selection based on finer detail. These selections can then be transferred to a single collection point: where all the filtered items from the whole space converge.

The importance of this abstraction is that it highlights the fact that the whole process is organized through a hierarchy of humans who use nothing more than the unique ability of the human brain to differentiate between patterns in a complex environment. There are very few instructions, no complicated procedures or algorithms. The whole system relies on the processing power of the human brain to extract a range of specific items from a very large variety of unsorted possibilities.

Even more interesting is the ease and efficiency by which such a human system can be controlled and directed. It can be made to respond and adapt almost immediately to any changes in demand. For example, it was very easy to modify the garment-filtering system to find 1940s clothes when they became fashionable. Silk scarves, embroidered blouses, long skirts, etc. could all be filtered out when they were in demand. Just a few words of spoken instruction could cause the whole system of people to react almost immediately to any changes in customer demands or fashion trends.

With an abstraction of this system, it is easy to see how information can be substituted for garments. It is easy to see how the space of the country of England can be replaced by the space of the internet.

This provides yet another useful conceptual component to put into my solution space.

a real-life opportunity presents itself To illustrate how the

abstraction of this garment-sorting system might be applied to create an
e-business solution out of an opportunity, let's take a real-life opportunity that appeared in my solution space while I was writing Chapter 4
of this book.

The opportunity took the form of a problem presented by Tillman Pearce
– the medical director of an oncology business unit for a large
pharmaceutical company in France. Posting to a table of people in my
virtual café, he wrote:

I work in the pharmaceutical industry developing new cancer therapies. As
such, I am aware of current treatment options around the world and am aware
that most patients around the world are never presented with all the options
(this is as true in the US as elsewhere). I have therefore considered the
possibility of developing a web-based service for informing patients (or
doctors) of therapeutic options for specific patient/disease states.

Looking on the internet, one finds a profusion of sites purporting to provide
such services. All these services (ALL) provide standardized documentation on
basic categories of disease. For example, look up colon cancer – within a day
or two of effort you can find about 30 sites providing info on colon cancer. They
all state basically the same thing and 99% are based on what is currently
approved in the United States.

The problem is, nobody has 'generic' colon cancer. Rather, you are a male or
female of a certain age; your performance status and liver, heart, kidney
function are either excellent, good, poor, or other; your cancer has been
partially or completely removed; the histology is either of good or bad
prognosis; you have or have not received certain prior therapies (chemo
and/or radiation).

Depending on these (and other) variables, specific therapies are considered
highly recommended, possibly recommended or not recommended.
Furthermore, you might be interested in knowing what treatments are offered
not only in your country but in other parts of the world (a drug I work with has
been available in France since 1996 and for various reasons is not yet available
in the US; I am aware of about 150 studies around the world with this agent –

the 'gold standard' site, that of the US National Cancer Institute, lists about 15 studies).

A valuable service would necessarily CUSTOMIZE the recommendations to your particular situation and provide comprehensive information. One of the prior commentators suggested we might be heading to an e-consultancy. For me, this idea took hold since the café is composed of 'consultants' but also because we are in a position to provide customized advice. The above cancer consultancy could also be provided by a network of doctors and oncology nurses or by using decision algorithms backed up by modular software components (OOPS).

So, my main contribution at this point would be to point out a major anomaly today is that most services are providing standardized products rather than harnessing the power of OOPS to provide customized products in real time and at mass production costs. Furthermore, I would attribute this striking anomaly to the fact that those who have had the idea of health e-consultation services have not had a deep understanding of their customers' needs (tailored information to the specifics of the patient/disease state) but rather provided superficial services hoping to quickly capture eyeballs (revenues) to maybe later invest in something with more value added.

Similarly, consultancies have not really understood what is involved in providing meaningful advice to patients and hence have not understood how their technologies might satisfy the needs. [An aside, my problem is that people expect information to be free, so I haven't figured out a viable business model even if I think I understand the patient needs and technological solutions.] Can anyone provide other examples of internet services providing standardized products?

As soon as I read this post, an opportunity popped into my solution space. It was not that I could see an immediately profitable situation – it was that the conceptual components at my disposal could recognize a possible solution to this problem.

The reader might like to pause here for a moment before reading on, to see if this problem Tillman Pearce identifies also pops into their solution space. How would you solve this problem?

the first clue

I must admit that part of the solution was currently in my mind because, at the time I received Tillman Pearce's e-mail, I was making preparations for a talk I was to give at BOT 2001 (a seminar being organized by internet.com and taking place at the Fairmont Hotel in San Francisco in January 2001). The talk was to be entitled 'Using bots to create a living database'.

The principle behind a living database is that it consists of a system of people rather than information. This, as you might recognize, is similar to the rag-sorting business described above and is also a constantly recurring theme running through the books in this trilogy. The principal tenet is that people are needed where uncertainty, change and volatility render logical and algorithmic search techniques useless. Only the human brain can provide the kind of intelligence needed.

To appreciate the advantage of a living database, let's first examine a conventional database – an outline view of which is shown diagrammatically in Figure 9.1.

Information in a conventional database can be cleverly formatted and indexed to facilitate retrieval. Data can be sorted, mixed, matched, compared and selected using all manner of criteria and conditionals, but the algorithms used have to be pre-determined and require direct human reprogramming to change them.

Such databases are adequate as long as the data is reasonably long-lasting and can be maintained within a constant format. But if there are any chaotic or unpredictable elements of change, there will be problems because it will be extremely difficult to arrange for the database to question the validity of data, anticipate the possibility of error or check that it has become redundant or is incomplete.

Many important categories of information and knowledge – such as the expanding and evolving areas of technology – have such a high level of unpredictable volatility that reliable output is prohibitively expensive to maintain. The databases quickly become choked with redundant and conflicting information, the efficiency soon declining to a point where the information that is retrieved has very little practical value. This is the

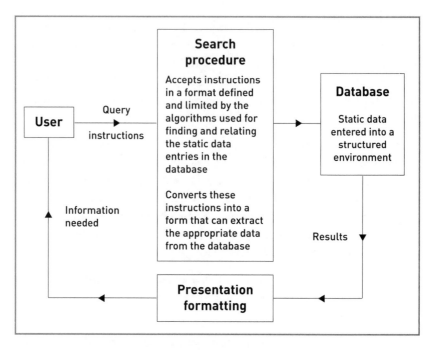

FIG 9.1 Outline of a conventional database

problem confronting anyone who would want to create the kind of database that Tillman Pearce is looking for.

In these situations, when accurate information and knowledge are not readily available, people resort to the age-old custom of asking around: finding somebody who may have the information they need. This involves a bottom-up strategy – following a trail, routed through person-to-person contact, with one piece of information leading to the discovery of another until the information or the solution to a problem is found.

In pre-internet days, the telephone was perfectly adequate for this kind of strategy. Databases could take the form of directories, yellow pages, etc. that listed contact names, where bottom-up, seek-to-find strategies could begin a search for people who might point to any kind of ill-defined, fuzzy or elusive types of information that might be needed.

Such a strategy is illustrated in a generic form in Figure 9.2.

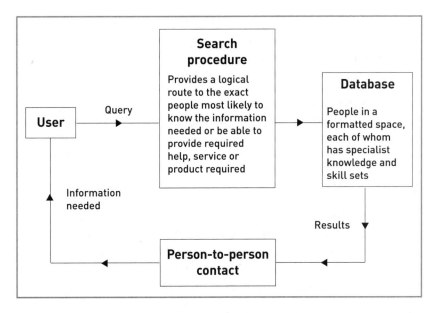

FIG 9.2 A strategy to find ill-defined, fuzzy or elusive types of information must involve asking people. A system needs to be devised to locate the appropriate people to ask

Figure 9.2 shows how it is necessary to have some method of formatting the space where people can be found and a procedure for finding the most suitable people to provide any required information. In pre-internet times the database would be a directory of names, separated into various categories. The search procedure would involve nothing more complicated than choosing people in an appropriate category to question.

Viewed in the diagrammatic form, it becomes obvious that in the massive communication environment of the internet and with the rapidly changing and evolving nature of knowledge and information, similar problems will occur as with a conventional database.

The number of people needing to be included in the people space would be impossibly large. There would be too many categories and the categories chosen would have to be constantly changed and added to. There would be too many ways in which the people space could be formatted. Even for

66 IT BECOMES OBVIOUS THAT IN THE MASSIVE COMMUNICATION ENVIRONMENT OF THE INTERNET AND WITH THE RAPIDLY CHANGING AND EVOLVING NATURE OF KNOWLEDGE AND INFORMATION, SIMILAR PROBLEMS WILL OCCUR AS WITH A CONVENTIONAL DATABASE 99

the people that could be listed and categorized, there would be no certainty that they could provide currently accurate or up-to-date information. There would be no precise way of determining who knew what and the extent and exact nature of their knowledge.

With these thoughts in mind, let's turn to the opportunity offered by the problem of creating a treatment database for cancer patients as outlined by Tillman Pearce.

creating a database of cancer treatment options

As Tillman Pearce explained, the requirement is for a fully comprehensive, universal cancer treatment database covering the very many different kinds of options and treatment strategies available in different clinics and hospitals in different parts of the world. Both the medical profession and cancer patients have a great need for such a resource.

The main reasons why such a much-needed resource hasn't emerged yet are:

1   There are too many variables involved: type of cancer; location and size of cancer; progression of cancer; age and sex of patient; health of patient; genetic variation of patient; prior therapies; combination therapies; trial treatment strategies; etc.

2   Technology and scientific knowledge relating to cancer treatment are continuously changing and evolving.

3   There are a very large number of people involved in the treatment of cancer. They are moving around in different areas of speciality as new types of treatment become available through research and new technologies.

These reasons suggest that an effective, efficient, universal cancer treatment information resource would require a massive and highly complex database, where the content would have to be continuously updated. The costs and the organization necessary for the establishment and maintenance of a conventional database would certainly prove prohibitive.

Clearly, a conventional solution is out of the question. If there is to be any solution at all it will require a radically new approach. This is where we can start to think in terms of using some of the unique properties of the internet to create a database that will be self-organizing and self-maintaining.

similarity to the problems facing all e-businesses

The cancer treatment database problem is very similar to the information-seeking problems encountered in the technological world of e-business. In e-business also, there is a great need for up-to-date information that is frustrated by large numbers of variables and the rapidly expanding and evolving knowledge base; not to mention the large number of technical experts and specialists involved.

Despite the vast capacity of the world wide web and the low cost of internet communication and information transfer, the creation of a universal knowledge database has similarly proved impossibly difficult and prohibitively costly to implement.

As an alternative to conventional database solutions, the internet has naturally evolved networks of people who, as interacting communities, provide living databases of up-to-date information and knowledge. Direct information exchange between humans, rather than algorithms, seems to be the most efficient and cost-effective way to search, sort and obtain the type of volatile information involved in electronic communication technology.

This suggests that a solution to the cancer treatment database problem might be to set up a similar living system of information exchange to serve doctors and patients. The trick will be to organize a suitably formatted people space, where people can find each other and which will be economical to build and maintain.

helping people to do it for themselves One of the most common mistakes made by e-businesses is to think from a bricks and mortar

perspective and try to build an internet presence based on the notion of providing a fully comprehensive and efficient service for customers or clients. Such an approach to doing business is so universally accepted that it is seldom even considered that there might be a better way. After all, what could be better than using all possible means to find out what customers want and then make every effort to give it to them?

However, the environment of the internet is not the same as that of the world of bricks and mortar. It is possible to go one better than provide customers with what they want – it is possible to enable customers to provide for themselves.

A service to provide information about cancer treatments is a case in point, where to think solely from the provider's viewpoint clearly highlights the limitations of the quality of service that it is possible to provide. Conventional business thinking would conclude that it is not commercially viable to satisfy fully a customer's need for complete information about available cancer treatments.

However, because of the uniqueness of the communication environment of the internet, it is possible to do things that wouldn't even be considered in the conventional bricks and mortar world. For example, you wouldn't expect an old-economy business to tell their customers they can't help them, but if the customers got together they could help each other. Yet this is exactly the kind of thinking that is appropriate in many areas of e-business.

Take this problem of supplying cancer treatment information to patients: a conventional approach to supplying such a service would assume that such a service is impractical because there is too much knowledge to be recorded and even if it could be recorded it would rapidly become outdated. Yet it must be a fact that all current, up-to-date information must be known somewhere in the world by someone. Isn't it possible to find a way to connect those who know with those who need to know?

Structural organization, formal rules and procedures are not appropriate for solutions to this kind of problem. It will need an informal, dynamic system that is self-building and self-maintaining. Such a system might be possible to arrange if natural human motivations can be harnessed to create and drive a self-organizing process.

In the world of the internet, such systems are appearing all the time, as the need for speciality information causes special interest e-mail discussion forums to form spontaneously. It is just such a natural consequence of mass connectivity that can be called into service to create a database for cancer treatment.

The trick is to provide a suitable framework for this self-organization process to take place. To this end, we can use the abstraction of the system used to extract 1920s and 1930s garments from the mass of garments discarded every week in England.

The reader might want to pause again here, to contemplate how this model might be applied to the problem of making patients aware of available cancer treatments. It is a useful exercise in applying abstractions to seemingly intractable real-world problems.

formatting a people space
In the bricks and mortar world example of using rag merchants in a system to extract 1920s and 1930s clothing from all the garments discarded every week in England, it is natural to think of the entrepreneur as the sole collector and organizer. All garments would be selectively filtered to the entrepreneur's central base for redistribution to the customers.

Using a paradigm shift, now imagine that it is not the organizing entrepreneur who is using such a system to filter garments, but the customers – each of whom would have their own set of rag merchants to obtain garments exclusively for themselves. In this way, the customers would be able to order exactly what they wanted without having to be limited to the selections made by the entrepreneur.

If the customers used the system themselves, the entrepreneur wouldn't have to deal with the rag merchants, nor the customers or their orders. In fact the entrepreneur wouldn't even have to know what the customer wanted or what the rag merchants were supplying. The entrepreneur would be completely outside the system. It would be completely self-organizing, with customers going directly to the rag merchants and the rag merchants supplying directly to the customers.

This begs the question: 'What would be the role of the entrepreneur?'

To answer this question, it is necessary to consider the main problem each customer would have to face before they could take advantage of this system. How would they find and make contact with rag merchants on their own? Where would they find those that would be interested in sorting out the particular garments they wanted? The rag merchants would have a similar problem: how would they find the customers who were wanting the kind of garments they were sorting?

From this viewpoint, it is easy to see that the role of an entrepreneur in such a self-organizing system of supply and demand would be to provide an infrastructure to make it easy for people to find each other.

In the bricks and mortar world of real rag merchants, customers would be able to find rag merchants if an entrepreneur created a directory: listing all rag merchants and their contact details, together with a description of the garments they were sorting. This could be represented as a table: a two-dimensional space divided up into rows and columns, as illustrated in Figure 9.3. Dots in this diagram represent either:

1   the garments each merchant sorts, or

2   the rag merchants that sort any particular listed garment.

The trick now is to imagine each dot in this space as representing a merchant. Conceptually, the diagram then stops being a table and becomes a number of boxes that contain merchants. For example, the part of the space reserved for blouses (the blouses column) becomes a box that contains every rag merchant who sorts out blouses.

If somebody wants blouses, they can be imagined as visiting the box allocated to blouses (the blouse column), where they will find all the merchants in the country who are sorting out blouses.

	Dresses	Blouses	Skirts	Jeans	Furs	Hats	Coats
Merchant 1	●		●				●
Merchant 2		●	●		●		
Merchant 3			●				●
Merchant 4		●		●		●	
Merchant 5	●			●		●	●
Merchant 6		●			●		
Merchant 7	●				●	●	
Merchant 8		●		●			●

FIG 9.3 Using rows and columns, a two-dimensional space is created. Each dot in the space represents a merchant (identified by the name in the row) who is sorting out a particular type of article (specified by the description of the column)

This situation is illustrated in Figure 9.4, where the rag merchants are identified with a reference number (eliminating the need to have them represented as rows in a table).

In the same way as a merchant can be represented as a dot in a garment space, so can a buyer. Figure 9.5 shows a mixture of merchants and buyers visiting the space allocated to a type of garment that is being sorted or bought. Merchants are identified with numbers and buyers are identified with letters. Using these identifications to obtain the necessary contact details, merchants and buyers can visit an appropriate box to communicate with each other directly.

Conceptually, it is as if the people in each of these garment spaces (boxes) were together in a virtual café, where they'd each be free to wander around and talk to each other. Thus, instead of seeing a tabular

Dresses	Blouses	Skirts	Jeans	Furs	Hats	Coats
● 1		● 1				● 1
	● 2	● 2		● 2		
		● 3				● 3
	● 4		● 4		● 4	
● 5			● 5		● 5	● 5
	● 6			● 6		
● 7				● 7	● 7	
	● 8		● 8			● 8

FIG 9.4 Each category of garment can be thought of as a box that contains several rag merchants. Any rag merchant (each identified by a reference number) can be in several boxes at the same time

representation, you have a picture in your mind of a number of cafés – each attracting a uniquely different group of people who have a particular niche interest.

Using conventional thinking, it is impossible to imagine a database without algorithms that store, sort and search for information. It would seem impossible that a database could construct itself without a team of people entering all the data. Yet, from Figure 9.5, it is easy to see how there wouldn't be any need for algorithms or management – if only rag merchants and buyers were given facilities to enter their own presence in any of the garment spaces.

For example, new rag merchants starting up in business could simply enter their presence into the spaces associated with the articles they were sorting. It would immediately put them into contact with all the buyers

Dresses	Blouses	Skirts	Jeans	Furs	Hats	Coats
● 1	○ D	● 1	○ F	○ G	○ C	● 1
○ A	○ F			○ R		○ D
○ D	● 2	● 2	○ E	● 2	○ F	
○ M		● 3	○ G	○ G	○ R	○ J
○ P	○ K	○ B	○ B	○		● 3
○ J	○ N	○ L	○ V	○ A	○ M	○ H
	● 4	○ K	● 4	○ B	● 4	○ M
● 5	○ X	○ Q	● 5	○ J	● 5	● 5
○ H	○ W				○ L	○ K
○ Q	● 6	○ E	○ T	● 6	○ U	○ Y
	○ L		○ S			
● 7	○ S	○ M	○ Y	● 7	● 7	○ Z
	○ X			○ V	○ T	
○ N	● 8	○ Z	● 8	○ U		● 8
		● Rag merchants		○ Customers		

FIG 9.5 Buyers can be thought of as visiting garment spaces to find rag merchants. Rag merchants can be thought of as visiting the spaces to find buyers for the garments they are sorting. Each garment space can be thought of as a virtual café where those present can talk to each other

who would be looking for those particular garments. They could also enter garment spaces to find out how many people were looking for particular types of garment, giving them a guide as to what garments would be the most profitable to sort.

Similarly, a buyer could enter their presence into the spaces associated with the garments they were interested in obtaining. This would put them in contact with all the rag merchants who were sorting those items.

There wouldn't be a requirement for sorting or searching algorithms on the database side because all the entering and retrieving of data would be done by the rag merchants and buyers when they decided where to enter their presence. Merchants and buyers could add or remove their presence from various garment spaces, as and when their respective sorting or buying patterns changed.

If merchants and customers are also allowed to add extra columns, to specify additional garments that are being sorted or are wanted, the whole database could be run by the users themselves without the need for any building or maintenance from the server side. In fact, the server side needn't even have any direct contact with the users – because through a self-organization process they would be able to make all the appropriate contacts themselves.

Would such a system work? There is a very good precedent. Napster, the peer-to-peer networking phenomenon that threatened to bring down the entire music publishing industry, worked on a similar principle. During the dot-com bubble at the turn of the century, while other start-ups were obtaining millions of dollars in funding and failing spectacularly to create viable information systems, Napster, with virtually no capital and little organization, attracted 12 million people who used Napster's very simple peer-to-peer networking system to exchange music with each other. Napster did very little more than provide a way for people of similar interests to get in contact with each other directly – and they didn't even format the people space.

scaling up
The hypothetical example described above assumes a limited number of rag merchants and garment buyers. The number of rag merchants in each garment space is assumed to be quite modest, such that it would be possible for buyers in the space to contact all of them easily to sort out who is the best to deal with.

However, if this were extended worldwide, to include every rag merchant on the planet and everyone in the world is allowed to join in, the system would soon become overcrowded. There might be hundreds of rag merchants in the garment spaces and it would be very difficult for buyers to choose between them.

To make life easier, it might be sensible if each garment space were divided up further. Perhaps divided by geographic location, according to where rag merchants were geographically situated. This would reduce the numbers in any particular space and at the same time ensure that buyers didn't waste time trying to deal with merchants whose warehouses were further away from them than they were prepared to travel.

By splitting up the garment spaces in this way the total space would take the form of a two-dimensional grid, as shown in Figure 9.6. In this diagram, there are 12 garment spaces (columns) divided up into 12 geographic locations (rows). This creates 144 different spaces where rag merchants and buyers can meet.

In each of these areas, there will be fewer people, but they will each know that they are interested in the same kind of garment and are geographically close to each other.

Even though there might be a large number of garment categories and a large number of geographic locations, some of the contact areas might still be overcrowded. This problem is easily overcome by adding yet another dimension to the overall meeting space.

Let's say that the type of locality where the rag merchant's warehouse is situated is also an important buying consideration. Some buyers might prefer the unsorted garments to be drawn from one type of locality, while

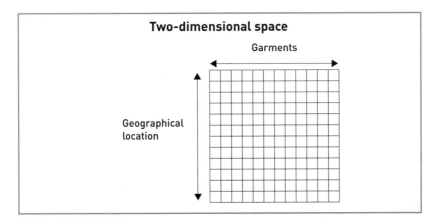

FIG 9.6 Contact places, where rag merchants and buyers meet, can be spread over a two-dimensional grid to increase the efficiency of finding the best contacts

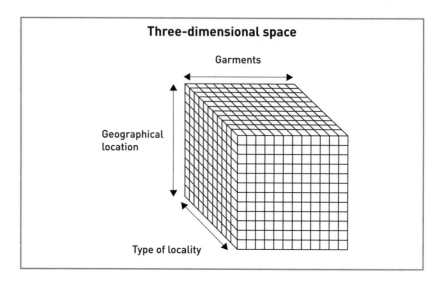

FIG 9.7 By adding a third dimension, the possible contact places have increased from 144 to 1,728

others might prefer another. This distinction could provide a third dimension to divide up the total meeting space. This is illustrated in Figure 9.7 where, by adding 12 categories of locality, the total number of possible contact points is increased from the two-dimensional number of 144 to a three-dimensional number 1,728.

Adding this third dimension not only reduces the overcrowding but also ensures that buyers and sellers are more likely to be compatible. In this three-dimensional space, every buyer will know that the rag merchants, who will be in a particular meeting area they choose, will not only be sorting the type of garments they need and be geographically near to them, they will also be drawing stock from the right kind of locality.

Imagine now that there are thousands of different rag merchants of many different nationalities and the customer speaks only one language. They would obviously prefer to deal with only the rag merchants they can speak with. This can be accommodated by adding a fourth dimension, which will create a different three-dimensional space for every language. This four-dimensional space is illustrated in Figure 9.8, where the three-

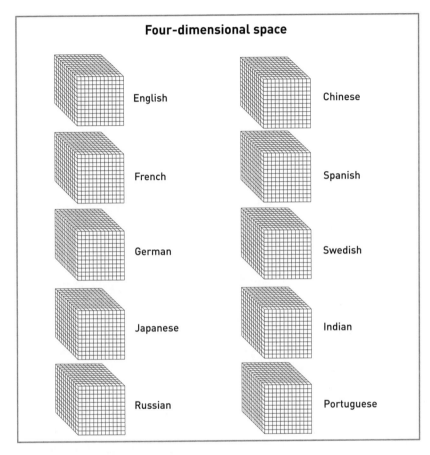

Four-dimensional space

English

French

German

Japanese

Russian

Chinese

Spanish

Swedish

Indian

Portuguese

FIG 9.8 By adding a fourth dimension, customers can go to the spaces where they'll meet only the merchants who speak their language

dimensional space is re-created ten times: each to cater for a different language that the merchants and customers might prefer to speak.

This fourth dimension will have the effect of increasing the number of different possible meeting places to 17,280. This will greatly reduce the effect of overcrowding and at the same time improve the compatibility of buyers and sellers.

There may be other preferences that a customer might have. If there are

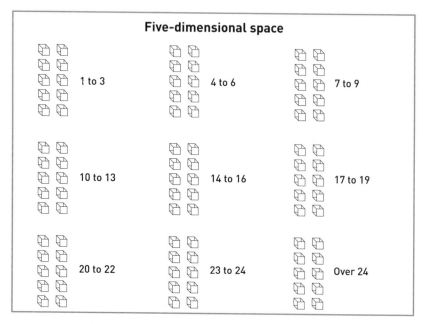

FIG 9.9 A fifth dimension might separate out the rag merchants by the number of sorters they use, as well as by garments sorted, geographic location, type of locality and language spoken. In this diagram, it shows this fifth dimension as consisting of nine groups, each with ten three-dimensional areas

so many merchants that that there is still overcrowding, a new dimension can be added for every important category. Figure 9.9 shows a fifth dimension being added to allow the customers to choose also the size of the merchants they deal with.

This fifth dimension will increase the number of different places a rag merchant or a buyer can establish a presence to 155,520. This may seem ludicrously excessive for finding rag merchants, but this is only a simplistic example used to explain the principle. What is of interest is that this same principle can be applied to areas where there are millions of people involved. Then, 155,520 different possible meeting places might seem very sensible indeed.

These diagrams graphically illustrate how the parameters associated with choice can be used to format a people space to increase the efficiency of finding suitable contacts. The significance of this model cannot be under-estimated. This is a powerful way to divide up a super-large population in order to seek out valuable contacts for information or help.

the creation of such a scenario At first thoughts, this would seem to be an impossibly complex scenario to set up, involving much organization and considerable capital expenditure. However, every entrepreneur has their own little speciality knowledge that can be applied to situations – the equivalent of Sherlock Holmes' treatise on the one hundred and fourteen varieties of tobacco ash. My particular speciality is clones and intelligent agents. These can be used to build and maintain such an environment inexpensively and to adapt it for all kinds of information-gathering situations where conventional databases would not be viable solutions.

10

A DIFFERENT WAY OF LOOKING AT DATABASES

visualizing a living database

Using a virtual café, for readers to comment upon each chapter as it is written, is a good way for an author to appreciate how people can interpret explanations in different ways. A case in point is the conceptualization of a living database, where almost everyone who read the last chapter saw it in a different light.

After reading the last chapter, one reviewer wrote:

I'm still not quite clear on what Peter is proposing – to keep track of the people generating the data (like a net phone book), or the data they are generating...?

Depending on what is shared, surely the data that is uploaded to the database (or a pointer to it, at least) would take a similar form to that data which is already on the web – in which case the standard problem of relevance and quality of information is going to be a major issue.

Current search engines are getting better all the time, and we've already hit the 'search engine of search engines' barrier. Thus, I think Peter will require a different type/source of information for this project to work (if he's going to do what I think he's going to do...!)

This reviewer seems to be thinking in terms of a conventional database, where either the names of people, or the information they provide, are recorded by a database management system. This would see the purpose of the database as being a depository of information that is accessed by the users.

Although a living database can be visualized as working in this way, the conceptualization is totally different. The function of the computer needs to be seen as providing only an infrastructure – a formatted, but otherwise empty space – where users can insert their presence.

The action would consist of users inserting their presence in places where they would be most likely to find people who can provide them with exactly the kind of service, help or information they need. In other words, the computer programming of the database isn't concerned with storing and providing information, it is about providing a landscape in which people can move around to meet each other.

This point was appreciated by another reviewer, Hubert Spall, an English website developer, who wrote:

The advantage of the internet seems to be in the speed with which communication takes place, so, by using e-mail effectively, we can network our business more easily. This is the case even if our main business is off-line. The website then becomes a repository for information too vast to be discussed with each contact, customer or partner individually. The website itself may have nothing directly to do with the business – no online selling involved, the product or service itself existing outside of any computer-related area – but simply provides an information point for the real business.

In order to bring in business via a website it is often necessary to provide a free information service about a whole lot of stuff RELATED to your business, but not leading directly to any sales – providing a façade of objectivity, the appearance (real or imagined) of a free service. And this is where costs begin to escalate...

The alternative model [the living database] provides a virtual environment which enables people in the specialized area we are interested in to find and communicate with others who have some knowledge or service they need. The use of intelligent agents allows searching for the relevant people to be personalized and specific.

Another reviewer, Mary Rickman-Taylor from the Arizona Institute of Business and Technology, also realized that Chapter 9 was about providing an environment where people could find each other. She viewed the living database in a more abstract form:

Chapter 9 pulls into tangible reality what perhaps many of us have been doing as we have been going along. In a sense the n-dimensional people space will become the 'super group' that writers have promoted for years as being one of the tools for success. That is, the collection of people that can help one move in the direction of successful endeavors, of solutions to problems that are not amenable to easy solutions by the limited means of a small group, but that can be approached in the people space referred to in Chapter 9.

Mary Rickman-Taylor had realized that Chapter 9 hadn't been about storing information, but about devising a strategy to find useful contacts. Throughout this trilogy, constant stress has been laid on the need to deal with people rather than information. This is because information and knowledge in the world of technology are continuously changing, expanding and evolving. It has the appearance of a fractal: the more you know, the more you find there is to know. Every branch of knowledge has innumerable niches and every niche has innumerable branches. Only humans can deal with this kind of dynamic complexity and they do this by interacting with each other and sharing knowledge.

Computers are undoubtedly ideal devices for handling vast amounts of information. Hierarchical branching can be employed to store and retrieve data according to specified categories or divisions of categories. However, if the information is undergoing continuous evolutionary change or the organizing structure becomes unstable, intractable problems arise.

Considering the bricks and mortar example described in the last chapter, the system of retrieving particular garments from piles of miscellaneous cast-offs looks as if it can be modelled in the form of a regular database. Suppliers, buyers and products can be listed and categorized, and it would seem relatively straightforward to create relational links between them. However, if such a database were to be used in a real-world situation it would be subject to continuous dynamic change due to unpredictable fashion swings.

To explain, think of fashion creating a demand for long skirts. This would create a concentration of interest in that particular garment area, with buyers looking for rag merchants sorting out long skirts and rag merchants responding to the market demand by selectively sorting for them. Then, for no logical reason, fashion might suddenly switch to short skirts. This would cause all information concerning long skirts to become redundant and the database would have to start reflecting the new interest in short skirts.

Then, skirts might go out of fashion altogether as ladies turned to wearing dresses. Interest in skirts would evaporate, as people would then want to know everything there is to know about dresses. If this volatility of interests is happening all the time, it would be totally frustrating for database managers, who would be continually revising and updating the content and organization of their systems.

The paradigm shift of visualizing a people space instead of a conventional database would completely remove all problems associated with information volatility because there would be no information to change. Instead, there would be just a framework of designated areas where people meet. When information needs change, people simply move their presence to new areas in the space where their new information needs can be met. For example, if interest changes from skirts to dresses, people would simply move their presence from the areas where skirts are being discussed to the areas where people are discussing dresses.

The database function would be minimal: simply to register the current locational presence of people as they choose to move between different areas of interest. These locational changes would be instigated by the people themselves, the database simply recording their current choices.

keeping up with trends and fashion

It is probably easier to visualize this not as a conventional database but as a formatted space of initially empty areas. When a new topic of interest emerges, anyone can spontaneously label a new empty area with the name of that new topic. Anyone else interested in the new topic can then move their presence into that area so as to be in contact with others interested in discussing it.

In this way, the overall people space would see new areas of interest continuously coming into existence, as and when fashion changes or new trends emerge. People could move between these areas according to their changing interests, leaving one area to go to another. In this way, it wouldn't matter how dynamic or changeable the information base is; the conceptual framework would simply reflect a population of people moving around to different areas within a formatted space.

Treating this situation as a conventional database would see it as being similar to that of trying to publish a book that listed all the trendy meeting places in London. It could be up to date at only one particular moment in time. By the time the book was printed, new meeting places might have become fashionable and those listed in the book might be out of fashion. This would cause the book to be an inaccurate source of reference. Imagine now trying to create such a book that tried to record the currently trendy meeting places of every town and city in the world; this would be nearer to the scale of the problem that we are trying to deal with.

Despite the near impossibility of being able to create up-to-date directories of currently trendy places where people are meeting in various parts of the world, these gatherings do take place and quite obviously the people who are there have discovered where they are being held. It is this enigmatic process of knowing where things are currently happening that needs to be accommodated in the formatted structure of a living database.

London can be viewed as a formatted space, where trendy meeting places suddenly and unpredictably become popular. This view would see movements of people as they moved *en masse* and for no apparent reason from one venue to another. The only certain way to keep track of the movements of any particular group would be to be part of that group, so that you can move with it when it moves on.

It is the essence of this dynamic scenario that needs to be created to ensure that people can find out where the current action they are interested in is happening. The information is irrelevant. The most important issue is being in the right place at the right time. This will have to involve being in regular contact with the right kind of people.

from the general to the particular

Let's look now at the problem posed by Tillman Pearce. How can cancer patients be helped in finding out about all the treatments that might be available to help their condition?

The treatment of cancer is a typical example of a rapidly expanding technological field where new research is continuously creating an abundance of new developments in many different parts of the world. For a patient seeking treatment, it would be impossible to keep track of all the activities taking place. Realistically, a cancer patient couldn't be expected to study all the technical papers relating to their condition. Neither could it be expected that they'd be able to discuss matters with many specialists. As discussed already, any databases available to them on the subject would almost certainly be incomplete, probably out of date and unlikely to address their specific individual situation.

66 THE MOST IMPORTANT ISSUE IS BEING IN THE RIGHT PLACE AT THE RIGHT TIME 99

The only option left open for them is to mix with other cancer patients who have a similar condition and find out what is happening to them. This is where they can be helped: by providing them with a formatted space where they can get together in niche groupings to pool their knowledge. After all, collectively as a group, the patients are as much aware of all the possible treatments as the physicians.

If a conceptual framework can be designed to arrange for cancer patients with a similar condition to find each other, this would be far more valuable to them than any informational database. They can compare treatments, swap information. Many of them will have built up specialist knowledge on their condition that they can share with the others. Perhaps some of them will have websites, where they have recorded the extent of their knowledge within the niche area of their particular condition. Between them, the patients are likely to have more experience and knowledge of treatments and outcomes relating to their condition than most individual cancer specialists.

If special areas of interest are created in a people space – relating to different types of cancer, types of treatment and other associated topics – it is likely to attract more than just the patients themselves. It will also attract friends and relatives who use the internet to help find the best treatment for their loved ones. It will be of interest to researchers, drug companies, doctors and surgeons who will have a professional interest in knowing about the work of others and the treatment options outside of their own particular approach.

Visualizing these communities as forming spontaneously in a formatted space – with changing circumstances and new technological develop-ments causing them to move around, dividing them up into more specialized grouping as their number increases – would seem to be a far more realistic approach to obtaining knowledge than trying to create a conventional database of information.

As we shall see later, this approach can be usefully applied to many other areas of technology – especially where there is an impossibly large knowledge base that is continuously changing, expanding and evolving.

the ubiquity of empty formatted space
The idea of starting with an empty formatted space and allowing areas of interest to form spontaneously through the activity of users may seem somewhat esoteric, but this is the principle behind a living database. To begin the explanation, let's start with the formatting of a space.

In the world of computing, the formatting of an empty space is common to all computer hardware and software applications that deal with memory and information storage. The most well-known example is the formatting of a hard disk. The general idea is that a certain volume of memory space is available or allocated and this is divided up into small sections that are individually identified and kept in some form of order so that each section can be accessed irrespective of its label or content.

After the formatting process, any information that is put onto the hard disk is divided up between a number of these small sections. The identification numbers and sequence of these sections are recorded by the operating system, so that it knows where to retrieve the pieces and put them back together again whenever it is called on to do so.

With this system of pre-formatting the disk with small empty sections, files and applications can be broken up and stored on the disk using any sections that are currently free. This method of storage might seem bizarre, but it is an efficient way to store information that is constantly being changed, added to, deleted or replaced because the storage can be distributed instead of being confined to a fixed area. The operating system has no problem with a file being broken up and distributed in different places all over the disk because it knows where every section is located, so any file can be retrieved as easily as if it were stored in one single section of memory.

Software applications that need to create their own formatting system can overlay the formatting of the operating system with its own ordering arrangement, i. e. the operating system allows an application to create its own formatting and will then transparently convert this to its own system when saving to disk. When the application wants to access the information, the operating system will retrieve the data in a way that preserves the formatting arranged by the application.

This method of storing files allows all applications to use their own formatting systems, so databases can hold information in a format that is most convenient for the algorithms they use.

More sophisticated formatting can attach little computer programs to each of the separate formatted areas that are created by an application. This can be seen in spreadsheet programs which, although they appear initially to a user as completely empty grids of rectangles, are in fact formatted arrangements of complex cells that are able to communicate with each other and be linked in highly complex ways.

Computer programming languages always have facilities for formatting a memory space in any way defined by the programmer. High-level, multimedia authoring programs present the developer with a pre-formatted empty space into which can be slotted software modules, text, graphics and sounds. It is the existence of pre-formatted space that makes it possible to use object-oriented design strategies, because through the arrangement of the formatting, objects know where to send messages to each other.

These are just a few examples of the ubiquity of the concept of a formatted empty space and the various ways in which it can be employed. The essential idea to grasp is that the way in which a formatted space can be used is limited only by the imagination.

growing into a space

A conventional database design approach will be to create a formatted space to suit algorithms that will be used to sort, search and form relationships between the data items. A human database designer will work out what the categories and sub-categories of the formatted areas should be, so that data and information can be inserted into places where the algorithms are designed to expect it.

> **THE ESSENTIAL IDEA TO GRASP IS THAT THE WAY IN WHICH A FORMATTED SPACE CAN BE USED IS LIMITED ONLY BY THE IMAGINATION**

A living database cannot be constructed in this way because the initial assumption would be that no one has any idea at the start as to what kind of information the living database would be dealing with, let alone knowing all the categories through several levels of subdivision.

My own approach to the construction of a living database was first to create an empty list of 26 lines – each of the 26 lines being identified by the letters of the alphabet: A to Z. This then became the template for the formatting of the entire living database.

When any line is clicked on, it will either point to a particular area of the formatted space described by the line, or present another different but identical-looking list of 26 lines identified by the letters A to Z. These lines can then be used as subdivisions of the topic described by the line that has been clicked on.

Presenting new lists of lines when categories need to be subdivided allows the database to expand at a second level to a total of 26 × 26, equalling 676 lines. Clicking on any of these 676 lines can present yet another different but identical list of 26 lines, allowing a total number of lines at this third level of $26 \times 26 \times 26$, equalling 17,576 lines. Extending this to five levels would allow a total of 11,881,376 lines, creating a structure that can format any space into nearly 12 million different possible topic areas.

Of course, it is extremely unlikely that any area of knowledge would need 12 million categories, but that is not the point. The idea is that this formatting technique allows ample room in which to expand the content of a living database in many different directions according to the most appropriate way to divide it up.

For example, one level may use only two or three of its possible 26 sub-categories. Many sub-categories may not extend to the full five levels. However, with such a large possible space in which the content can extend, the content has the freedom to grow to any size and shape of tree-like structure that conveniently divides up the total subject matter. Figure 10.1 illustrates a typical tree-like structure expanding into a formatted space from a first level that uses only four of the possible 26 categories available at that starting level.

Figure 10.1 shows a database consisting of just four categories at level one. Each of these subdivides. Some of these subdivisions divide several times, creating new levels where, at each level, there might be more subdivisions. Category 'A' of the first level through the route of sub-divisions 'A,A,A, A' points to seven subdivisions at level five.

From this figure, it is easy to see how billions of possible subdivision arrangements can be grown in this formatted space, which has 26 possible subdivisions at every branch at every level.

The advantage of this system is its elegant simplicity. Any tree-like structure that might grow as a result of adding and subdividing categories of the content will be constructed of multiples of exactly the same simple template of 26 lines. Using an object-oriented environment that can use a template to create components on demand, there will be no need to create these lists until they are actually needed.

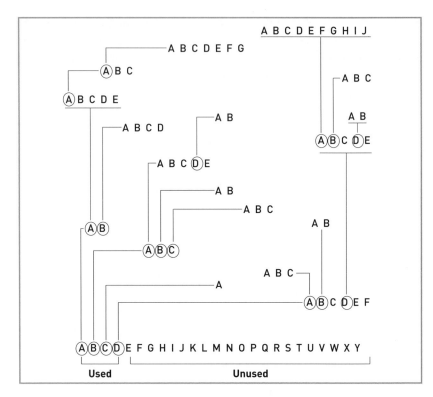

FIG 10.1 A living database where subdivision of categories is creating a tree-like structure within a formatted space. The circled categories are those that are subdivided. The others are pointers to particular areas in the space which contain information (or people)

It might seem that there would be a problem in addressing or trying to locate any particular area in a space containing up to 12 million areas. However, the modular nature of the formatting of the total space allows an elegantly simple solution to this problem. Each of the areas can be described by the route taken to reach the area from the first level.

Addressing any of the 12 million separate possible areas in this space requires a maximum of five letters: the route description from the first level. For example, an area at level five in this 12 million area space might be described as 'CKRAY'. This would indicate that category 'C' was chosen at the first level, category 'K' at the second, category 'R' at the third, category 'A' at the fourth and category 'Y' at the fifth. This address would identify one particular area out of the possible total of 12 million.

If this formatting scheme were used to describe areas where people could meet to discuss a particular topic, this simple addressing system would not only define a particular place to meet to discuss one out of a possible 12 million topics, it would also describe how anyone could reach that meeting place to insert their presence and to find out who else was there.

With such a simple addressing system, it is possible to string several addresses together to describe being at several meeting places simultaneously. It is also a convenient form of addressing to include in the construction of a bot, so that it knows what places to visit on behalf of its owner.

Notice also that anyone can find a particular topic that interests them by making selections at each level: a maximum of five decision points. This is best explained with an example.

finding a way through thousands of spaces

Trying to visualize a people space with 12 million different possible meeting places might seem impossibly complex. How, for instance, would people find the best areas to establish a presence, i.e. find the virtual meeting places where they could make just the right kind of contacts? Surprisingly, it is very easy: it involves nothing more complicated than answering a few multi-choice questions: one for each level (note: the levels correspond to the different dimensions of a multi-dimensional space as described in the last chapter).

In the hypothetical example described in the last chapter, rag merchants could establish a presence at meeting places in a people space – where customers would be looking for the garments they were sorting – by answering the following five multi-choice questions (selecting by clicking on a single line in each of five given lists – with each click bringing up the list for the next question):

1 What items do you sort? (12 items listed – A to L)

2 What is your geographical location? (12 items listed – A to L)

3 What is the type of locality you draw stock from? (12 items listed – A to L)

4 What languages do you speak? (10 items listed – A to J)

5 How many sorters do you use? (9 items listed – A to I)

The answers to these questions (requiring only five clicks) would automatically create a unique address at one of the possible 155,520 places in the people space. By repeating this simple procedure, a rag merchant can establish a presence at every meeting place where there are customers looking for someone like them and wanting to buy the products they are sorting.

In an identical way, buyers can establish their presence in the most suitable places to meet the right kind of rag merchants who are sorting out the garments they need – simply by answering five similar multi-choice questions (again by clicking on lines in lists):

1 Select the type of garments you are interested in (12 items listed – A to L).

2 Select the geographic areas you can travel to (12 items listed – A to L).

3 Select the type of locality you want the garments to come from (12 items listed – A to L).

4 Select the languages you speak (10 items listed – A to J).

5 Select the size of company you want to deal with (number of sorters) (9 items listed – A to I).

Again, each meeting place chosen would require no more than five clicks, each click bringing up the next set of lists. This could be repeated for as many meeting places as the buyer wishes to go to meet appropriate rag dealers.

There will be no sense of the complexity of the formatted space; the users probably won't even realize it exists. They will simply be answering the questions and as a result find themselves automatically connected to the people they need to know.

This system matches suppliers to customers. As it is a virtual space, both suppliers and customers can go into as many spaces as they like, so a rag merchant can appear simultaneously in several different places if they sort several different kinds of garment, or speak several different languages.

Similarly, a customer can appear in many different areas if they need a number of different garments, speak several languages, are prepared to travel to several different geographic areas and don't care how many sorters the rag merchant employs. This exploits the unique property of the internet to allow people to be in multiple virtual places at the same time.

Although this is a hypothetical and probably not very practical example, it illustrates the essence of the general idea. It is not hard to adapt the conceptual framework to all manner of subject areas where it is useful for people to meet others. This will apply particularly where people need to meet others to be able to share information and knowledge.

abstracting this model for other purposes
The rag-sorting example involves the transfer of physical goods. But this same structure can be used to bring people together for the purpose of exchanging information or finding collaborative partners.

Imagine, now, all the millions of people on the internet. Imagine them each needing a special piece of information that somewhere some of the other millions of people on the internet might have. Wouldn't such a structure be useful for bringing together those who need to have a particular piece of information with those who might have it?

Such a structured space could also be used to bring people who want to create e-businesses together with people who can help them. It can be used to bring people with software products together with those who have a need for those products. It can bring service providers together with those who have a need for those services. It can bring experts and specialists together with the people who need their specialist help. It can bring together people with money with those who need it.

Returning to Tillman Pearce's initial problem of creating a database for cancer treatment, wouldn't this be a useful infrastructure to facilitate the flow of information in this particular subject area? Patients with similar types of cancer could meet to share experiences, exchange knowledge about treatment strategies, costs and locations of specialist treatment centres. As this could be made available to anyone in the world, it could bring in opinions and knowledge of practices and treatment facilities from every corner of the planet.

Meeting places could be established based upon any number of criteria, so that patients could go to special areas to discuss a particular treatment option, a promising line of research, methods of coping with pain, drug testing programmes, etc. All it would take to set up a new meeting area would be to add a new category to one of the lists. This could be done by the users themselves if they are given the facility (this would be the function of a bot, as we shall see in the next chapter).

Similarly, in any area where there are too many people or too much information to deal with, a tree-like structure can be created in a people space to filter out fast and efficient routes through the confusion and noise to where solutions to problems can be found.

what happens at the meeting places?

Every route through a tree-like structure in a people space will end at a meeting place where people can establish a presence and have an opportunity to communicate and interact with the others who are present.

For the moment, we'll skip over the questions of making sure there are enough people there to make it interesting, or of getting the details of those who are present – these questions will be dealt with in the next chapter when we cover bots and overall system organization and house-keeping. First, we need to establish what form these meeting places might take.

As there could be any number of meeting places, they would have to be able to be created on demand, from a single template. Just like the list modules from which the trees are constructed, these meeting places would need to be produced as and when they are needed without having to use custom programming or call upon any human management system to make the necessary arrangements. When a user sees a need for a new topic to be discussed, they should be able to create a new meeting place simply by giving it a topic name and clicking on a button.

Having to use a single format for all the meeting places, it will be necessary for the design to offer a wide range of options for people to be able to communicate with each other in a variety of ways. Many options can be covered by bots on the client side, but for the moment let's look at the kind of template that can be provided to create meeting places on a website.

At a minimum, the meeting place would have to provide the following facilities:

1 a list of the people who have currently established a presence;

2 an e-mail discussion forum;

3 a message bulletin board;

4 a news group;

5 facilities for instant messaging (peer to peer or chat rooms);

6 list of associated meeting places;

7 list of relevant websites.

This arrangement is illustrated in Figure 10.2.

At any particular meeting place, different facilities might be used according to the preferences of the people who have established a presence there. There is no way of being able to determine in advance what these preferences might be, so all options must be offered so as to allow each meeting place to evolve on its own.

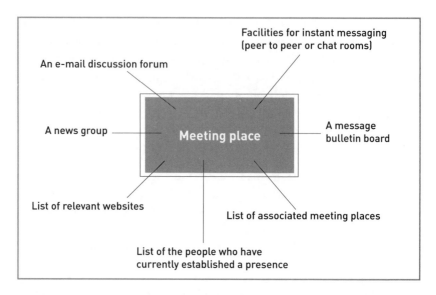

FIG 10.2 Each meeting place in the formatted people space will take the form of an environment in its own right, with various types of communication facilities provided. This environment will have to be designed as a template so that it can be re-created for every meeting place needed

individual communication strategies

The picture presented so far is of an open environment that anyone is free to join. Meetings and communications are public affairs with no apparent facility for mixing groups or for anyone to be able to choose people from different groups to have private discussions. This omission needs to be addressed.

The simple solution is to combine the concept of the people space with the concept of a personal café of contacts. In this way, anyone can use the public meeting places to acquire contacts and then use the conceptual environment of their own café to have more private discussions outside of the public people space. This is illustrated in Figure 10.3, which shows how an individual can acquire a number of contacts from various public meeting places, then add them to the list of special contacts they communicate with privately in the conceptual area of their own personal café.

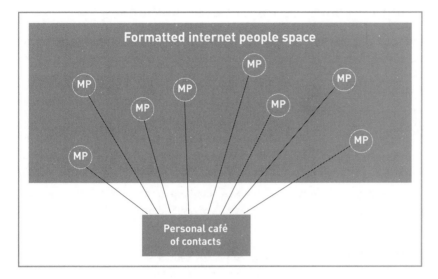

FIG 10.3 By visiting various meeting places in a formatted people space, a variety of personal contacts can be acquired. These can then be conceptualized as appearing in a private café within the space of a personal computer

Although this café can be purely conceptual – with the café existing as no more than simply a list of people to communicate with privately – the café can be given a definitive form and substance. This has already been discussed, with a more detailed explanation given in the second book of this trilogy (*The Ultimate Game of Strategy*). In essence, this involves creating a major list of all known contacts, out of which 50 special contacts are chosen who might be useful or directly involved in current activities.

If people use bots, created as clones of their owners, it is possible to insert these as presences in the meeting areas. This would allow direct transference of these bots, with all the information they might contain about their owners, directly into a personal café environment where they can be examined in private. Technically, this is fairly easy to arrange – as will be discussed in the next chapter.

using components to produce solutions The concept of a

living database would seem to be a likely candidate for a basic component in a solution to help patients locate suitable cancer treatments. It is worth taking it further at this stage because this structure could become a very useful component in all kinds of e-businesses that involve putting people in touch with each other.

Biological evolution works in this same way. It is a continuous process of finding and developing new components that are then combined in different ways to create complex organisms. Few, if any, of the biological organisms we recognize today have evolved from scratch; they are all made up of components that have evolved independently in a previous evolutionary structure.

Biologists have discovered the same biological components being used over and over again in different contexts and in different organisms. Looked at in this way, we would see Mother Nature's evolutionary strategy as primarily that of developing components and then using them in different combinations for opportunistic purposes.

This takes us back to Sherlock Holmes' method of detection. He had built up a number of components he used for detection. One of these was his speciality knowledge of cigarette ash. He had this knowledge to call upon where it became opportune in helping to find a solution to the problem of who committed a crime. In a similar way, a fully developed, living database structure could be just the key component needed to turn an opportunity into a viable e-business solution.

Working in this way to create e-businesses, it isn't sufficient to have components that are just conceptual ideas. For a component to have any real value it must have been developed and perfected to the extent that it can be put to work immediately when an opportunity comes along.

In the fast-moving world of e-business, this component building is happening all the time. The vast sums of investment money thrown at the early dot coms at the turn of the century may have been a complete loss to the investors, but what this money did was to create many little tried and tested modules that designers are able to reuse later by applying them to new situations.

Most professional programmers work this way. They never build software solutions entirely from scratch. They progressively build up libraries of modules that they can use whenever an opportunity presents itself. Most importantly, these modules have been tried and tested – even though it may have been at the expense of a client.

This is why it pays to use experienced programmers. It's not so much that they have learned to become cleverer and cleverer at programming (although this happens as well); their greatest value is that they can put together previously developed modules that can be quickly and efficiently combined and adapted to suit a new project.

Looking at the living database as a component – for me, this idea evolved out of a number of different life experiences. These experiences tell me that the concept is not complete or viable in itself as it can only be of value if used with a strategy to achieve a condition known as 'critical mass'.

critical mass
With practically all web-based businesses, the key to being successful is to achieve critical mass. This has many definitions but they all boil down to the following:

Critical mass is the point at which there are sufficient users or customers for the business to be profitable, self-running and self-maintaining.

Perversely, many of the failed dot coms relentlessly pursued the goal of attracting as many visitors to their websites as possible in the mistaken belief that this would lead automatically to commercial success. It doesn't. This is not what critical mass is about. The only people who count towards critical mass are those who are benefiting from the site and also adding to the profitability of the business. It is the need to achieve this double goal with all visitors that makes it so hard to reach critical mass.

The only way this double goal – of both visitors and the e-business benefiting – can be achieved is by building a system that creates wealth, i.e. developing a non-zero-sum game situation where everyone can gain.

In the design of a web-based business, the primary consideration should be that the visitors, customers or clients should benefit substantially and directly. If this condition is fully satisfied, stability of the business can be assured. Only after this condition is fully satisfied can the business owners start to consider how they themselves might benefit.

If the system is creating sufficient benefit or wealth, there is bound to be some way in which the business can find some way of profiting. After all, if someone establishes a wealth-creating situation it is only right and fair that they have a share. If there is not sufficient wealth created for both customers and the business to benefit substantially, then critical mass cannot be achieved – a point often ignored by those who create websites whose main objective is to attract eyeballs.

Benefit for customers or clients must be immediate, but the benefit for the business often comes later – once the conditions for critical mass have been fulfilled. This will involve an initial capital expenditure, which will be needed to cover the burn rate (excess of outgoings over income) while attempting to reach critical mass. A prudent strategist would see this as the most important area to concentrate on, even taking precedence over the technical aspects of the solution. This suggests a strategy of starting simple and leaving as much of the complexity as possible until after critical mass has been achieved.

Achievement of critical mass with systems like the living database is particularly difficult because it depends upon self-fulfilment for success: a 'chicken and egg' situation. Obviously, a business based on a living database would have a great chance of success if the people who used the system could click their way to a meeting place and be guaranteed to find a useful group of contacts waiting for them when they arrived. However, the first people to arrive at a meeting place will be disappointed because there won't be many there.

Clearly, a strategy has to be devised such that in the beginning a sufficiently large number of people arrive at a meeting place at the same time. In other words, every meeting place will have an individual critical mass that has to be achieved and maintained before it can be deemed successful.

This again points to the advantage of starting with a very small niche grouping where marketing can be narrowly targeted and timing more easily controlled. Having successfully achieved one synchronized start for a meeting place, others can be added – one at a time – to gradually increase the number of meeting places which have exceeded the point of critical mass.

The necessity for every meeting place to have critical mass means having to wait until the number at a meeting place reaches some multiple of critical mass before it can be subdivided to create new categories or levels. Consequentially, the tree-like structures within a people space must be grown rather than be predetermined or planned. This requires a bottom-up strategy, which is fundamentally different from the top-down way in which conventional databases are designed, where the branching and categories are mostly planned in advance of data being entered.

This makes sense because if 100 categories were pre-planned to create 100 meeting places, the average attendance would be only 1 per cent of the people using the system. This might see the first hundred people using the database all going to different areas and finding themselves the only person there. Even a thousand people visiting a living database would find the meeting places they chose to visit fairly empty and might conclude that the system wasn't worth bothering with.

A similar but slightly different problem occurs when an e-business tries to be too clever. Many e-businesses have failed to achieve critical mass because their system offers too many features, or too many options, which confuses the users. A complex system that makes perfect sense to the designers might be totally unfathomable to the intended clients. It is fair to conclude, therefore, that any web-based business has to be as simple as possible to use, with all the technology completely transparent. Anything more complicated than clicking a mouse on easy-to-understand buttons is likely to put users off and lessen the chances of achieving critical mass.

This leads to the most crucial challenge for all e-businesses: getting potential customers actively involved. Or, to put it another way, why should any customer or client be motivated to use whatever service or product is offered? And, even before that, how do you get customers or clients to become aware of the service or product in the first place? These are not questions to be dealt with after a product or service has been developed. These will be critical issues that have to be included in the strategy right from the very beginning.

There is much to learn from the failures of the early dot coms. Many of them developed an e-business solution and then spent heavily on advertising, only to discover that the system they'd so expensively developed wasn't customer friendly, or was so full of flaws that customers soon gave up on it. Many of them, in desperation, threw good money after bad by increasing their advertising or tried to patch up a system that was fundamentally wrong.

The living database concept described above offers an important advantage in this respect because it allows business systems to grow from a small base – a bottom-up strategy. If you look back at Figure 10.1, it can be seen to consist of many routes that lead to different areas of interest. This suggests that small sections can be isolated and developed independently of all the others.

A good strategy, therefore, would be to start very simply with one small section and develop this to a state of satisfaction before moving on to add others. This would allow concentration of marketing effort to be confined initially to one small niche area, which could be strategically chosen as being a group that is highly motivated to take part and is not expensive to contact.

When several meeting places have been established, more sophistication can be introduced. Experimental trials, of improvements or added facilities, can be tried out on single meeting places before using them on a wider scale. This, again, is a bottom-up strategy of system development, which ensures that if intended improvements do not work out as expected, the success of the whole project isn't jeopardized.

competition for critical mass
In the massively connected communication environment of the internet, critical mass cannot be treated as a permanent asset. It is highly vulnerable to competition and changing circumstances and can disappear virtually overnight.

Unlike the world of bricks and mortar, people can easily and rapidly change their patronage if a new technological development outdates a business system or a competitor offers something better or cheaper. The only way to safeguard against this eventuality is to have a system that has low overheads and is extremely flexible and adaptable.

Low overheads will make it difficult for a competitor to compete on price. It will also reduce burn rate if the system has to adapt to any new and unexpected turn of events where critical mass is temporarily lost.

If a business system has a modular structure – such as a living database with many different meeting places – it is unlikely that all the modular sections will be affected simultaneously if critical mass is threatened. This will provide some stability to keep the business running while a strategy of recovery or adaptation is taking place.

11

THE ENIGMATIC WORLD OF BOTS AND PERSONAL AGENTS

a hybrid solution needed The main message of the last two chapters is that there are some very important areas of knowledge that cannot be handled by database solutions. These are the information areas where there is so much volatility and change that the costs of maintaining up-to-date, accurate and complete records are prohibitively expensive. Without appropriate databases, the only practical way such knowledge can be shared is through personal contact between people.

Unfortunately, dealing with people is far more complex than accessing information from a database. People are not machines, so they aren't amenable to being simply information sources. It takes time to get to know someone well enough to be able to ask them questions. It takes time to know if they have sufficient knowledge to provide the answers. It takes time to transfer information. It takes time to explain a problem to someone else and it takes time for them to understand the problem and provide an answer. It takes time to check out if the information given is correct. This is not a very efficient form of information transfer.

Somewhere, in between a database and a person-to-person exchange of information, there needs to be a hybrid solution that combines the advantages of person-to-person contact with the ease of accessing a database. Such a hybrid solution is possible by combining the concept of a living database with the concept of bots and personal agents. This solution may not be suitable for every kind of situation, but where bots and personal agents can be used, the efficiency of human interaction can be substantially improved.

This chapter is about using bots and personal agents in this hybrid role, but first, it is necessary to have a more abstract view of a people space, so as not to confuse this concept with the rigidity of conventional database thinking.

summarizing the last two chapters

To try to get away from a people space being a conventional database structure, let's consider what a people space actually does. This has been very well expressed by one of the readers in the virtual café of reviewers, Vic Harper, who sent in his summary of the current position as it stood at the end of the last chapter:

I already know there is...

too much information out there to gather or sort

too little time to read all that you want to

too little energy to absorb all that is useful

too much technology to master

too much useless dribble masking the useful

too much redundant effort

too much lost stuff

I have just learned of a solution that provides...

a choice of many useful meeting places to meet others that are the 'right' ones for whatever my reason/need

a way to organize the location (addressability) of these places

a nice easy way to create a new space if the need arises (bottom-up and object-oriented, sweet) a way to facilitate me when I'm in that neat little space

a way to put a virtual me into that virtual space

a way to have my clone in many places at once

a way to sort out what is actually useful to me without a lot of energy

a way to save time

Vic Harper isn't visualizing a database structure, he is seeing a mental picture of a space that can help him to meet people who might be of value to him.

visualizing a people space

From the comments of the various people who read the last two chapters, there seemed to be a sharp polarization of views as to what a people space represents. Those who saw it in terms of a database thought the concept highly impractical and fraught with problems associated with the choosing of categories and the freedom given to users to construct it in a random way.

Others saw it quite differently. They didn't think of the people space in terms of categorized compartments, but as a valuable conceptual model from which to think about meeting people who could help them obtain hard-to-find knowledge or assist them with e-business problems. Seeing a people space in this more abstract form requires a considerable paradigm shift that is not easy to make – and is even more difficult to explain.

In writing the book *Magical A-Life Avatars*, I had a similar problem when explaining the concept of object-oriented programming. Some programmers could think only in terms of the syntax and structure of the programming and couldn't catch on to the idea of object-oriented design strategy at all. Others saw beyond the code and thought about the memory space in the computer that the code would fit into. They realized they could divide that area up into self-contained areas into which they could place little code modules that could function completely independently of any of the other code in the memory space.

Having this higher-level view of the programming environment allowed the programmers to think in terms of small code modules that interacted with each other. They could then rise above the level of the detail of the coding to concentrate on the functions themselves. In this way they could construct high-level systems that called on functions, without having their thinking cluttered up with how the functions were performing their tasks.

To explain this idea of thinking about a formatted space in memory, I used the following dialogue which appears in Chapter 4 of *Magical A-Life Avatars*:

Presenting a new concept:

Time: Early 1970s

Place: The president's office in a large electronics company in California

'The president will see you now.'

The young man was ushered into the president's sumptuous office and shown to a seat in front of the huge desk dominating the room. He waited nervously for the president to finish reading through the pile of papers on his desk. The president looked up at him.

'You the guy with the killer app for these new-fangled computer things?'

'I think so,' replied the young man nervously.

'What is it, then?'

'Well, it's sort of difficult to describe,' began the young man hesitantly. 'It consists of a grid of rectangles covering a computer screen.'

'What's in the rectangles?'

'Nothing.'

'Nothing?'

'Well, not until the user puts something into them.'

'What sort of things?'

'Text and figures, but figures mostly, because the rectangles are used to do mathematical operations on the figures.'

'So each rectangle is programmed to act like a calculator?'

'Well, they could be. It depends how the user programs them.'

'You mean these empty rectangles have to be programmed by the user?'

'Yes, that's right. The rectangles are connected to each other by some kind of formula.'

'What's the formula you use to connect up these rectangles?'

'I don't provide the formula.'

'Who does?'

'The user.'

'How are these rectangles connected to each other, then?'

'They aren't connected until the user supplies the connections.'

'So, this killer app of yours consists of a grid of empty, unrelated rectangles that the user has to fill up with figures and connect together with their own programming and formulae.'

'That's right.'

'What are you going to call this killer app of yours?'

'I thought of calling it a spreadsheet.'

'Nice name. Thank you for coming along.'

'Thank you for seeing me.'

'Goodbye.'

'Goodbye.'

The above scene seems humorous to us now because we know what a spreadsheet is and we can see how easy it would have been for somebody without previous knowledge to miss the point of having empty rectangles in a spreadsheet. The idea that you can model a business or a manufacturing process on a spreadsheet consisting of nothing but empty cells isn't instantly obvious. However, as the Taoists say, 'The usefulness of a bowl comes exactly from its emptiness.'

The dialogue illustrates the conceptual hurdle that has to be overcome before a living database, or a people space, can be usefully employed in the creation of an e-business. It isn't about planning the meeting areas, or classifying them. It's about creating a structure where useful meeting places can appear spontaneously in a formatted space. In this way, any details of the structure are irrelevant – only the benefits that manifest within this space are important.

The example used in the last two chapters – of a people space being used by cancer patients to find available treatments – illustrates how the space can be used without the need for any rules or algorithms. Users just click their way to a meeting place where they have an opportunity to meet others who have a special interest in the same particular narrow area of knowledge as themselves.

There were reservations from some readers about the success of some of these meeting places. Would they attract a viable number of people? The answer is: nobody knows. The outcome is statistical. Some will work, others will fail.

This can be compared to many nightclubs opening at the same time in the centre of a large city. Each nightclub owner would have planned to make their establishment successful and popular, but it is unlikely that they would all succeed. Probably, nobody would be able to predict in advance which would be successful and which would fail, but to the people who go to nightclubs this is irrelevant, as they will be visiting only those that succeed.

A people space with designated meeting places should be looked at in this same way. To view any particular meeting place in isolation would see all kinds of reasons why it could fail, but from a statistical standpoint, it is unlikely that they would all fail (conditional of course on there being a real need for the kind of information that the people space can provide).

For instance, a people space designed to create meeting places for people with various types of cancer could not be expected to succeed in every category. Some categories might not click at all, while others, for no accountable reason, might be a roaring success. The fact that there might be failures in amongst the successes does not invalidate the overall concept.

focus of attention

Another interesting viewpoint came out of a correspondence I had with Richard Ross, a Brit working in San Francisco. I'd met Richard some three years previously when I'd given a talk at the Hub Club in London about using agents that could represent people on the web. When Richard heard that I would be visiting San Francisco to present a paper at BOT2001 (the annual event for all those interested in bots and intelligent agents), he suggested we met up for a chat.

To explain what I'd be talking about at BOT2001, I sent him a copy of the paper, which included a description of a living database as described in the previous two chapters. He wrote back:

I have just read the paper. What I like about it is that it suggests an approach for that old problem so rarely recognized in DP [data processing] of dealing with qualitative as opposed to quantitative information and recognizes the expertise of the individual perspective in this domain.

I must say though, I'd rather see a description of the data domain less hierarchically structured. Instead of describing the data field as a tree with fixed hierarchies as implied by the address system you describe for 'navigating' it (this sounds suspiciously hypertextual), I'd rather see a metaphor of the address description being a non-hierarchical one that configures the data field around me, i.e. it just offers me a particular perspective.

I could plug in things like location, language, volume etc. and I would find myself at the same café table as before but with having imposed rather fewer assumptions about the nature of the information in this domain. I suppose it's more like data visualization than navigation. It's ultimately about how I can reconfigure the way I might see the world so that it allows me to do some useful work.

Interesting stuff though, and yes, I have always thought the real power of the web was people.

What I had failed to do was to provide Richard with any of the details of the personal virtual café. He could only visualize one half of the story: the moving around in the space, to meeting places where he could make contact with people. This view sees all the person-to-person interaction as happening only at meeting places on the server side of the web.

The full story, however, sees the meetings as happening not only in a shared space but in a personal and private space: within the confines of a café created in the memory of every user's own computer. These meetings will then be under individual control, where additional contacts can be brought in from anywhere in the formatted space.

This effectively reconfigures the people space individually, for every person using it, making them the centre of a non-hierarchical information network that allows them to include only the people and contacts relevant to their interests.

In other words, a people space isn't set up to be the sole infrastructure for interpersonal communication and interaction: its main purpose is to allow people to find appropriate others whom they can then bring into their own private information network. This is organized through their personal virtual café where the interactions are outside of and apart from the formal structure of the people space (see Figure 11.1).

With this visualization of the concept, the user of a people space is not restricted at all by its formatting. The formatting has only the same significance in a people space as lines of latitude and longitude have on a map of the world: they provide a grid reference.

This can be appreciated once you realize that the route to any meeting place need not be through the hierarchies of categories. A meeting place may be recommended by somebody. This recommendation would simply provide a reference of the form 'BHEAC', which would allow anyone to navigate straight to a meeting place without even being aware of the hierarchical nature of the formatting.

the necessary paradigm shift
Richard Ross wasn't the only person to whom I sent a copy of my BOT2001 paper: I also sent it to many of the reviewers of my book in the virtual café. I asked them to read through it to see if they could anticipate any awkward questions I

> " A PEOPLE SPACE ISN'T SET UP TO BE THE SOLE INFRASTRUCTURE FOR INTERPERSONAL COMMUNICATION AND INTERACTION "

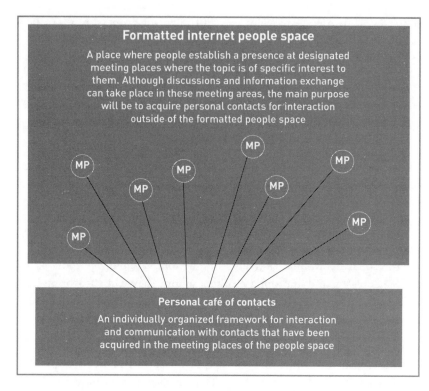

FIG 11.1 Showing diagrammatically how a formatted people space is used primarily as a source of acquiring personal contacts for a private communication network

might receive when I explained the concept of a living database to the audience in San Francisco.

I was quite alarmed when I received their responses. It seemed that no two of them were seeing the same picture. Many of them were suggesting problems with the model that shouldn't be relevant. It was a puzzle. Why should so many people not be seeing the living database as I'd been visualizing it?

As I went through the various comments, it suddenly clicked what was going wrong. Most of the readers were viewing the living database from a server-side perspective and not looking at it from the client side. From the server side, the meeting places might seem to be clearly defined topic areas, where the people meeting at these places would communicate with each other only around that narrow area of interest.

However, from a client-side perspective, the meeting places represent only a place of contact. The topic of interest at any particular meeting place is not a restraint upon the range of communication, but simply serves as an indicator that those present share a single common interest. It doesn't necessarily mean that their whole range of interests is in alignment.

This can be likened to an antique dealer going to a meeting where the subject matter is snuffboxes. The antique dealer goes there to broaden her knowledge and isn't there to develop a major interest in snuffboxes. In the course of mixing with the people at the meeting she might meet another antique dealer, who tells her about another meeting that is taking place where the discussion is about old fountain pens which are becoming a popular collector's item.

This illustrates how from the organizer's perspective (the server-side view) the meeting is supposed to be about snuffboxes, but to the antique dealers who attend the meeting, it is about old fountain pens and, for one, the discovery of a new area of interest.

This is the difference between server-side and client-side perspectives. From the server side the categories that divide up a people space would appear to be rigid. From the client side, there is no rigidity at all – as the categories can unpredictably merge with each other. The topics are not seen as communication restraints, but as small points of common interest that unexpectedly link people together, providing a catalyst for what might turn out to be a useful association.

One of the readers of the BOT2001 paper – William Ethridge, an internet payment systems consultant from San Diego County in Southern California – had grasped this client-side perspective of the living database, writing:

Might you be familiar with the writings of Robert Fritz? His books include *The Path of Least Resistance* and *Creating*. I believe his core ideas are relevant to

> **"** ONCE YOU COME TO REALIZE HOW MUCH VITAL 'NEED TO KNOW' INFORMATION THERE IS AND TO APPRECIATE THAT YOU CANNOT HOPE TO LEARN IT ALL, IT BECOMES OBVIOUS THAT A SPECIAL STRATEGY IS NEEDED **"**

your work. (And how I wish I had more time to elaborate!) He makes a meticulous argument that the way to successfully achieve the desired end result is to 'follow the path of least resistance' and discusses how to create the structures that make it easier – in motivation and in action – to follow those paths.

Fritz outlines the psychological patterns, and how to develop them consciously, that tend to satisfy an initially inchoate desire. No cheesy motivational writer, Fritz is an acute observer of people who successfully achieve satisfaction in their lives.

Much of what he says, I believe, has application in gathering information that one is initially unaware exists. For example, a person seeking information about a specific type of disease (to pick up on an example you used) has a specific set of motivations – however inchoate or disorganized – to gather information about that disease.

S/he may discover that the most important or useful piece of information is about how to emotionally manage the disease and treatment process, even though that was not a conscious goal. In the process of learning from others – how best to manage the disease and its treatment process – the person learns about treatment methodologies, physical effects, etc. So, the information which the person originally saw as being the desired end result becomes simply a step towards more valuable information.

Of course, all sorts of variable results can be had, depending upon the person and the myriad specifics of the situation. The point is that the goal sought is often of lesser importance than the goal actually reached – however little this fact is initially recognized.

Thus, intrinsically, the process is open-ended. Any search that is non-trivial – speaks to the most vital human concerns – cannot have a predetermined aim. Fritz writes with great insight about the 'structure' (a word he often uses in a specific manner) of the process of creating, not attaining, our goals.

William Ethridge's comments illustrate the kind of paradigm shift needed in order to appreciate the value of a people space. It isn't about seeing a formatted space that is designed and categorized by others. It is simply a valuable construct that allows people to make contact and, if these contacts are of special interest, bring them into their own private communication space. This private information space will be individually different for every person who uses the people space.

A people space might be imagined as a city with a large number of places where different interest groups meet for specific reasons. Instead of going to these places to join in the discussions, you might simply go there to observe and find a few people you can invite back to your own home for a private party: a party where there are only people you like and can get along with – talking always about the things you are interested in. The magic of this concept is that this ideal situation can exist for everybody simultaneously: for everybody who is using the people space to make contact with others.

structure of a meeting place

At the end of the last chapter, the reader might have formed some kind of an idea as to what form a meeting place in a people space might take. It would probably be imagined as an area on a website where there are various options allowing the visitors to join an e-mail discussion forum, a news group or a chat room. Certainly a meeting place can be structured in this way, but this would be a conventional server-side view where all these facilities were laid on. This is illustrated in Figure 11.2 which shows the meeting place as it was depicted in the last chapter.

However, this idea of a meeting place doesn't accord with the notion of every individual having their own private meeting place within their own computer, where they have complete control of the topics of discussion. This is where another sharp paradigm shift is needed.

Return now to the vision of meeting places in a large city where you go just to observe and find people you like the look of. You then invite these selected people back to your place for a party. At this party, you find out what their interests are and what interesting places they frequent. If the places they go to sound interesting you might arrange to meet them at these places. You might get their telephone number in order to have private conversations with them. You might invite them to a small dinner party

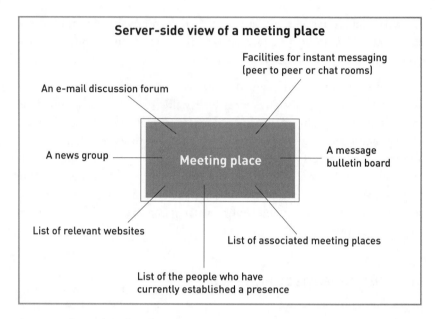

FIG 11.2 A meeting place in a people space as it might be viewed with a server-side perspective

you arrange for a selected few, like-minded people. This is the way social contacts are created and cultivated in the social world of bricks and mortar.

This scenario can easily be emulated in the virtual world of the internet. If the meeting places in the people space are treated as contact areas where people with a particular common interest establish a presence, everyone has an opportunity to invite any of the people who are there back to their place to maybe develop further contact and associations.

In this way, it isn't essential for the server side to arrange discussion forums, news groups or chat rooms. People could just tell each other of the e-mail forums, news groups or chat rooms they frequent. In other words, the people themselves could provide links to existing facilities for communication that are already in existence outside of the people space – established anywhere in the vast landscape of the internet environment.

The people can swap e-mail addresses for one-to-one correspondence. They can arrange to be on each other's lists for peer-to-peer instant messaging. They can form small groups for discussions in the way tables in a virtual café are designed to operate. Seen in this way, the people at the meeting places are capable of combining to create their own communication environments, which would be far richer and more extensive than any that could be organized on the server side.

It takes quite a radical paradigm shift to see what is happening here, as the idea of a publicly shared meeting place is transformed into a variety of individual meeting places in the virtual cafés in people's own computers.

Consider: every person at a meeting place is likely to have their own personal communication environment. When people are invited into a private café environment outside of the people space, their individual communication environments would have to move with them because it is part of them. Thus by bringing several contacts into a personal virtual café, you are effectively creating a rich communication environment which includes all of the personal communication environments of all the people invited.

This is illustrated in Figure 11.3, where the contacts brought into a personal client-side café can provide the client with a far richer environment of possible meeting places and facilities to communicate than would be available at the meeting places provided by the organizers of the people space.

Having a conventional, bricks and mortar world perspective makes it very difficult to appreciate the full significance of this arrangement. The medium of the internet allows a phenomenon to take place that would be impossible in the real world: people can have multiple presences such that they can be at a meeting place in their own computer and at the same time be at meeting places in the computers of lots of other people. The magic of the net allows people to be at many places at the same time.

Not only this, everyone can create their own individual communication environment according to who they invite into their personal café of contacts. This is because a contact represents not only themselves but all the people they know, the news groups they belong to and the discussion forums they take part in.

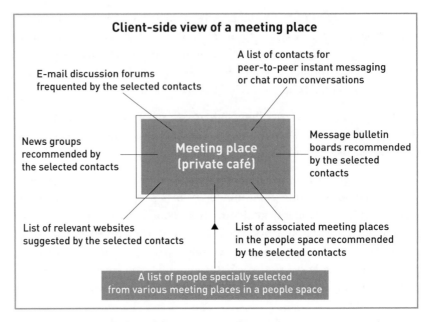

FIG 11.3 A client-side meeting place that is filled with contacts obtained from various meeting places in a people space. The client now has a far richer environment and choice of communication facilities available

This ties up with the ideas that were introduced at the beginning of the book – in Chapters 1 and 2 – where, by having a suitable group of people in a personal café of contacts, an ordinary individual can become a 'super individual'. Not so much through direct communication with the contacts themselves, but by having indirect access to all of their communication environments.

meeting people online

The above scenario of creating client-side meeting places must involve some kind of interaction between the owner of a client-side café and the contacts that are brought in from a public meeting place. This presents a major problem because quite obviously, people can't just be yanked out of a people space and compelled to cooperate with the café owner's wishes; they would have to have a strong reason or motivation for wanting to communicate and cooperate with the café owner.

The key to any cooperation is the shared common interest. This can be both the ice-breaker and the glue that holds any mutually beneficial communications together. If communication is beneficial to both parties then communication can take place. If either party does not benefit, then cooperation will not be possible. This makes the success of finding suitable contacts in a people space a statistical exercise because only an unknown proportion of the other people at a meeting place will be suitably compatible with each other.

Let's say that a people space has been created for the purpose of bringing people together to help each other create websites. There are many possible categories that might include all manner of technical aspects of website solutions. Say one of these categories was designated for interest in payment solutions. This would attract people who provided solutions and those who needed them.

The people who needed them would be a little wary of dealing with any particular payment solution provider and might want to discuss with some of the others the relative values of the solutions on offer. By striking up private dialogues with each other the people who need the solutions can compare notes and experiences and help each other out in deciding who might be the best of the payment solution providers to get into conversation with. Such collaborative discussions would take place outside of the people space and in the private cafés of the people involved. The trick is to find somebody suitable to talk to and then persuade them to enter into personal dialogue.

However, as anyone who has engaged in this kind of internet activity knows, it isn't a simple matter to get to really know people in internet environments. It's something like going to a conference where you know there must be lots of interesting people who would be valuable to know but you don't actually get to talk to them. The only people you get to know about are the speakers and this is a one-way dialogue with no interaction.

There is a similar problem with large cocktail parties. There might be interesting people present but there never seems to be enough time to speak to everybody to find out who they are and what it is exactly they

> **THE KEY TO ANY COOPERATION IS THE SHARED COMMON INTEREST**

do. What you'd like to be able to do is to have a list of pertinent questions that you can quickly ask everyone present so you can decide who best to spend your time talking to. Unfortunately, society frowns upon this kind of behaviour.

From time to time, some of the e-mail discussion forums I belong to arrange real-life meetings, usually in a wine bar or a convenient English pub, where we get together for a drink and informal chat. Invariably, these meetings fragment into small groups who engage in specific discussion concerning particular topics. There are always very interesting people at these meetings, but it is extremely difficult to wander around to find out who everybody is, what skill sets they have and what type of projects they are involved in. The same society norms prevail, preventing people asking each other direct and personal questions and then moving on to ask the same questions of everyone else.

These meetings are not held on a regular basis. They occur when somebody declares it is time for another meeting, others agree and then somebody takes the initiative to name a time, date and place for the meeting to be held. On one occasion, in a forum of web design freelancers to which I belong, somebody called for a meeting to be held in London. Nobody came forward to organize the meeting so I called up a friend of mine who organizes meetings for another online forum, using the premises of a private club he belongs to in London, suggesting we might organize a joint meeting between the two groups.

As the people from one group wouldn't know anything at all about the people in the other group, I asked all those who would be going to the meeting to send me a short biography, which I then put on a website. This worked extremely well as people could then know beforehand who everybody was, their interests and work experiences. This allowed people to seek out those who might be of specific interest to them and led to several useful collaborative project-sharing arrangements.

It is not difficult to see how such a similar arrangement might be beneficial to people who meet at virtual meeting places in a people space. This might be a key element in bringing people together.

knowing who everyone else is

If we now consider a people space, where there might be hundreds of meeting places, the idea of everyone having a bio posted up on a website for everyone else to view isn't very practical. It would require organizing. Some people wouldn't be bothered to describe themselves. In any case, it would be a daunting task to read through everybody's bio every time you entered a meeting place, to find out what kind of people were there and who would be interesting to communicate with.

What would be convenient, though, would be to be able to send some kind of intelligent agent into a meeting place, to find out about everyone there and then report back to you with a list of who might be of particular interest.

Such a possibility might seem to be in the realms of science fiction, but it is perfectly feasible in the world of bots and personal electronic agents.

what is a bot or personal electronic agent?

Sitting in the Fairmont Hotel in San Francisco, the evening before the BOT2001 seminar, with Brian Proffitt – Managing Editor of BotSpot, the bi-weekly e-magazine on bots – and Dr Stephen Thaler, one of the other speakers whose speciality was neural nets and bot intelligence, the question arose as to what exactly was the definition of a bot. None of us could provide a definitive answer.

The speakers at the seminar were interpreting bots in a number of different ways. Some saw bots as web crawlers or spiders that travelled around websites picking up selected information. Others saw them as search engines that identified locations on the web where information, described by key words or phrases, could be found. There were those who thought of bots as online avatars, who had a pictorial representation as a real person or cartoon character on a website and could answer questions in an animated way: some responding in text, others speaking with voices, even some with animated emotional expressions.

There were several varieties of intelligent bots that could search through posts sent in to list servers and news groups, searching for rude words and phrases, or detecting the spread of rumours and spam messages. Dr Thaler was introducing learning capabilities into bots, to give them an ability to deal with vague instructions and fuzzy logic.

With all the huge variety of forms that bots could take, it was very hard to come up with a description that fitted all categories of bots and electronic agents. It then occurred to me that this problem of bot definition was the same frustrating difficulty I'd encountered when trying to explain what an object was in object-oriented programming. It's not that the concept is at all complex to understand, it's just that it requires a paradigm shift.

In the book *Lingo Sorcery – the magic of lists, objects and intelligent agents*, I'd explained the experience of understanding objects in an object-oriented world as being similar to that of learning to ride a bicycle. When you begin learning to ride a bike, it seems impossible to be able to cycle along on two wheels because, every time you start off, you fall to one side or the other. Then suddenly, for some unaccountable reason, you find yourself cycling along and not being able to understand how you had ever thought it was so very difficult.

The problem with cycling, objects and bots is that they are impossible to explain because of their simplicity rather than their difficulty. In cycling, it is momentum that keeps you upright, which cannot be appreciated until you are actually moving. With objects, the understanding comes not through looking at the complex ways in which objects can be used, but by realizing that they can be anything you want them to be. This can be as simple as giving a space in memory a name, putting a program that performs a function into that space and arranging for that function to be performed when a particular message is sent to the named space. Whatever name you give that space then becomes the object that can perform a function when you (or another object) tells it to.

For example, you can give a space in memory a name like 'greenFrog'. You can then put into that memory space a little program that will put a picture of a little green frog on the screen when a message is sent to that memory space: 'greenFrog showYourself'. You could do things like putting a program in that 'greenFrog' memory space that will turn off the computer when you send it the message: 'greenFrog turnComputerOff'.

By adding all kinds of little functional programs into this 'greenFrog' memory space you can make this 'green Frog' perform all kinds of useful functions on your computer. Then, when a neighbour pops into your house and sees you working at your computer and tells you they wish they could learn how to use a computer, you can tell them that you don't know yourself, but you've got a little green frog in there that does everything for you.

This is the conceptual breakthrough that has to be made with objects and bots. They are an illusion that is used to obscure underlying complexity. Once you fill your computer memory space with green frogs, pink elephants, alien life forms or any other object you care to imagine, you can think about what they do rather than how they do it.

Bots and personal agents are like the objects that can be created in the memory space of a computer. They are simple images that can be used to get away from the underlying complexity to be able to think about the functions they perform.

In my talk at BOT2001, I tried to convey this concept by telling a joke that was going around in the 1970s when computing was largely confined to mainframes:

A man is at an airport waiting for his flight to be called when he notices a woman opposite him fiddling around with her wristwatch. The wristwatch looks unusual and instead of a clock face it has a little screen.

Curiosity gets the better of him and he goes over to the woman and asks her about this strange-looking watch she is fiddling with. She then explains it is not a watch but a computer. She asks him to give her a difficult mathematical calculation to solve. The man does this and after a few taps on her wristwatch she shows him the screen and it gives the right answer.

The man is astounded (it is at a time before microchips). 'What else can it do?', he asks. She then tells him to ask her a few general knowledge questions. He does this and every time she taps around on her wristwatch and up comes the answer on the little screen.

> " BOTS AND PERSONAL AGENTS ARE SIMPLE IMAGES THAT CAN BE USED TO GET AWAY FROM THE UNDERLYING COMPLEXITY TO BE ABLE TO THINK ABOUT THE FUNCTIONS THEY PERFORM "

'I must have this wristwatch,' he tells the woman. 'I'm a very rich man and I'll give you any price you name.' She names a price and he writes her a cheque on the spot and puts the wristwatch on his wrist.

At that moment, the man's flight is called. 'Sorry,' he says to the woman. 'I have to go now,' and starts towards the boarding gates. She calls out to him, 'you've forgotten to take these' and points to two large suitcases on the floor. 'They are not mine,' he calls back. 'Yes they are,' she tells him. 'You've just bought them. You need to connect the wristwatch to the electronic equipment in these cases to be able to get the computer to perform its functions.'

Nobody laughed at my joke. I then explained that this wristwatch was an analogy for a bot. It was the visible interface to a complex programming environment – from which it is not possible to be separated. For bots, the equivalent of the two heavy suitcases is always some kind of database or information source, together with sophisticated algorithms to search, sort and process data.

As was discussed in the last chapter, databases are very inefficient and expensive to maintain when dealing with volatile information. This is the wristwatch equivalent of having suitcases that are too heavy to carry. Thus when thinking about bots, you have to look beyond the neat little image they convey and think about what has to go into the suitcases that allows them to function properly.

Think now of a little green frog on your wrist that is connected up to a set of algorithms, a large database and the web. In theory you could ask the little green frog on your wrist to find all kinds of information for you on the web, but in most areas of technical knowledge, where the knowledge base is continuously evolving and expanding, the little green frog will give you unsatisfactory information no matter how big the suitcases to which it is connected.

It is this limitation of bots only being able to deal with information that has some kind of order and permanence that greatly limits what can be done with them. Sure, you can use artificial intelligence techniques, rule-based systems, fuzzy logic, neural nets and genetic algorithms, but nobody has yet succeeded in giving bots or electronic agents any real intelligence:

at least, not of the kind that can deal with conflicting data, uncertainty or ambiguity.

This gives rise to a paradox – because you can let bots or intelligent agents be anything you want them to be, you can use bots to help solve problems that bots are not very good at solving. To resolve this paradox, we need another paradigm shift that would see a database record as a personal agent that can represent a person on the web.

the missing link

As discussed above, all bots and personal agents are illusions. They don't wander around the web searching for targeted information or executing intelligent decisions. Mostly, they are simply a contrived means of inputting a request into a search engine or relational database. Even the animated agents that appear as personal assistants or customer service avatars are simply novel interfaces to database files.

Unfortunately, most of the information on the internet is disorganized, not categorized and extremely volatile in nature. It is soon outdated and there are far too many changes happening and too much information to keep track of. Even the most sophisticated of search engines or databases are not efficient when it comes to dealing with this kind of volatility. As bots and electronic agents are totally reliant upon search engines or database-type algorithms, this same limitation must apply to them also – because it isn't possible to incorporate into their design enough intelligence to handle uncertainty, ambiguity and excessive volatility. Only humans can do this.

Databases and bots can provide pockets of order, but are inherently incapable of dealing with the chaotic confusion of vast quantities of changing information. What is needed is a totally new paradigm – a different way of looking at databases, search engines, bots and personal electronic agents – a way in which these problems might be overcome.

It's time now to step back and take an overview of the internet. It's a vast conglomeration of information and knowledge of gargantuan proportions; quite beyond the capability of the human mind to comprehend in its entirety. Alone, the task of dealing with all the knowledge available is too daunting even to contemplate, but by people taking different areas of knowledge and collaborating, the task of making use of an unimaginably large knowledge base can become a practical reality.

The proposal here is that we forget about using databases for dealing with information and instead use them to create an environment for people to meet each other to exchange information. We also give up on the idea of bots and personal electronic agents as having any inherent intelligence and view them simply as message carriers – with humans providing any intelligence that might be needed. In this way, we can contemplate a living database – where all the information is held in the heads of people – where the human brain can be used strategically, to do all the clever sorting stuff.

" INSTEAD OF DEVELOPING PROGRAMS AND SYSTEMS THAT DO OUR THINKING FOR US, WE THINK IN TERMS OF PROGRAMS AND SYSTEMS THAT ARE PERSONAL TO INDIVIDUALS "

What this paradigm shift implies is that instead of developing programs and systems that do our thinking for us, we think in terms of programs and systems that are personal to individuals: systems that act as if they were extensions to the human brain. In this way, we shouldn't be thinking about creating universal founts of knowledge but of people, with extended powers to communicate and assist each other to take individual advantage of the knowledge that is available.

From this viewpoint, it doesn't make sense to have bots or intelligent agents go out into the internet environment to mine knowledge or select appropriate information for us to use. They aren't up to the job. It would make more sense to have bots or personal agents go out into the internet to find people with whom an individual might be able to have useful collaborative communication.

As we have seen, there are two basic structures that can help us to do this: on the server side, a formatted space that can provide areas of contact; on the client side, the personal café which can be used to filter out the most appropriate contacts and provide an organized way of communicating with them. What we are looking for now is the link between the two.

THE CREATION OF
AN E-BUSINESS

THIS FINAL PART OF THE BOOK DESCRIBES the structuring of the e-business I finally decided upon. In keeping with the philosophy of the whole trilogy it has no specific plan, there is no managerial structure and it requires very little start-up capital. It is also designed to have a minimum of overheads and running costs.

Above all, the business was designed to be able to grow organically, from the bottom up. It consists of modular components and loosely associated collaborators to provide the maximum of flexibility and adaptability.

The choice of business was determined by a rule that came out of an analysis of the many dot-com failures: 'If it is already being done in the non-internet world, then it is liable to fail.' This meant looking for a business that not only isn't being done in the world of bricks and mortar, but is not possible there. In other words, a business was selected that makes use of the unique characteristics of the internet environment.

Despite all the many attempts to use the internet to supply goods and information, in the vast majority of cases they have been failures. The businesses that have been most successful have been those based on enabling more efficient person-to-person communication. It was this aspect of the internet that was used as the core idea.

Another important criterion was that the business should not be reliant on any particular business venture: it must be able to be applied over a range of different kinds of opportunity. Not only must it be applicable to a wide range of possibilities, it should be able to cover many different business situations simultaneously. In this way, risks and discontinuities can be accommodated.

Chapter 12 describes the essence of the software components that will be needed and how they fit together to empower people to make optimal use of the internet.

Chapter 13 describes the esoteric concept of 'stigmergy'. Borrowed from the insect world, this concept forms the basic philosophy of the business. It is the subtle strategy used by ants to coordinate their activities with the utmost efficiency. It is ideally suited to the environment of the internet and can produce self-organizing information structures that require little supervision or control.

Chapter 14 is the conclusion of the book. It provides a game theory strategy: a set of heuristic rules consisting of essential criteria that need to be applied when choosing a business opportunity. These criteria are used to select an actual business opportunity to pursue. It is a real-life example, demonstrating a low-cost business solution to a problem that is too costly to be solved using conventional methods and techniques.

12

ENHANCING THE HUMAN BRAIN

an example emerges Just after I'd sent out the last chapter to the people in the virtual café, I had a real-life meeting with one of the readers, Dan Winchester. Dan lives just a few miles from me and we often meet for a beer and a chat in a local pub. Dan's speciality is databases and the design of back-end systems that provide websites with their organization.

Dan was somewhat bemused by the strategy I was suggesting. He didn't see the need for bots or personal agents as he felt everything that needed to be done could be handled from the server side. He considered it would be far less complicated if clients simply complete a form on a web page and leave everything else up to the website – which could use a suitable suite of programs, coupled to a database, to provide all the functions the clients would need.

When I explained how it might be preferable to put the programming on the client side if the client's help were needed in obtaining the solution they wanted, he immediately raised the objection that this was different from the way everyone else was using the web. He was of the opinion that because the approach would involve having to teach clients to do something new, there would be a resistance to its use. As he explained, 'People don't want to learn anything new. They like intuitive applications that are simple to use and to understand. They want everything done for them.'

Although this is a valid argument, it applies only where it is possible for computer programs and algorithms to perform satisfactorily the tasks that are needed by a client. For many client needs, particularly those involving highly volatile data, it just isn't economically possible to create a server-side solution because too much human input is required. This makes it imperative that the solution is handled on the client side, where a human is available to handle the parts of a solution that are not amenable to any algorithmic approach.

Dan Winchester wasn't convinced. He couldn't imagine a situation where clients would need to be an integral part of a solution – and, at the time, I had no specific example to give him. However, the very next week, an ideal example arose: when I was invited along to a special meeting in the UK Houses of Parliament.

Here was an instance of developments that seemingly arise out of the blue when pursuing an opportunity. Prior to starting work on this book, I'd never had any contact with the medical business. Yet, after the question about a cancer database coming up in the virtual café, I'd found myself discussing with several people in the oncology division of a major drug company the possibility of applying the people space concept to help cancer patients find cancer treatment trials. These contacts saw a great value in this approach, not only from the point of view of the patients but also from that of the drug companies, which were having to spend quite considerable sums of money trying to find suitable patients for their treatment trials. These communications with the drug company resulted in an invitation to the meeting in the UK Houses of Parliament.

The meeting was called for 5 pm, Tuesday 27 February 2001, in committee room 21 in the House of Commons. It was entitled 'Developments in Information Technology and Cancer Care' and the subject matter to be discussed was 'How developments in information technology will affect the quality of care received by cancer patients'. In the chair was a Member of Parliament: Dr Ian Gibson MP.

These kinds of meetings are regularly used as one of the means by which the British government obtains information about the various areas of speciality that the government has to deal with. At this particular time, there had been much press comment on reports that the standard of care and treatment for cancer in Britain had fallen below that of some of the other countries in the European Union and the government had declared their intention to catch up within five years.

There were three main speakers who had been invited to the meeting to describe the approaches they were taking in using information technology to help improve the quality of cancer patient care.

One of these speakers described how his department was in the process of creating a registry of all cancer patients in the UK. They had recorded the details of some 8 million patients already and were attempting to add to this registry the 250,000 new cases that occurred every year. The speaker produced some graphs to illustrate how they'd used their database to deduce that patients who were treated by more experienced physicians did rather better than patients who were treated by less experienced physicians. Not exactly a startling revelation to come out of such a gargantuan amount of data.

Another speaker, who was a project manager for the National Health Service Information Authority, described how they were setting up a database to record the treatment of every cancer patient in the country. An outline was given of the many practical difficulties that were involved in getting this information into a database.

The most ambitious scheme was proposed by the third speaker, who was attempting to set up a website to advise cancer patients of the various treatment options that were available. It was explained that many patients wanted to be informed enough to play a part in the decision making concerning their own treatment and needed a reliable source of up-to-date information.

The literature handed out by this speaker to the attendees of the meeting explained that there were 20,000 medical journals in various languages that between them publish 2 million papers every year. These papers were said to contain details of many clinical trials but some were too small to give clear answers and most reviews of the evidence presented in the papers tended to be highly biased. Additionally, it was pointed out that a search for 'cancer' on the internet search engine GOOGLE.COM produced 5,960,000 references. The speaker told the meeting that this amount of information would be confusing and too ambiguous for most patients to be able to make any use of it.

The speaker explained that there were multiple decision points in a patient's journey. Questions needed to be driven by patients as well as their carers. There would be a requirement for various levels of information to allow shared decision making between patients and their physicians. This would create a need for unbiased, systematic reviews of all cancer treatments, which would have to be continuously kept up to date. The suggestion was for there to be 'kite marks' given to papers, to provide indications of their authenticity.

All through these presentations there were murmurs of support and approval for this work, with many of the attendees making copious notes. Nobody seemed to be aware of the practical limitations of these proposals. It seemed to be assumed that the mysterious power of the computer could overcome the horrendous problems associated with dealing in enormous numbers of people and vast quantities of volatile data.

> **IT SEEMED TO BE ASSUMED THAT THE MYSTERIOUS POWER OF THE COMPUTER COULD OVERCOME THE HORRENDOUS PROBLEMS ASSOCIATED WITH DEALING IN ENORMOUS NUMBERS OF PEOPLE AND VAST QUANTITIES OF VOLATILE DATA**

After the presentations there was a question and answer session, where I was able to ask the speakers about the practical realities. I asked about the costs of collecting and categorizing all this information. It may be cheap to manipulate once it is in a database, but didn't every single piece of information have to originate from a human entry? I asked if the proposers of these schemes were taking into account that the nature of most patients' condition was continuously changing as their disease progressed or went into remission as they were put onto different treatment schedules. Could this highly volatile information be kept up to date on millions of different patient files?

I asked about the practicality of any organization being able to judge the contents of 20,000 journals, differentiating between the merits of 2 million articles every year, removing bias and selecting those to kite mark. There was a stunned silence as the reality of the situation dawned upon everyone at the meeting. They weren't dealing with a finite amount of stable data. All this data was highly volatile and even if it could be put into a database it was likely to be out of date by the time it came to be used. This would seriously compromise the value of any conclusions that could be drawn from any analysis.

I pointed out that what they were proposing as new British initiatives in the fight against cancer appeared to be new initiatives only because there was little evidence that any of these proposals were already in existence. However, it was extremely unlikely that nobody had thought of these ideas before. And, if they had been proposed, surely the funding would have been available if the proposals had been viable? Certainly these ideas would have been an attractive proposition for venture capitalists if they were practical possibilities. The fact that these proposals weren't already in existence would seem to indicate that the cost and the practical problems involved had ruled them out as realistic approaches to improving the quality of patient care.

The inescapable conclusion must be that an organized, server-side approach cannot provide a solution. The only possible way for this information to be organized and made useful would be if it were possible to engage the coordinated help of millions of people, sharing the work such that each could look after just one small section of the database to keep it up to date and make sure that it interacts appropriately with all the other information in the database.

Here was a real-world example to explain to Dan Winchester the need for a client-side solution. If every patient handled their own data and if each could individually control the database to get results specific to them, then it would be possible to deal with this vast amount of volatile inform-ation and use it to make a difference to patient care and treatment.

The trick would be to get such a system into operation. Clearly, trying to organize such huge numbers of people would be an administrative nightmare. The only possibility of success is to create a self-organizing system of self-motivated people, where people take part because it is in their best interests to do so.

Client-side control versus server-side control

To appreciate what is involved in handing over the running and control of a database to clients, it might help to have a few diagrams. Figure 12.1 illustrates a conventional website where data is collected, categorized, stored, sorted and processed on the server side. Clients receive the processed information upon making requests to the website.

In situations where there are vast amounts of volatile data, the Achilles heel of this kind of system is the cost and practicality of collecting the data and keeping it up to date. This weakness can be overcome if the responsibility for entering and updating the data can be transferred to the client side.

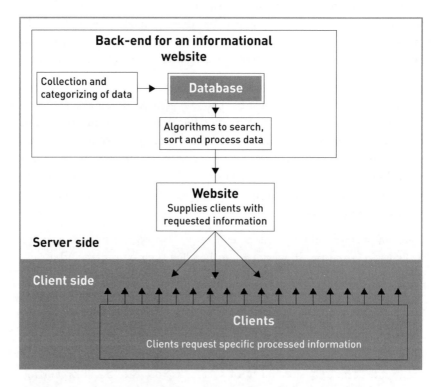

FIG 12.1 A conventional website providing clients with sorted and processed information from the server side

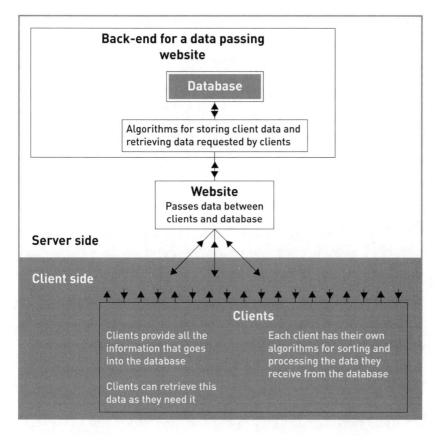

FIG 12.2 A website that stores client information for them to retrieve and process for themselves

Such an arrangement is shown in Figure 12.2, where the database on the server side does very little other than hold data provided by clients and allows them to retrieve this data without any added processing.

If each client is responsible for their own data and their own processing, all the work necessary to create and maintain a database of volatile data will be shared amongst many. More importantly, each client's specific needs can be catered for individually because each client will be able to take part in the processing of their own information: able to control and customize their own results.

The paradigm shift is to see how the total system has acquired real intelligence. It is no longer a robotic system that relies entirely on non-intelligent algorithms. Humans are now included in the system, to take care of any parts of the data processing that computers and algorithms are not able to handle satisfactorily.

The pertinent question then seems to be, 'How can we train clients to use databases and to process their own informational requirements?' The answer is surprisingly simple: we make it as easy as filling in a form on the page of a website. To illustrate, let's go through an example.

bot parties

In *Magical A-Life Avatars*, I described a scenario where it would be possible to clone your personality and character onto a bot and send it out across the web to look for other bot clones and bring them back to your own computer for a party. At these virtual parties, your own bot clone could socialize with these other bot clones to find those whose owners would be the kind of people you would like to be friends with or who might make useful contacts.

Although this might sound highly implausible, it was based on an actual business experiment I'd tried out a few years previously. As this will apply directly to the linking of a client-side application and a server-side formatted space, it may be worthwhile running through the background and some of the details of this idea.

how it started

In the mid-1960s, I was watching a science programme on television where they were describing imaginative new uses for the latest wonder of modern science, the electronic computer. The application being described was an experiment in computer dating that was being carried out at Harvard University (this was at a time when the only computers in existence were at government research establishments, universities and a few very large companies).

As I'd been involved in computer research (at a government research and development establishment as part of my student training), I could easily understand how such a system could be programmed and immediately recognized the commercial possibilities. In those days, computers were designed with thermionic tubes and low-level programs were fed in via punched cards. It was all very primitive but quite capable of reading in the results of questionnaires, then comparing and matching the answers.

I decided that this might make an interesting entrepreneurial business venture and set to work to design an appropriate questionnaire and a suitable computer program. The questionnaire was quite lengthy and asked many questions, but in practice the basis of matching the people was limited to very basic considerations such as sex, age, height, interests and educational background. Although it was not a great commercial success for me as a pioneer, others took up the idea later and turned it into highly profitable businesses.

In fact, somebody who started a computer dating agency by copying my questionnaire went on to turn the business into an international company with a turnover of several million dollars a year. I was always a little peeved that I'd missed out on this great opportunity, but the idea of matching people by means of a series of punched holes in cards continued to fascinate me.

the biological connection

Several years later, I became interested in evolutionary biology. I was amazed to find that the complete design of the human body, including the human brain, was described by a biological form of punched card – the human genome. The human genome may look very different, but in essence it contains nothing other than binary information – equivalent to the holes and spaces on a punched card, albeit a punched card that contains three billion holes.

Three billion holes isn't that big a deal in the current world of computer technology. It's only 750 megabytes: not much more than the information-carrying capacity of a CD-ROM (650 megabytes) and easily contained on the gigabyte hard disks of even the cheapest of today's home computer systems.

The thought then struck me that somewhere on the human genome there had to be a series of binary digits that described a neural arrangement in the brain that would help a human to choose a partner to mate with. Assuming there are no metaphysical phenomena involved, the design specification of this neural mechanism must be totally describable using no more than a punched card (or bits in computer memory).

The thought intrigued me. I then set out to try to find the connection between a series of binaries and the complex set of emotions that cause people to be attracted to one another.

Kurt Gödel and John Holland

The first clue came from the work of Kurt Gödel, a Czech mathematician who in 1930 described how statements and rules could be represented by numbers. Together with the rules of logic, Gödel showed how it was possible to represent any complex, rule-based processing system solely by numbers. It was this work that had inspired Alan Turing to build the Turing machine: the basic mechanism underlying the design of all modern-day computers.

Gödel's work also described how tangible as well as intangible entities could be represented as numbers, allowing any kind of system to be modelled in binary form as a computer program. The inference to me was that this could also include neural mechanisms and the esoteric and intangible phenomena we describe as emotions.

The second clue came from the work of John Holland, a computer scientist, who in the 1980s discovered the mathematical mechanism that causes biological organisms to evolve. He called his mathematical device a *genetic algorithm*. The essence of this deceptively simple mathematical mechanism is that it provides a fast way of optimizing any system comprised of a large number of dependent variables: a task impossibly difficult for conventional mathematics.

The principle of genetic algorithms is that you start off by making wild guesses at what the variables of a system should be and then breed different versions of the system to see which work best. At regular intervals (generations) the systems that work best are selected to 'breed', whereby new systems are created using various mixes of the most promising variable values.

It is similar to the way biological organisms evolve – survival of the fittest – where the fittest get to pass their genes onto the next generation. In the case of John Holland's genetic algorithms it is numbers that survive to reproduce, but thanks to Gödel's theories, these numbers can represent any kind of entity, both tangible and intangible, from physical assemblies to rules and statements.

There is no question that this technique is effective because variations of genetic algorithms are now used extensively in the design of all manner of complex systems.

representing emotions on a computer

Gödel's work suggests that you can represent emotions by numbers. Holland's work suggests that you can evolve these numbers to respond appropriately to any given situation. It was with these thoughts in mind that I set out to design a bot that would have a mechanism to emulate the human brain's ability to emotionally choose a suitable partner.

The idea is very simple. You represent an emotion by a variable. Whatever number is put into this variable represents the strength of that emotion felt by the system. If the number is positive the emotion is positive. If the number is negative the emotion is negative. To obtain a range of different emotions you simply have a number of different variables. Figure 12.3 shows a bot with ten different emotions, each of which can be focused on a particular characteristic or feature of a target.

As an example, let's consider a bot that is looking at the profiles of many different people. One of its emotions might be specifically allocated to provide a response to people's heights. An emotional profile would arrange for a suitable value to be placed into the 'height response' emotion according to what height is 'seen'. Perhaps this might be strongly positive to one particular height, but variously less strongly to others and in some cases even negative (see Figure 12.4).

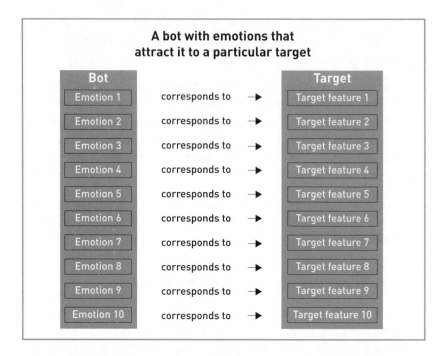

FIG 12.3 If we provide a bot with ten variables, we are effectively giving the bot the ability to express ten emotions. These can each be tuned to correspond to a particular quality or characteristic that the bot is looking out for. In other words, a bot can be trained to have emotions relating to ten features of a target

Another emotion might be set to respond to age. Similarly, it can be set to respond strongly positive to one particular age range, variously less positively to others and some variously negative. Combining the two 'emotional' variables, the bot will respond in a characteristic way to all combinations of ages and heights. If the bot encounters an age and height that together correspond to a maximum positive emotional value, the total emotional response would be at a maximum: telling the bot that it had found someone with an optimum combination of age and height.

By setting other 'emotions' to respond to other significant features or characteristics, the bot's aggregate emotional response can be obtained as a summation of all of the emotions. This can be explained by means of an example.

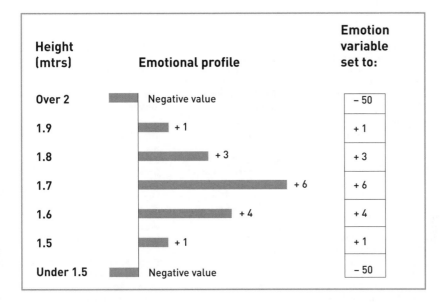

Height (mtrs)	Emotional profile	Emotion variable set to:
Over 2	Negative value	– 50
1.9	+ 1	+ 1
1.8	+ 3	+ 3
1.7	+ 6	+ 6
1.6	+ 4	+ 4
1.5	+ 1	+ 1
Under 1.5	Negative value	– 50

FIG 12.4 A bot can be set up with a profile to respond to height. When it 'sees' a height, this emotional profile will place an appropriate value in the emotion variable corresponding to its 'reaction' to height. In this example, the bot's profile is set to 'like' people of height 1.7 metres in preference to people of other heights

creating a clone

In 1993, I decided to test out these ideas in real life. I advertised in my local newspaper for single people looking for partners to try out a computer experiment where they could use a personal digital agent in a computer program designed to bring compatible people together. The experiment involved each participant creating a digital clone of themselves to mix with other clones to search for optimum partners.

To create the clones, a questionnaire was devised to allow people to provide various details about themselves. Besides the obvious physical and tangible characteristics, the questionnaire also carried many questions that might provide clues as to their attitudes and personalities. This questionnaire is shown in Figure 12.5.

The applicants were asked to tick the characteristics on this questionnaire they thought applied to them. From these responses, an array

Male	Impetuous	Career orientated
Female	Territorial	Enjoys cooking
Average intelligence	Decisive	Enjoys family life
Above average intelligence	Carefree	Likes animals
Highly intelligent	Open-minded	Likes children
Basic education	Lives for the future	Considerate
Advanced education	Lives for the moment	Doesn't mind being alone
Graduate	Extrovert	Easy to live with
Trendy	Reads a lot	Outgoing
Fashion conscious	Appreciates antiques	Thoughtful
Casual	Philosophical	Sensitive
Cultured	Academic	Sense of humour
Sophisticated	Likes current affairs	Critical
Enjoys dressing up	Enjoys cultural arts	Talker
Enjoys formal occasions	Likes scientific subjects	Listener
Conventional	Likes foreign travel	Serious
Enjoys participation sports	Enthusiastic	Gregarious
Enjoys outdoor life	Laid back	Enjoys conversation
Enjoys staying at home	Efficient	Enjoys gossip
Enjoys eating out	Leader/Follower	Enjoys talking about business
Enjoys theatre	Fastidious	Enjoys entertaining
Enjoys intellectual games	Competitive	Enjoys dancing
Enjoys dinner parties	Creative	Enjoys pop music
Enjoys watching television	Practical	Enjoys classical music
Gambler	Cooperative	Enjoys taking risks
Smoker	Punctual	Spendthrift/Saver
Enjoys drinking	Planner	Highly principled
Vegetarian	Has common sense	Always in debt
Believes in star signs	Intellectual	Hates figures
Religious	Artistic	Reserved
House proud	Progressive	Hates dealing with authority
Self-employed	Values security	Optimist

FIG 12.5 An example of the personality and attitude questions on the questionnaire. The responses to these questions are then turned into a binary string

record could be created to correspond to the way people had answered the questionnaire. This record is shown in Figure 12.6.

Figure 12.6 is the computer record of a person called Jane Morrison. It codes for her age (born 11 November 1962) and height (5 feet 8 inches) together with her answers to the questionnaire which are recorded in binary form. It is effectively an electronic clone of this person, representing many of her physical characteristics, attitudes, tastes and preferences.

```
F1504
Jane Morrison
11,11,62
5,8
0,1,0,1,0,0,1,0,0,1,0,1,0,
1,1,1,0,1,1,1,1,0,1,0,0,1,
1,0,1,0,1,0,1,1,1,1,1,1,1,
1,1,1,1,1,1,1,0,1,1,0,1,1,
0,0,1,1,1,1,1,1,1,1,1,1,1,
1,1,1,1,1,1,1,1,1,1,1,0,1,
1,1,1,1,0,1,1,1,1,1,1,1,0,
0,0,0,1,1
```

Trendy	54
Sophisticated	55
Homely	54
Sporty	67
Academic	53
Reprobate	43
Confident	60
Strategist	60
Tactician	68
Niceness	75
Neg factors	44
Mother's rating	30

FIG 12.6 An example of the record that is created from a questionnaire. Besides carrying information coded for physical and tangible characteristics, it carries a series of binaries to indicate how a person had responded to the personality and attitude questions

FIG 12.7 A generalized clone personality, arrived at by grouping the answers from the questionnaire into various categories

creating a personality

It is unlikely that single questions would be reliable guides to a person's overall personality and character, but the average of a number of questions might be more significant. The questions were arranged into groupings according to very broad categories. It was then very easy for a computer program to count the positive or negative responses to the questions in a particular category and give that category a score or rating. Such a record for a particular person is shown in Figure 12.7, where the marks in each category are expressed as a percentile.

Once you have a clone defined in this form, it is easy to make rules relating to the categories and give weightings to those rules. This is shown in Figure 12.8.

Once you have a system that can describe people by means of categories, you can set up rules of attraction (or repulsion) based on these categories and use weightings to specify the strengths of the rules (using negative

Rule	Weight
Trendy people like trendy people	3
Sophisticated people like sophisticated people	1
Homely people like homely people	−1
Sporty people like sporty people	2
Academic people like academic people	3
Reprobates like reprobates	−2
Confident people like confident people	−3
Strategists like strategists	−2
Tacticians like tacticians	1

FIG 12.8 By grouping questions into categories, you can devise rules to relate those categories to attractions between different people. The relative importance of each category matching rule can be specified by giving each rule a weighting

weights to reverse the rules where necessary). This can easily be translated into the form of variables that represent emotional responses to the characteristic profiles of different people. In other words, bot clones can be designed to 'feel attractions' to other bot clones, analogous to the way humans are attracted to each other, i.e. a complex set of emotions that when summed together give an overall impression of liking or not liking a person.

human and computer combinations

Common sense tells us that such an automated system of computer matchmaking would have a limited amount of success. There would be many other factors that would need to be taken into account besides those included in the questionnaire. Even if it were possible to incorporate an extensive questionnaire with thousands of questions, the system would still be reliant on the rules and the weightings – which have no logical basis and certainly wouldn't be universally applicable.

The situation could be greatly improved if humans were introduced into this system of matchmaking to assist in processing their own results. For example, if clients were able to choose their own rules and provide their own weightings, they could arrange for the system to select potential partners who were more specifically matched to their unique, individual requirements. Using the principle of Holland's genetic algorithms, they could then try out different combinations of rules and weightings to see which delivered the best results. This would undoubtedly give better accuracy than a universal set of rules and weightings that applied to all.

For a conventional website, the problem with this arrangement would be in dealing with the complexity of having thousands of clients effectively running their own programs on the same computer system. This would require sophisticated website programming and hardware, and would be a nightmare to organize and control.

The alternative would be to give everyone their own copy of the database, and provide them with the necessary software to run the selection process on their own computers. In this way, everyone would be free to create any rules they liked and to play around with the weightings to see which combinations gave them the best results in their search for a suitable partner.

On first thoughts, this might seem totally unrealistic. If there were very many people involved, transferring a copy of the complete database to every single person over the internet would be impossible. However, it could be practical if some form of preselection were made on the server side: reducing everyone's choice to a chosen sub-section of the full database that included only the candidates most likely to be of interest to them. By reducing the number of choices each person would have to consider, the size and sophistication of the client-side database could be drastically reduced (Figure 12.9).

Perhaps the reader might see the connection here between these sub-sections of a database and the meeting places in the people space described in the previous chapter. The meeting places are effectively sub-sections of the total database that group together people who are most likely to be of interest to each other. This saves the client having to consider every single person in the database.

Having only a few people to deal with at a time, the data processing facilities needed on the client side can be relatively uncomplicated. Such a

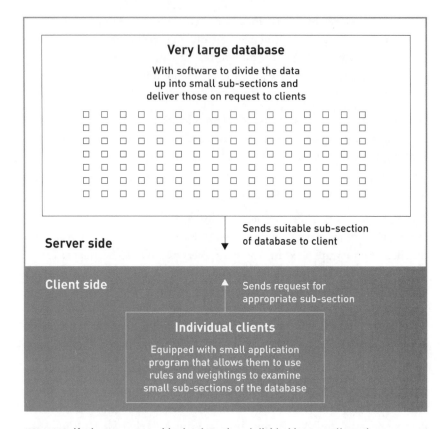

FIG 12.9 If a large server-side database is subdivided into small sections, appropriate sections can be sent to clients for them to carry out their own custom processing

database could then be incorporated into a small client-side application – something like the virtual café – that will help the client make final selections.

the problem of the final choice

The idea of dividing a database up into small sections of people who might be of interest to each other might be more clearly understood with another example. For this, let's return to the real-world, matchmaking experiment I tried out in my home town.

In that experiment, it wasn't possible to provide client-side data processing and selection software because very few of the people owned computers. There was also the problem that in human matchmaking there is no program that can be devised to replace the natural way humans can judge each other through face-to-face interactions in real life.

As a solution to this problem, a space was created in the memory of my own computer to simulate the local town. Into this space were placed representations of all the town's pubs, bars and other social meeting places. I then randomly distributed all the clones (records of questionnaires) into these virtual meeting places.

A program was then devised to arrange for each clone to 'look' at the records of all the other clones in the meeting place it had been assigned to and compare them with its own. Through a system of rules and weightings, the clones could assign a compatibility value to each of the other clones they were grouped with – calculated in much the same way as described for emotional responses (see Figures 12.3 to 12.8).

By adding together all the compatibility values and dividing by the number of people at the meeting place, each clone would be able to calculate a value to indicate how generally compatible it was with the average of the whole group. Those clones whose compatibilities were furthest away from the average were judged as 'feeling out of place' at the meeting place and were moved on to a different meeting place where they might find clones that were more compatible.

By repeating this process with all the clones in every meeting place, moving the misfits around and repeating the whole sequence many times over, the population of clones in the simulation gradually sorted themselves out into compatible groupings: each clone moving around the meeting places until it found itself in a 'comfortable' environment.

This is very similar to real life. People sample various social venues and choose to frequent those where they feel most attuned to the people present. This results in social meeting places becoming 'cliquey': catering for people of a similar type.

The idea was that at the end of this computer processing, the owners of all the clones would be told which of the meeting places their clone had ended up in. The owners could then be given a specific date to visit the real-life meeting place to meet the owners of all the other clones that had favoured that particular venue. In this way, the clones were making a rough selection based on rules and weightings, but the final choice was left to the humans.

This real-life example illustrates the principle of a people space that is divided up into compatible groupings. Computer programs cannot make a final choice, but they can do the donkey work, helping to create short lists of the most promising prospects from a large number of possible choices. This makes it possible for a human to concentrate on only a relatively small number of people: a number low enough for the human brain to be capable of dealing with efficiently.

It was with this experiment in mind that I started to write *Magical A-Life Avatars*. It led to a completely new way of thinking about the internet.

a system of objects

In 1997, when I began working on *Magical A-Life Avatars*, I had no idea what the contents would turn out to be. I simply set out on an adventure of exploration into the world of the internet – writing about it as I went along.

My starting position was a good grasp of object-oriented computer programming, which I'd developed while writing *Lingo Sorcery*. This saw me starting with an empty space in the memory of my computer. The idea was that I could fill this space with software objects to perform various functions.

I began to experiment by creating simple objects that passed messages to each other. I got them to ask each other questions such as 'What is the time?' and 'What is the date?'. The objects could answer these questions by getting information from system software. This was quite easy

TECHNICAL NOTE Although this may appear to be very technical, it is surprisingly simple once you begin to get the hang of it. An object is created by going to a menu and selecting a menu item called 'New Object'. This will create a space in memory which can be given a name. Let's say the name is 'greenFrog'. Having created this 'greenFrog' memory space (known as the object), it can be sent a message simply by adding the name 'greenFrog' after the message name. For example, you can ask this 'greenFrog' object to tell you the time by including the following message in a code that is activated when a button is clicked on the screen:

tellMeTheTime greenFrog

This 'tellMeTheTime' message will go to the place in memory that has been allocated to the 'greenFrog' object.

For the object to be able to respond to this message you have to place into the object's memory space a little description of what the object has to do when it receives this 'tellMeTheTime' message. This takes the form:

on tellMeTheTime

put the time into field 'greenFrogsReply'

end

When the message 'tellMeTheTime' reaches the object space in memory, this little bit of code is triggered, causing the object to get the time from the system software and put it into a box on the screen (the box is given the name 'greenFrogsReply').

The beauty of this object-style programming is that you don't have to worry about how objects do whatever it is you want them to do. You just send them messages that contain key words (built-in functions). Hidden software, from behind-the-scenes, does all the difficult part for you – so you don't have to know how it is done. In this instance, the key words are 'the time'. The behind-the-scenes software recognizes this phrase and knows that it has to supply the object with the current time. The behind-the-scenes software also recognizes the phrase 'into field' and will place the time into the field named after this phrase. It is all very pedantic and mechanical, but does not require any arcane techno-wizardry.

With these authoring packages, which may contain thousands of built-in functions, you can create objects that will do almost anything. In essence, all the programmer needs to do is remember the names of the key words that call the functions.

because I was programming in the formatted space of a multimedia authoring package (Macromedia's Director), which has hundreds of ready-made functions that software objects could use.

Before very long, I was getting the objects to tell each other jokes and play simple card games with each other. I got them to carry out mathematical calculations, sometimes splitting a problem between the objects (so they had to cooperate with each other to produce a result).

As I got more ambitious, I started to investigate the built-in functions that allowed software objects to communicate with a website. I set up a website with a local ISP and although it took a couple of frustrating hours, sorting out the right parameters and passwords to include with the functions, I soon had objects creating files on my website. I then created other objects to download them back again onto my hard disk.

Then I found I could get my objects to download files from anywhere on the web. All I had to do was to send a message to an object giving it the URL (web address) of the file and it would use the necessary built-in functions to place the file in a designated folder on my hard disk. Experimenting further, I had one object download a file from the web and then pass it on to another object to process the contents. I then found I could set up an object to download a list of different web pages and send these pages to different objects where they could process the contents in different ways.

It then dawned on me that I was creating a system that was extending out beyond my computer to the whole of the internet. In effect, the internet had become an extension to my hard disk and I could create all kinds of objects to process and deal with information from anywhere on the web.

I began to introduce e-mails into this system I'd created. Objects were arranged to read the contents of e-mails and act upon any messages they contained. I then made myself part of the system. I'd read e-mails and if I found something of particular interest, I'd drag my mouse across the text and send the selected piece to an object that would either act on any instructions it contained or file the content away under any category I chose to define.

Taking an overview of what I was doing with my computer, I was using the computer as an artificial extension of my brain to communicate with the web. This gave me a new perspective on this world of objects I was creating. I was enhancing the capability of my brain to deal with the vast information environment of the internet.

I didn't have sufficient natural mental ability to sort rapidly through the information on hundreds of websites without some kind of aid; I hadn't the memory to record and categorize thousands of facts. I couldn't remember hundreds of names and relevant details of the people I was exchanging e-mails with. I had a normal human brain – a brain that hadn't evolved to deal with information of this magnitude – but my software objects were helping me to overcome this handicap.

This perspective is illustrated in Figures 12.10 and 12.11. The conventional notion of using a computer to access processed data from the web is replaced with the idea that information is downloaded from the web to be processed by the client – with the aid of client-side software objects.

Once I'd made the paradigm shift to see these objects I'd created in my computer memory as an extension to the capabilities of a normal human brain, I began to explore further possibilities. I created an object that simulated a café, which could keep a list of everyone I knew and selectively choose amongst them to sit at tables where I could have [e-mail] discussions with them.

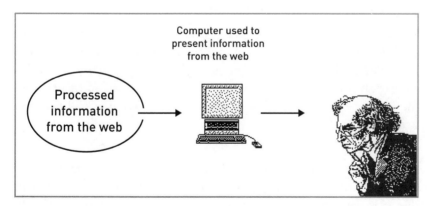

FIG 12.10 The conventional idea of using the web is that the client side is passive, with all processing arranged on the server side

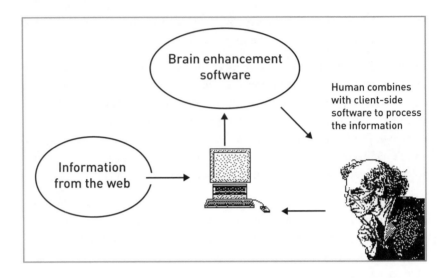

FIG 12.11 Client-side software can be thought of as an enhancement to the human brain, assisting the client to process the information available on the web

NOTE Conventional database matching techniques involve selecting against particular criteria. Each step of the selection process considers one criterion at a time, eliminating part of the database at each step until it gets down to just a few possibilities. This is a fast way to select but allows only a relatively small number of criteria to be used and doesn't balance out good points with bad. Using the 'simulated emotion' technique of selecting or matching allows any number of criteria to be taken into consideration at the same time, selecting for the best compromise between all the factors taken into consideration.

If I wanted to speak to programmers, I'd have an object search through my list of contacts and bring all the programmers into the café. Similarly with business contacts, social friends and a host of other categories: all I needed to do was to ask an object to produce a particular group of contacts according to a number of selection criteria and they'd be placed at a table ready for me to communicate with.

The advantage of using this object-based system was that I could design objects to look out for profiles of particular types of people in much the same way as the matchmaking program described previously looked for partners. It would be different from conventional database searches because the profile searches could choose people on the basis of overall nearness to a fit (rather than be limited to an exact match that would greatly limit the number of criteria that can be used in a selection process).

Despite the apparent complexity of this system of objects, the programming used a fairly small amount of memory. This meant that I could send this brain enhancement software across the web for others to use. I could also use it as the basis for myriad different business ventures.

cafés, objects and parallel worlds

Working within the environment of the internet, there can be far too many possible contacts for our brain to cope with efficiently. We need help to remember all the names and the different ways in which different people might be of interest to us. We need an efficient way to bring the right contacts to our attention whenever there is a need for particular assistance or information. Such help can be arranged by making appropriate use of the computer.

As humans and computers have totally different ways of dealing with information, an interface is necessary for humans and computers to be able to communicate with each other. Computers communicate across this interface using sound and visual images on a screen; humans by using a keyboard and mouse.

As most humans cannot communicate with computers at a programming level, the interface has to take the form of a metaphor of something that a human can easily relate to in the real world. Clever programming and graphics can create these metaphors and translate the human interactions into the binary language that computers can understand.

The virtual café is such a metaphor. It is a conceptual image that helps in the handling of a large number of internet contacts. After all, it is far easier to think of inviting people into a café to have discussions than to think about a complex environment of records and algorithms. This is illustrated in Figure 12.12, where an auteur (director of operations) or an entrepreneur visualizes themselves in a café where, at the various tables, sit the contacts they need to help them create an e-business.

An on-screen representation of a virtual café may look quite different from the mental model carried by the auteur. It might consist of a list of contacts and a means of bringing selected people into a 'café' area, which may be represented as a grid. Particular choices of people selected to sit at 'tables' would be names highlighted in this grid. Such a screen view of a café is shown in Figure 12.13.

In reality, the virtual café is a sophisticated database. Each listed contact name is created as a record. Software objects can search these records to

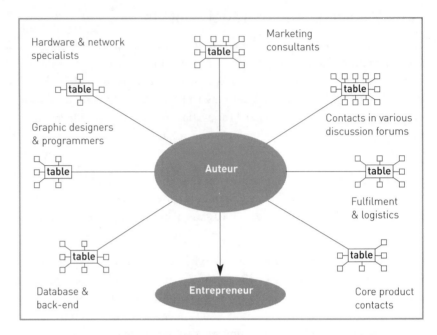

FIG 12.12 This is how the café might appear to an auteur or entrepreneur whose contacts are selected to help create an e-business

find people whose interest or knowledge coincides with any particular subject the café owner is interested in discussing.

Each record in the café database will contain a list of attributes and characteristics that have been assigned to a particular contact. Effectively, these records are clones of the contacts, representing who they are, what they know and what makes them interesting. Seeing these records as clones of the people they represent, it is then only a short step to think of these individual records as separate files that can exist independently of the database. As separate files, they can be sent to a software object, which can then send them to a website or include them in an e-mail to send to other people.

Visualizing these records as transportable clones, if a person created a record of their own characteristics, they could send this record to their friends and contacts. Figure 12.14 illustrates such a facility that might be

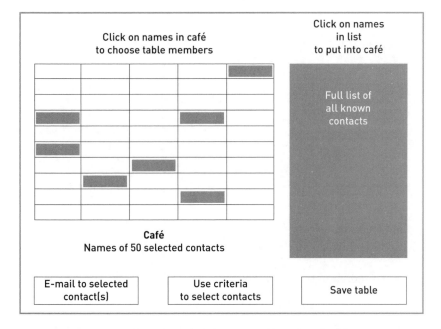

FIG 12.13 On-screen view of a table being created in a virtual café

included with the virtual café software to enable café owners to make a clone record of themselves that they can send out to all their contacts.

Such a cloned record would be created in a way similar to that in which the clones were created in the matchmaking experiment previously described. People would simply answer some form of questionnaire – with the questions chosen to relate to a specific area of interest depending on the purpose of the clone.

If the people who receive a clone record also have a virtual café – with a software object that can insert clones' records into their virtual café's database – it would save them the trouble of entering that clone owner's details themselves. Figure 12.15 illustrates a café with an object that can accept clone records from other people and insert them into a virtual café's database.

A software object on the client side can also be designed to transfer clone records to a website. This is illustrated in Figure 12.16, where an individual

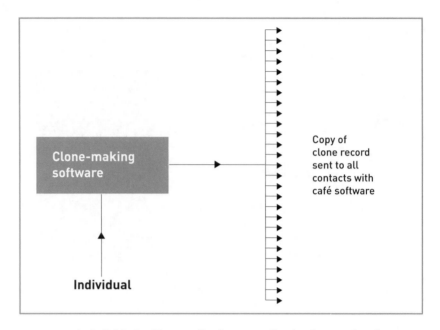

FIG 12.14 An individual, with a small software application for creating clone records, can send copies to all friends and contacts

creates a clone record of him or herself which is then passed to an object that will send it to a website. In this way, it can be arranged for many different café owners to send their clone records to particular meeting places in a people space (which might exist as a file on a website). Such gathering of clone records can be organized completely from the client side by the café owners themselves without the server side having to be involved at all (other than to facilitate the inclusion of a clone record in the designated file).

If café owners have objects that can send their clone records to a particular meeting place in a people space, they can equally have objects that download the clones at a meeting place into a virtual café in their own computer. This is illustrated in Figure 12.17, where one object downloads copies of the clone records at a particular meeting place, then passes these to another object to insert into the café database.

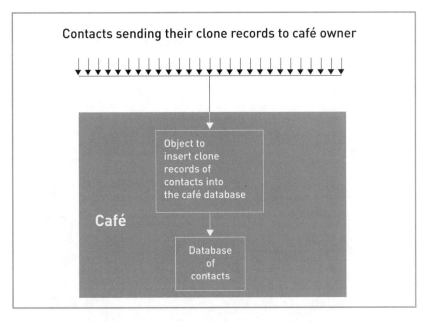

FIG 12.15 A virtual café with a software object that can insert clone records into its database

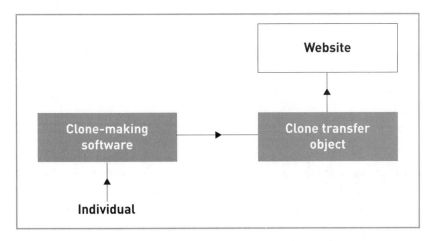

FIG 12.16 Individuals can make clone records of themselves that can be sent to designated websites. If the website is a people space, these clone records can be sent to selected meeting places

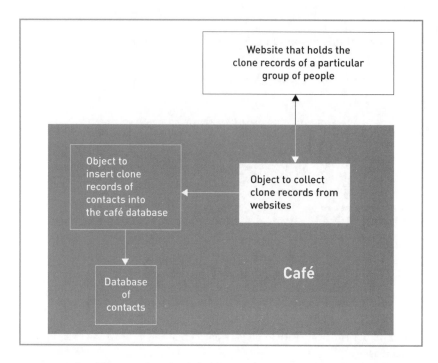

FIG 12.17 An object can download the clone records of a particular group of people and pass them to another object to insert into the virtual café database

In the matchmaking experiment I tried out in my home town, people had to physically go to the meeting places in real life to make their final personal selections. In this virtual world, the meeting place can be transferred to everyone's own computer, for them to inspect the clone records of everyone else and decide who to make actual contact with.

Just as in real-life meeting places, one-to-one communications can take place or small groups can be brought together for discussions. The big difference is that everyone has their own personal copy of the meeting place and can use it in any way they wish. It is this aspect of virtual meeting places that is so difficult to comprehend because there is no equivalent of this situation in the world of bricks and mortar.

The conceptual jump is to get away from the idea of there being a single meeting place and imagine each meeting place as being duplicated in a number of parallel worlds, where the interactions may take all kinds of different forms and directions. This may seem like something out of science fiction, but it is through understanding the bizarre and counter-intuitive nature of the internet that breakthroughs can be made.

a self-organizing system

Understanding how software objects on the client side can create clone records and send them to designated meeting places makes it possible to appreciate how a low-cost, self-organizing database can be created through all the users entering their own data.

The server side need not cross-link any of the records; the users themselves can create appropriate links by sending duplicate records to different meeting places where appropriate. A simple addition to a clone record can be used to cancel its appearance at a particular meeting place, thus eliminating the need for any server-side housekeeping duties. Alterations to records can also be arranged by the users themselves, simply by modifying their own clone record and sending it off to replace the previous record. Thus no updating need be carried out on the server side.

The only creative work required on the server side is in deciding on the initial questions that are used by the clone-making objects (these correspond to the initial categories decided on when creating the people space). It is this seed that starts off the process of self-organization and is the initial input provided by the entrepreneur.

an extension to the brain

Figure 12.18 shows how all these elements fit together. Although the tasks may be carried out by different software objects, this division of tasks would be transparent to the users. They would simply see a single application that allows them to send out clones to meeting places and bring back clones of other people into their cafés. On-screen buttons would activate the various objects, allowing the users to examine, sort and select amongst the records to find a particular

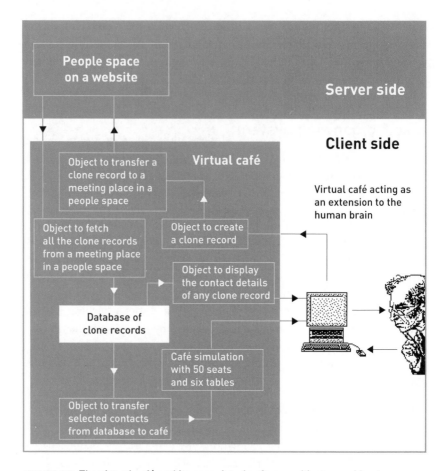

FIG 12.18 The virtual café and its associated software objects combine to enhance the ability of the human brain to cope with the complexity of the internet environment

contact or group of contacts they might need to help them solve a problem – or create a business.

From the user's point of view, this virtual café would not be seen as a complicated programming construct but as a useful aid that allows them to take full advantage of the internet to build and organize a powerful network of contacts. It will be like an extension to their brain, allowing them to use the internet environment efficiently to turn them into super individuals who are positioned at the centre of a personal hub of 'need to know' information sources. Thus, Figure 4.4 will now be transformed into Figure 12.19.

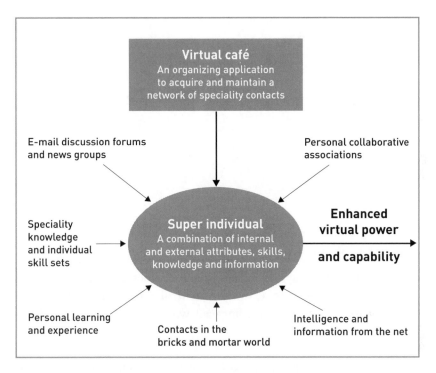

FIG 12.19 An individual's power and capability can be substantially enhanced by having an application that allows them to take full advantage of the internet to acquire and maintain a network of contacts

13

STIGMERGY

two ways of looking at a database In the previous chapter, I thought I'd done enough to explain the mechanics behind the business situation I was developing. It came as something of a surprise when one of the readers expressed disappointment with the explanation I'd given. He wrote:

'I still think that what I brought up back in Chapter 10 is missing. Basically, my point is that a non-negligible challenge in Peter's proposal is to establish and maintain (or rather, let evolve) an appropriate framework. Even if smart clients are installed on users' computers, to let them process their own set of attributes, the main data needs to be properly qualified first.

In Peter's matchmaking algorithm, 96 different Boolean attributes (they could have also been dimensions with fractional values) are used to model each individual. Adding, modifying or deleting individuals from the entire distributed network does not represent a big challenge. But how can the system be made to accept new attributes and to reject obsolete ones?

Worse than obsolescence, redundancy has to be dealt with. Not because it wastes data space, but because it leads to inconsistencies. Now, this has more to do with politics than technology.

In my previous posting, I mentioned two existing approaches: The Yahoo! approach: regardless of who is feeding the data, there is a small committee of designated people who constantly monitor the system and modify the framework accordingly, and the news group approach: self-designated users creating enough momentum to let the framework evolve one way or another. Regardless of how dictatorial or anarchic Peter's recommended system is, it has to tackle this political issue.

Vahé Kassardjian

This chapter, I hope, will answer most of Vahé Kassardjian's reservations. Firstly, it must be pointed out that Chapter 12 dealt with a very general overview of the idea. If it is to be applied to a specific situation for an e-business purpose, there would have to be an element of human control over the main categories of the people space. This will be explained later. However, the other difficulties envisaged would apply only if a server-side database were used in a conventional way.

At the same time as I received Vahé Kassardjian's post, I received a post from another reader, Kate Cooper, who has a senior fellowship at Warwick University – running their Innovation programmes for various MSc degrees in Engineering Management. Kate is not a database technologist but has been a consultant to UK blue-chip companies since 1983, mostly advising on human communication in large organizations. She saw beyond the nuts and bolts of the technicalities to visualize databases as part of an interactive system of communication. She wrote:

Think Experian/Acorn and how they're used by businesses – turn that on its head and think how individuals can use the same information ... now *that* is maybe a lucrative idea!!!

←snip→

Enable a user to latch into a known psychological construct – there are some human universals (e.g. an understanding of hierarchy is universal, probably because of family relationships, but knowing about Cinderella is parochial). A hugely pervasive and successfully exploited construct is that of a 'journey' –

already used of course on the net with terms such as 'path' and 'navigation tools'. There are many others that could be used – see stigmergy later. Also metaphors to assure people – signposts, junctions, fastroutes, superhighway, meandering path, etc. etc. PLUS you are, I presume, familiar with the social network stuff, 'small worlds'.

←snip→

I have a theory that stigmergy trails (as I think of it) within an internet system might identify the equivalent of the mavens, connectors and salespeople that Gladwell talks of – now imagine that the *geometry* of such trails was evident to the observer of this hive mind *and* that an individual could be both participant in the mind and observer of it. Some kind of stigmergy-driven search engine???

←snip→

An aside: humans find it very difficult, if not impossible, to 'see' the dynamics of a system. So we create geometries to help us – Poincaré's 'phase space' – and, as highly visual primates, that suits us. The only 'geometry' of the internet that most of us have is 'bricks and mortar' – we need, obviously, a new model that reflects the dynamics – hence my 'stigmergy' idea in which the rate of change of the trail matters more than the trail itself; fashion fashions itself. That we can handle these kinds of dynamic geometries as representations is evident in our nightly view of the TV weather forecast ... Whatever, the internet could do with a geometric model ...

Here was a view from somebody who claims to be non-technical but is an expert in business systems. Kate's mental model wasn't influenced by the technicalities of database design; she was seeing a more abstract represent-ation that eliminated all the problems anticipated by the database expert.

The two key models that came into Kate's mind when she read the previous chapters were Experian/Acorn and stigmergy. Let's take a look at these.

the Experian/Acorn model
These are models well known to the marketing experts of large companies. They represent the techniques

used by two of the largest players in the so-called 'geodemographic and lifestyles industries'. In effect, these models are people spaces that seek to map the relevant details of large populations of people in an n-dimensional space for marketing purposes.

Experian (now a subsidiary of Great Universal Stores), with annual sales around £1 billion ($1.5 billion) and employing more than 12,000 people, maintain records on millions of consumers. Through a variety of sources, they create socio-economic profiles of consumers, categorizing them according to age, income, family status, credit rating and all manner of other classifications that turn up on the billions of records that are sourced for information.

This huge volume of data can then be subjected to exploratory analysis, or 'data mining', using sophisticated programming tools – such as automated cluster analysis, probability modelling, neural networks, genetic algorithms, etc.

Founded on simulation technology in 1962, CACI International Inc. (www.caci.com) have developed a system called ACORN (A Classification of Residential Neighborhoods) to underpin many of their various services. It is a demographic information system, based on a people space that categorizes people according to where they live. The general idea is that residential localities can give indications of lifestyle and spending patterns. This allows businesses to target particular sections of the community more efficiently. From this people space, CACI have evolved a diverse solutions portfolio for the net economy. With approximately 5,000 employees and more than 90 offices in the US and Europe, CACI integrate the networks, systems and software for telecommunications, e-commerce and marketing information.

Clearly, such customer profiling and lifestyle databases are immensely costly to build and maintain. They require large revenue streams, so the benefits can be made available only to very large organizations that can afford to pay the necessary fees. Customers benefit from this system only indirectly, through the questionable advantage of having their needs targeted more specifically. The disadvantage is that these needs are approximated to cater for the statistically significant averages and are biased heavily towards the products of the suppliers who can afford to use these customer targeting services.

Turning this system on its head would involve handing the construction, control and running of such a system over to the customers: letting them enter their own data and choosing for themselves the suppliers who would be most likely to satisfy their needs. This is what we are proposing to do.

stigmergy

The idea that clients, acting independently, could work together to create anything so complex and highly organized as the giant databases created by the geodemographic and lifestyles industries might seem highly fanciful. Yet, similarly complex structures are a feature of many insect colonies. Ants, termites and bees are examples of insects that create elaborate nests with intricate architecture, create bridges, use complex food-gathering strategies, coordinate their activities to find new nest sites and defend them against intruders or invaders.

There are no central databases in these systems of complex insect organization; there is no central control, no leaders, no algorithms. Quite independently of each other, every insect plays some small part in a system of organization without any training, learning or instructions.

It is only in recent times that scientists have understood how this seemingly mysterious process of unorganized organization comes about. The trick, it seems, is to see the environment as part of the system. Individuals make changes to the environment and these changes affect the behaviour of the individuals. It is a feedback loop between the insects and their environment, not, as previously thought, a process of communication between the insects themselves.

> **INDIVIDUALS MAKE CHANGES TO THE ENVIRONMENT AND THESE CHANGES AFFECT THE BEHAVIOUR OF THE INDIVIDUALS**

The name 'stigmergy' was given to this process in the 1950s by Pierre-Paul Grasse, who used it to describe the indirect communication taking place among termites as they built their nests. He explained how the regulation and coordination of the building activities do not depend on the termites themselves, but are the result of responses being triggered in the termite workers by the structures of the nest: as the nest evolves. Changes in the structure induce different worker activity, sometimes in the same termite.

Appreciating how an insect can alter the environment to affect the behaviour of other insects, a new light was thrown on the pheromone (chemical complex) trails laid by ants. Instead of seeing pheromones as messages that are passed from one ant to another, they are seen as contributing to a large chemical infrastructure, overlaying the landscape, to which ants are genetically programmed to respond.

When this paradigm shift was first pointed out by Grasse, it seemed of little consequence. Now, however, in the age of information technology, it has been rediscovered and is being employed in a wide variety of applications. (Note: If a web search for 'stigmergy' is made with the GOOGLE.COM search engine, it will reveal 282 references; many of these illustrate novel internet applications for this concept.)

decentralized control

It seems that stigmergy is a powerful way to coordinate activity over both time and space in a variety of systems. It requires no planning, no leadership, no direct communication between participants. It is self-organizing. This sets it apart from the conventional organizational methods usually associated with human cooperative activity. Let's see how this maps across to a system of organization for an e-business environment.

The main features of a stigmergic system are:

► Individuals do not rely on instructions.

► Each individual gathers information itself and decides for itself what it should do.

► Information is gathered from a shared environment.

► There is no centralized decision making.

► Individuals need only a few elementary rules.

In an ant colony, the ants will lay down a trail of pheromones. They will

> IT SEEMS THAT STIGMERGY IS A POWERFUL WAY TO COORDINATE ACTIVITY OVER BOTH TIME AND SPACE IN A VARIETY OF SYSTEMS. IT REQUIRES NO PLANNING, NO LEADERSHIP, NO DIRECT COMMUNICATION BETWEEN PARTICIPANTS

have receptors to recognize the pheromones of other ants. There will be a decision function that activates appropriate ant behaviour when it encounters pheromone trails. The components used by the ants are genetic, the genes being supplied to each worker by the queen ant.

Translating this to the system of clone agents and people space as described in the previous chapter:

▶ The queen ant would be represented by a business that would create a questionnaire based on the needs of people who would benefit by being able to be put in contact with each other. The questions would equate with the genes that a queen ant passes on to the worker ants, which enable them to create pheromones. The pattern of pheromones laid down by the ants would equate with the digitized answers that a client would produce when completing the questionnaire. These records would be deposited in a people space in a way analogous to an ant laying a pheromone trail.

▶ Ants can sense the pheromones laid down by other ants and this would equate with individual bots detecting the records deposited in the people space by other individuals. The ants will be equipped – through genes provided by the queen ant – by a computing mechanism to interpret the pheromones of other ants. This would equate with the café software – provided by the business – that would allow an individual to identify suitably interesting contacts from the many records that would be deposited in the people space.

> THE MOST DIFFICULT CONCEPT TO GRASP IS THAT SUCH A SYSTEM IS NOT ORGANIZED OR CONTROLLED FROM A CENTRAL SOURCE

When translating this into human activity, the most difficult concept to grasp is that such a system is not organized or controlled from a central source. Every individual acts independently. The information provided does not come directly from the business but from the environment of records created by the individuals making use of the service. This is far outside of the concepts covered by conventional business strategies. It can only happen in the unique environment of the internet.

You do not have to look hard to see this process of stigmergy already taking place on the internet. Newsgroups and discussion forums manifest in this same way, where people find places of interest where they discover messages that are useful to them. The messages prompt other people to respond, by adding their own messages. People will move from one group to another, choosing to participate only in those where the messages are of specific interest to them.

There has been no centralized, organizing body to create the tens of thousands of news groups and discussion forums that have spontaneously birthed on the internet. Organizations do not provide content. People do not collude with each other as to what messages will be sent. The whole system has evolved organically and is driven by people acting independently.

It is this strange phenomenon of stigmergy that is now becoming of increasing interest to e-businesses. It can be employed to create self-organizing databases that cost little to build and maintain, yet provide a service and efficiency that far outstrip anything that can be created through rational design and control.

Two prime examples of stigmergic systems, growing and evolving without central control or organization, are The Open Source Movement and Napster. Both of these phenomena appeared almost spontaneously, growing to such power and influence that they out-compete the industry giants.

Even with its vast organization and huge financial resources, Microsoft is no match against the cumulative efforts of tens of thousands of independent programmers in the battle for supremacy in the server market. Building upon each other's efforts, the unorganized, independent programmers have created a free and highly flexible system known as Linux which has consistently held Microsoft at bay in providing the server of choice for ISPs and maintaining UNIX as the preferred operating system.

Similarly with Napster; a simple system devised by students evolved into a people space that created a distributed database spread over hundreds of thousands of private computers. The combined efforts of the whole of the music industry had to resort to legal action to stop the free distribution of its copyright-protected musical assets. Even so, the system adapted and evolved into new forms that had no central control for the legal injunctions to aim at.

This demonstrates the enormous potential of stigmergic systems. However, these systems have one vital omission that puts them a step behind the stigmergic systems of the insects: the ability to update automatically, to rid themselves of duplication, redundancy and out-of-date information. This essential feature is provided in the insect world by evaporation.

evaporation

There is one further feature of a stigmergic environment that needs to be emphasized. This is its impermanence. Stigmergic environments are designed to be short-lived, continuously self-updating through a process of evaporation. For instance, when an ant lays a trail of pheromones across a landscape, the pheromones last for only a short time before they evaporate. This ensures that recent pheromone trails are not confused with older pheromone trails – which might relate to circumstances that have changed.

This is a critical element in the design of a stigmergic system. Any records deposited in a people space would have to be given an appropriate 'life span' such that they 'die' after the lapse of a certain period of time. This safeguards the environment against getting cluttered up with out-of-date information. This solves the problems of obsolescence and redundancy envisaged by the database expert, Vahé Kassardjian, at the beginning of this chapter.

using a stigmergic environment for an e-business solution

Although this concept of stigmergy may appear to be wildly esoteric, it is an extremely powerful construct to use in many e-business situations. It can bring buyers in contact with sellers, it can bring information to people who want to know, it can bring help to the needy, it can bring specialist assistance to developers, it can put job seekers in touch with employers.

The first step would be to create a boundary for a people space and give it a formatting appropriate to the requirements of the business. The boundary would be the overall subject area. For example, if the business were concerned with the matching of people to jobs, the boundary condition would be to limit the space only to job seekers and employers looking for suitable job applicants.

The first level of categorization might specify broad categories of industries. A second level in each of these primary categories might categorize according to specific job descriptions. A third level in each of these categories might divide into different areas of specialization within those categories. Other levels might divide each of these subdivisions even further. This process of hierarchical categorization would format the environment sufficient to provide job seekers and employers with appropriate meeting points in the people space – in which to deposit their records.

To create a record, a job seeker or employer would simply click on a button to have a questionnaire automatically downloaded from the web directly into their clone creation software where the questions would be presented on the computer screen. From the answers to the questions, a record would be created to represent them and their needs. This record would then be deposited in one or more of the categorized meeting points in the people space as chosen by a job seeker (or an employer).

NOTE The actual mechanics of this process would be invisible to the users. They would simply click on a button to get a list of questions. When they answer the questions, they click on another button to see a route map to guide them to appropriate areas of interest. When they reach a point of interest, they simply click another button. This click automatically inserts their record at this point and at the same time invisibly downloads all the other records that are there.

The records automatically downloaded from a selected point of interest would go directly into a client-side application – something like the virtual café software described in the previous chapter. With this client-side application, both employers and employees could use the search functions to further categorize their selections. In effect, this is extending the categorization process of the people space out to everyone's own computer – in a way that allows everyone to make the final selections according to their own specific needs.

These records can be designed to carry the URLs of a personal, or company, website, to provide more extensive details than can be covered by the records. Employee websites can hold CVs, examples of work, photographs, references, etc. Employer websites can show diagrams of the organization, photographs of working conditions, terms of service, etc. The overall effect would be that employees would be able to see what kind of employers would have need of their services and have sufficient information to be able to draw up a short list for person-to-person contact. Similarly, employees would be able to draw up a short list of candidates for direct communication or interviews.

The great advantages that a stigmergic system would have over any conventional employment agency are speed, cost and its ability to self-organize. There are advantages that an employment agency would have, but it is highly likely that an employment agency would use such a system themselves to source clients and to satisfy their needs.

a self-regulating system

An interesting aspect of such a system is that it would automatically evolve to become progressively more efficient. In this example, job seekers would get the records of employers who were looking for someone like them and employers would get the records of the type of employees they were looking for. But besides this, they would also see the records of their competitors in this categorized space.

This would create a competitive market situation in every category – where the superior will drive out the inferior or cause them to improve their offer or presentation. For example, a job seeker might see other job seekers using better websites to present themselves, offering better examples of work, etc. Similarly with employers, their presentation must be at least as good as the other employers to be able to attract the best available employees. By allowing each record a short life-span, it provides the opportunity for job seekers and employers to improve their offers or presentations at subsequent visits to a selected meeting place – or change to a different meeting place where there might be less severe competition.

This is the way marketplaces become progressively more efficient and organized – a self-regulating process that works far better than any human rules, controls, regulations or selection procedures.

the commercial advantage

Although there are a number of additional extras that could be added (such as making provisions for

NOTE This is where clients are able to make their own categorizations: customizing the people space to suit their own particular needs. As this is done on the client side, within the client's personal application, this has no effect on the ordered space on the server side. Clients simply choose or add their own criteria to be able to filter out a suitably short list of people to make actual contact with. With each record having a limited life-span – being removed after a certain number of days – all records would be fresh.

privacy and keeping out spammers), the great advantage of this stigmergic system is that it costs relatively little to set up and maintain. Not only this, the development costs would be minimal because exactly the same system of basic components could be used for a large variety of quite different situations where it would be useful for people to make contact with others. It is like a spreadsheet; the starting position is a grid of empty spaces. Any system can be created simply by labelling some of the spaces and devising an appropriate questionnaire.

For instance, the job-seeking example could easily be used by large companies to fill vacancies within their organization. It could be used to make optimum use of subcontractors and consultants. It could be used to leverage the use of specialist employees, allowing them to work in different parts of the business as and when they are needed.

The system could also be used in speciality areas of interest. For example, gardening: where gardeners could be put in touch with others who share a particular interest in a specific type of horticulture. Seed merchants and specialist gardening services could set up such systems to gain goodwill to help them sell their products.

It could be used in all kinds of ways to bring people together for the purpose of collaboration or information sharing. It could be used in education, to put students in touch with suitable courses of study.

Particularly, it would be a useful organizational structure to create areas for micro money trading. So far, very little use has been made of the ability of the internet to reduce transaction cost to practically zero. Given a low-cost infrastructure, such as can be provided by a stigmergic structure, 'penny bazaars' can be opened – where a variety of software components, MP3 files, tutorials, specialist information, etc. can be traded for pennies.

It wouldn't be viable for a single small trader to set up a website to trade in items selling for pennies, but collectively, many coming together within a stigmergic organizational structure could attract millions of visitors – enough to provide many small businesses with substantial remunerative cash flows.

> THE GREAT ADVANTAGE OF THIS STIGMERGIC SYSTEM IS THAT IT COSTS RELATIVELY LITTLE TO SET UP AND MAINTAIN

It may seem to go against the grain, charging money for small software applications, music clips, tutorials and information. But the originators of these kinds of products are the people we need to support. A few pennies' appreciation for their efforts, given by many thousands of people, may enable them to work on their creations full time. Let's support the small artisan. It is the only way we can prevent the web being dominated by large companies.

14

THE EMERGENT BUSINESS

the first rule The main purpose of this book, in fact the purpose of the whole trilogy, has been to arrive at a position to start an e-business. The various chapters reflect the tortuous route that has had to be taken to reach this final goal.

It should be clear by now that starting out with a business plan, based on a set business idea, is not a practical way to go about creating a business in a rapidly changing environment. It may be the right way to obtain finance, but as the dot-com crash proved, getting finance has very little relevance to creating a viable business.

Learning from the many failures of the e-business pioneers, it has become evident that the internet is mainly about enablement rather than selling. It is about communication rather than simply providing more information. While most of the ambitious e-business ventures – based on expensively constructed websites and powerful back-end databases – were proving to be white elephants, the simple concept of person-to-person communication was going from strength to strength.

Ignored by most of the main developers, e-mail became the 'killer app'.

The inherent tendency for human systems to self-organize put all deliberate human initiatives to shame. Online communities, costing virtually nothing to set up and maintain, had created as much, if not more, usefulness than the millions of websites that had squandered billions of dollars in human resources.

Anyone who has studied organic systems knows that they have a natural tendency to self-organize. They are driven by evolutionary mechanisms that act continuously to improve efficiencies at every level of organization. The internet is an organic system, not because it is based on computer technology but because it is based on human activity. It is as natural for the internet to create its own order, and progress towards increased efficiency, as it is for any other biological organization or ecosystem.

Observing the progress of the e-business environment over the rise and fall of the dot-com bubble, it became increasingly evident that rational human organization is like a small sailing ship in a storm. Pitted against the natural tendency of a dynamic system to self-organize, it is virtually powerless. Any human activity that does not make any real improvements towards efficiency is ruthlessly broken up or destroyed.

The instances where internet businesses seem to have had most success are where they have been allowed to self-organize: without the imposition of human control. This observation provided me with a first rule for deciding what kind of business situation to create:

1 The business should take advantage of a system's natural tendency to self-organize.

what makes for increased efficiency?

'Increased efficiency' is a glib term. What does it mean in a new and as yet relatively unexplored environment? How do you recognize it? How do you measure it?

In the context of any business situation, efficiency is easily recognized and measured. It is the amount of wealth that is being created or lost. In competitive environments the biggest winners are usually those who can achieve goals more efficiently.

This begs the question: 'How can you tell whether or not a business venture is going to be profitable and create wealth?' Reading through the obituaries of the many e-businesses that failed during the dot-com bubble, the conclusion seems to be that predicting future profitability is impossible. Even with the survivors, the difference between expectations and actual results makes a poor case for the ability to predict future profitability in an e-business environment.

It seems reasonable, then, if most companies can't predict the likelihood or extent of e-business profitability, to assume that profitability is unpredictable. This gives rise to a second rule:

2   The business should not rely on an ability to determine future profitability.

At first, this seems ridiculous. Surely no business venture should be started without having some estimate as to future profitability. However, this is far less ridiculous than estimating future profitability when there is clear evidence that it is impossible to do so.

The resolution of this paradoxical situation is to think in terms of strategies rather than plans. If you start with a lot of capital you are compelled to estimate future profitability to make sure you don't lose the money. This automatically puts you on the slippery slope of trying to use human reasoning, planning and forecasting the future, rather than taking advantage of a system's natural tendency to move towards efficiency by itself.

Conceptually, the idea of working without calculating future probability is difficult to appreciate. The trick is to think in terms of starting with a very small amount of money, where a mistake can see you knocked out of the game. This forces you to progress only in directions where you can reasonably expect to earn enough money to continue. In other words, all activity is confined to small steps that bring immediate rewards.

Using this simple strategy, progress is dictated by inputs of revenue rather than an amount of capital. Although this may seem nonsense to those who have been brainwashed by the stories of business angels and venture capital largesse, the undeniable fact is that a business that is

> IF YOU START WITH A LOT OF CAPITAL YOU ARE COMPELLED TO ESTIMATE FUTURE PROFITABILITY TO MAKE SURE YOU DON'T LOSE THE MONEY. THIS AUTOMATICALLY PUTS YOU ON THE SLIPPERY SLOPE OF TRYING TO USE HUMAN REASONING, PLANNING AND FORECASTING THE FUTURE, RATHER THAN TAKING ADVANTAGE OF A SYSTEM'S NATURAL TENDENCY TO MOVE TOWARDS EFFICIENCY BY ITSELF

restrained by income cannot do anything other than progress in the direction of profitability.

This provides a third rule:

3 The business must be capable of starting with a small amount of capital and be able to generate enough of an immediate revenue stream to make further progress.

creating a revenue stream

There is only one way to create a genuine revenue stream, and that is to provide value in return. This places a further restraint on the type of business that can be chosen and provides a fourth rule:

4 The business must be able to provide value right from the start.

Investment capital can only be treated as revenue if adequate returns can be guaranteed. However, as profitability cannot be predicted, this condition cannot be met, so investment capital shouldn't be used in an e-business venture where the outcome is uncertain.

Seed capital can qualify as revenue if the probability of gain heavily outweighs the risk of loss. As a rule of thumb, seed capital can only be treated as revenue if there would be a reasonable expectation that a business could advance to where the investor's share could increase in value by a multiple of between ten and twenty. To expect to obtain better terms than this for seed capital would be unrealistic.

A different approach to obtaining start-up capital is to be able to offer a solution to a difficult or unsolved problem. In this case, seed capital could be regarded by the finance provider as research and development costs – on the understanding that there is a reasonable chance that a problem can be solved. This provides a fifth rule for the choice of business:

5 The business must be such as to be able to solve immediate and real problems.

personal assets and contacts
Every business entrepreneur must have personal assets of some kind. These may be tangible or intangible. Any personal finance, property or equipment would count as an asset. So also would intellectual properties, experience, special expertise or talents. Even an ability to network or sell would constitute an asset.

These assets represent the core of the business, and the more of them that can be applied to a business situation the more efficient the business will be. This provides a sixth rule:

6 The business must be chosen such that it makes full and appropriate use of the founder'(s) assets.

As has been covered earlier in the book, an individual's ability and capability are enhanced by their choice of personal contacts. The quantity and quality of these contacts determine the range of business opportunities that can be considered. Also, they determine the effectiveness with which opportunities can be realized and the ability to expand the business. This choice of contacts applies not only to immediate contacts but also to the contacts of the contacts. These are equally as important because they will enhance the total value of the network of personal contacts.

This provides a seventh rule that will affect the choice of a business:

7 There must be enough suitable contacts, direct or indirect, available to cover all aspects of the chosen business situation.

Employees count as valuable contacts, but they come with a penalty attached. They represent a liability unless they are directly or indirectly responsible for increasing the efficiency or income of the business: creating real value. With a young business, particularly at start-up stage, it is not possible to keep employees gainfully employed all of the time. Any discontinuities, setbacks or changes in direction can dramatically change the efficiency of a business, maybe even throwing it into a loss-making situation.

The penalties associated with employees are heightened by the increase in overheads they generate: floor space, services, management time, training, taxes, government regulations, working practices, etc. These may be accommodated in a large organization that has a steady cash flow, but can greatly reduce the efficiency of a young business where income is uncertain and subject to unexpected changes.

This leads to an eighth rule:

8 All employees must be revenue producing and fully covered by a stable and reliable income.

advertising and marketing
Most conventional business strategy books will emphasize the obvious: reliable product or service, competitive pricing, customer satisfaction, after-sales support, clever advertising and marketing. Few make allowances for the influence of the internet and the speed with which information and knowledge can diffuse through an online population.

NOTE Many people assume that viral marketing applies only to the people who are online. This is not true because of another phenomenon known as small-world clustering. The essence of this theory is that because people online tend to transfer their knowledge and information to those in their immediate locality, almost everybody, whether they have a computer or not, is also influenced by the internet spread of information and knowledge.

In the second book of this trilogy, *The Ultimate Game of Strategy*, I devoted a whole chapter to the spread of information through the internet. This phenomenon is analogous to the spread of viruses throughout a population. Information, knowledge and gossip can spread from one person to another, and one person can affect many others so the spread is exponential. This exponential spreading is speeded up when it involves groups of people (such as online newsgroups and discussion forums).

Using this phenomenon for marketing purposes has acquired the name viral marketing. It is highly effective and costs very little, but it only works if the product or service is highly novel, breaks new ground or is of exceptionally good value. This provides another rule for the choice of business opportunity:

9 The product or service should be sufficiently distinctive to be able to take advantage of viral marketing.

critical mass
The essence of technological advance in the twentieth century was encapsulated in the phrase 'To know the future is to invent

it'. The dot-com bubble illustrated how this philosophy is not appropriate for the Information Age.

Inventing the future implies that clever people, with good ideas, can determine what the future holds. Many well-funded dot coms tried to do this and failed miserably. What they proved is that the future, in a rapidly expanding technological environment, is beyond the power of humans to control. The future may evolve out of inventions, but it isn't invented.

Perhaps a new phrase might be more appropriate for the Information Age: 'To know the future is to GROW it.' This would involve admitting that the future is unpredictable and basing business strategy on the notion of providing businesses with the ability to grow, adapt and evolve by themselves.

> " TO KNOW THE FUTURE IS TO GROW IT "

This philosophy is anathema to the twentieth-century, Industrial Age mindset. It suggests a lack of control, a lack of organization, a lack of leadership – an inefficient system that is random and aimless. But nothing is further from the truth: it is just a question of knowing how to control it.

The key to controlling a self-organizing, evolving business it to understand the concept of *critical mass*. Critical mass is a single number. It may be expressed as a number of participants, a number of customers or a number of orders. It is the number that defines the point at which a business breaks even.

For every business there is a break-even point, where the income is just sufficient to take care of the outgoings. If income is above this point, the business is profitable and can develop and evolve from its own resources. If income is below this point, the business runs the risk of spiralling downwards out of existence. This much is common sense, but somewhere in between, there is a quasi state: where a business might go through a period of negative cash flow during a transitional stage in its growth.

Negative cash flow – or capital burn rate – most commonly occurs at the start-up stage, or during a period of expansion, or at a time of redirection. The nature of e-business is such that it is continually in one of these three phases – due to constant technological change and unpredictable competition initiatives. This makes the haemorrhaging of a business's capital base the single most important problem an e-business strategist has to deal with, not least because it is an ever-present danger.

Seed capital, loans, past profits and various stages of equity capital are traditional sources of funding used to finance negative cash flows. Such funding is assumed to be bridging finance, used to achieve new levels of business profitability with sound business plans aiming to meet well-defined targets.

However, planning and making projections involves anticipating the future. This is not reliable in an environment as unpredictable as e-business. It puts the business strategist in much the same position as a marksman trying to fire at a fast, random-moving target. There is nothing stable to focus on.

The only predictable metric is critical mass. It is this, rather than future targets, that should form the focal point of an e-business strategy. Unlike targets, critical mass is not the aim of a strategy but represents a minimum acceptable performance. This requires a large paradigm shift for anyone used to conventional business planning because anticipated results are not specific, but vague and open ended. Not an easy thought for anyone with a managerial mindset.

The trick to understanding why critical mass is a better basis than targets for e-business strategies is to imagine a high-jumper, jumping over a bar. If the high-jumper isn't sure whether or not he can jump over it, he can spend more time training to perfect his technique. He may then succeed, but a far surer way of jumping over the bar would be to set the bar lower. The point is that critical mass is knowable. It can be calculated. It is also adjustable. If it seems too high, it can be lowered to a point that makes it easier to achieve profitability.

NOTE It must be emphasized that critical mass is the single most important metric in e-business. It is the only figure that is certain, controllable and calculable in a bottom-up strategy. Almost all other metrics are vague and unpredictable.

This provides a tenth rule to apply when deciding upon an e-business:

10 The critical mass must be easily adjustable.

business strategy

The dot-com bubble provided ample evidence that even the best-laid plans can fail or be thwarted by changing technology and unpredictable competitive action. The question then becomes, 'What takes the place of plans?' The answer is strategy.

Strategy isn't about trying to plan the future. It is about using concepts to achieve goals in situations of uncertainty and competition. Concepts are in the mind so they cannot easily be written down on a piece of paper. However, once the concepts are in place, strategies can be employed and orchestrated using very simple calculations. These are often described as 'back-of-the-envelope calculations'.

Back-of-the-envelope calculations are not inferior forms of planning. They represent top-level understanding and control that deal with only the most important and critical aspects of a business situation. This is particularly applicable in highly complex areas of business where vast amounts of information, and a plethora of incomprehensible detail, can easily cloud the more important issues. With bottom-up strategies – the essential approach in these conditions – back-of-the-envelope calculations are vital for fast-reacting control.

> **STRATEGY ISN'T ABOUT TRYING TO PLAN THE FUTURE. IT IS ABOUT USING CONCEPTS TO ACHIEVE GOALS IN SITUATIONS OF UNCERTAINTY AND COMPETITION**

The main focal point, for back-of-the-envelope calculations in e-business strategies, is critical mass. A business direction can be guided according to the ease of achieving critical mass: moving in directions where critical mass is most easily achievable and away from areas where it is not. Such a strategy can be controlled and monitored by means of a simple model that uses only three business metrics:

▶ total overheads (O);

▶ gross profit per sale (P);

▶ total sales costs (S).

The critical mass (number of customers or orders needed to break even) can then be calculated using the formula:

Critical mass = (O + S) divided by P

From this simple formula, it is easy to calculate the minimum number of customers or clients needed for a particular business opportunity to be viable. If this number seems achievable then the business opportunity is deemed worth pursuing. This obvious fact provides a means of choosing between various business options: the easier it is to achieve critical mass, the more likely the business is to succeed in being profitable. This allows a business to be steered through a route of development that offers the least chance of failure.

The value of this formula is that it can show where flexibility and adaptability are needed. It can be used to guide the company into more profitable business areas and take it out of hazardous situations. It will let you know when your overheads are too high; tell you when they have to be drastically reduced if a sticky patch or a discontinuity occurs. It will let you know if increased marketing or reduced prices are likely to improve results or whether it might be wisest to pull out of a situation altogether and move on to greener pastures.

In essence, this formula can be used to enable a company to be flexible, adaptive and fast reacting. If a more powerful competitor comes on the scene, it will tell you to move on. If a new opportunity arises, it will provide a way of judging whether or not to take advantage of it.

Although this is described as a 'back-of-the-envelope' calculation, it is more usefully employed as the basis for a simple spreadsheet model. This will provide a simulation of the business as various consequences of adjusting the metrics are observed.

The three adjustable metrics are overheads, gross profit and sales costs. These can be constantly monitored and adjusted to suit current conditions. Gross profits and sales costs are easily adjustable, but overheads can be more difficult to change. For this reason, a business infrastructure that requires the lowest possible overheads is preferred.

This provides an eleventh rule when deciding upon a suitable e-business opportunity:

11 The essential infrastructure required must be such as to entail very low overhead costs.

Having a low level of essential overheads does not rule out the possibility of strategic expansion in favourable conditions. However, it will facilitate rapid contraction in times of change or adversity.

competition

Although critical mass is the only metric that can be relied upon, it is subject to continuous change. For example, critical mass is affected by competition: if competition becomes intense, it becomes more costly to compete and critical mass goes up. If there is less competition, critical mass goes down.

Using the formula in a spreadsheet model, it is easy to estimate relative competitiveness. If a competitor has a smaller critical mass they will be in a stronger position. It will give them more scope for reducing their prices, increasing their marketing efforts, and improving customer service and support, or enable them to put more funds into product development.

By far the most threatening aspect of e-business is the ease with which competitors can come up with a superior or less expensive product or service. The difficulty of achieving critical mass offers some protection as it may require a substantial capital investment to persuade a large body of customers to switch loyalty. This would be particularly true if the customers themselves were an important part of the product or service (such as an employment agency).

In warfare, opposing sides may fight a war of attrition, where each side depletes the other side's resources at the expense of their own. Usually such wars are won by the side whose resources last out the longest. Similar battles can be fought in the arena of e-business, where businesses may be prepared to sustain heavy losses until they have won over all the clients. However, such victories carry a high penalty because the losses have the effect of increasing the winner's critical mass as these losses have to be recouped (or higher equity earnings allowed for).

In warfare, there will be an advantage to the side that has the more efficient armour or firing power. In e-business competition, the advantage will lie with the business that has the lowest critical mass. This provides another important rule:

> IN WARFARE, THERE WILL BE AN ADVANTAGE TO THE SIDE THAT HAS THE MORE EFFICIENT ARMOUR OR FIRING POWER. IN E-BUSINESS COMPETITION, THE ADVANTAGE WILL LIE WITH THE BUSINESS THAT HAS THE LOWEST CRITICAL MASS

12 The business should have a lower critical mass than its competitors.

initiatives

It is too obvious to spend much time discussing the importance of product or service reliability, competitive pricing, customer satisfaction and after-sales support. These are fundamental to any business situation. The only difference the internet makes is that any improvements in these areas are not only noticed by customers or clients, they are just as easily noticed by competitors. This allows them to catch up or surpass any new initiatives very quickly.

This puts early movers at a disadvantage because if their initiatives are seen to provide a competitive advantage, they can be copied by competitors who would have the distinct advantage of not having to carry the costs of development or educating the customers or clients. This provides another rule for choosing a suitable business opportunity:

13 There should be no substantial development or pioneering costs.

switching in and out of opportunities

A bottom-up strategy that follows the direction of lowest critical mass will require high flexibility and involve fast switching between situations. As already covered, this will require the business to have low overheads, with many of the business functions being outsourced rather than carried out internally.

However, even with low overheads and a flexible business organization, switching around can be costly in terms of the disruption it causes. Partners, affiliates and contractors need to be considered. New hardware, different techniques and software might be required. There may be a need for retraining or learning new areas of technology. Also, a change in direction might require different contacts, making some valuable contacts redundant. These are important matters to be taken into consideration.

The cost of switching out of an unprofitable area of business into another that holds out better prospects can be costly. This cost, and loss of efficiency during the change, might outweigh the advantages of moving on to greener pastures – effectively limiting flexibility and inhibiting strategic switching opportunities.

The only way to avoid these kinds of problems is to be involved in a business environment that offers many opportunities for switching into new opportunities without the need to make any major organizational changes. This provides a fourteenth rule to influence the kind of business opportunity to take:

14 The business environment must be such as to allow switches in direction without too much disruption.

potential for growth
As a business in an unpredictable environment necessitates a bottom-up strategy, it relies upon there being ample scope for evolutionary, organic growth. There has to be sufficient opportunity to expand. It is no good creating a business in a small niche because it would become trapped and limited in the ways it can expand or evolve. This sets a fifteenth rule to influence the choice of business opportunities that can be taken:

15 The business environment should offer ample scope for evolutionary growth and expansion.

funding
Bottom-up strategies follow the line of least resistance, so choice is determined more by facts and events than rational decision making. Particularly this applies to funding. Funding cannot be planned or predicted. It either happens or it doesn't and is always obtained on the basis of some understanding of what the business is about and how it is to be conducted.

A conventional business approach will be able to offer up a detailed plan, to let an investor see how their money is to be spent and how they can expect to see the results turn their investment into profit. An entrepreneur using a bottom-up strategy hasn't got this option as there is no plan and no way of predicting the course of events. In some ways, they are in the same position as the person trying to sell the idea of a spreadsheet, as depicted in the story in Chapter 11.

The late Sir 'Billy' Butlin, who became a multi-millionaire by creating the first packaged holidays in the UK just after World War II, had a dream of building 'holiday camps' that provided cheap accommodation around a purpose-built entertainment complex. He went to hundreds of different banks throughout the UK, looking for financial backing. They all turned him down until he came to a small bank in a run-down suburb of South London: Barclays Bank in Tooting Bec.

The manager of this bank recognized the potential and, probably at the risk of his career, loaned Billy Butlin the money to get his scheme off the ground. A decade later, when the Butlin Holiday Camps had spread all over the UK, Billy Butlin was still using this same small bank to handle the millions of pounds the business was turning over every week. Despite many advantageous offers from larger banks to handle his cash flow, Billy Butlin steadfastly refused to move his account away from the small bank that had given him his start.

> **IF AN IDEA HAS ANY REAL MERIT, THERE WILL BE A FINANCIAL SOURCE SOMEWHERE THAT WILL RECOGNIZE IT**

The point of this story is that if an idea has any real merit, there will be a financial source somewhere that will recognize it. The more possibilities for funding there are, the greater the chances of success. This provides another rule for choosing a business:

16 There must be a variety of funding possibilities available.

the full set of rules

This gives us 16 rules that can be used to select an appropriate business opportunity in the uncertain and unpredictable environment of e-business. They are not in any particular order, as some of them are interdependent. They simply provide a checklist of conditions that must be met when the final decision is made:

1 The business should take advantage of a system's natural tendency to self-organize.

2 The business should not rely on an ability to determine future profitability.

3 The business must be capable of starting with a small amount of capital and be able to generate enough of an immediate revenue stream to make further progress.

4 The business must be able to provide value right from the start.

5 The business must be such as to be able to solve immediate and real problems.

6 The business must be chosen such that it makes full and appropriate use of the founder's assets.

7 There must be enough suitable contacts, direct or indirect, available to cover all aspects of the chosen business situation.

8 All employees must be revenue producing and fully covered by a stable and reliable income.

9 The product or service should be sufficiently distinctive to be able to take advantage of viral marketing.

10 The critical mass must be easily adjustable.

11 The essential infrastructure required must be such as to entail very low overhead costs.

12 The business should have a lower critical mass than its competitors.

13 There should be no substantial development or pioneering costs.

14 The business environment must be such as to allow switches in direction without too much disruption.

15 The business environment should offer ample scope for evolutionary growth and expansion.

16 There must be a variety of funding possibilities available.

The end of the journey

These rules now bring us to the climactic end of the book, the point that the whole trilogy of books has been working towards: the choice of a business opportunity to pursue.

It's taken two years of contemplation and investigation; through the period of the dot-com bubble, where all kinds of mistakes have been made and lessons learned. The progress of hundreds of companies has been followed; thousands of web articles and hundreds of newsletters have been read. It has involved listening to and taking part in many different internet discussion forums; meeting all kinds of people in real life; attending seminars and exhibitions. These past two years have been very busy.

Of most value has been the book writing and the virtual café. It gave me the opportunity to express ideas, thoughts and observations and have intelligent and informed comments and opinions to criticize and modify them. Over 200 people have contributed to the conclusions reached. Not all agreed with them, but those opposing views and opinions have been taken into serious consideration.

Although I've tried to keep the content as generic as possible, it is unavoidably biased towards my own particular situation: a lifelong entrepreneur who is as much concerned with interest, lifestyle and personal freedom as with pursuing a profitable goal. This has meant that the content and conclusions are not universally applicable. However, there should be enough useful sections to offer some value to everyone, even though they may have no intention of creating their own business.

The final choice of business I finish up with is of course highly personal. It has to be, because, as will be obvious from the rules, it must take account of my personal situation and assets. It must involve the particular knowledge and experience I've acquired during my life. It reflects the personal contacts I've made and the opportunities that have come my way. It also takes into account my shortcomings, the limitations of my knowledge and expertise, my physical location and state of finances. Everyone will have a unique and different set of factors that influence their choice of business opportunity. For what it is worth, here is the choice I made.

the final choice of a business

During the course of writing this trilogy, many possibilities and tempting opportunities for creating an e-business emerged. All, except one, had to be eliminated because they broke one or more of the above rules. To be more accurate, I did not start with those rules: they evolved out of the reasons I had for aborting so many of the opportunities that came along.

The exception, which seemed to comply with all the rules, was a business based on helping cancer patients locate treatment trials. This particularly appealed to me because it was a business that was based on providing help to people with needs rather than being concerned solely with the amoral pursuit of making profits.

As you will have gathered from previous chapters, this was not an idea I came up with myself. It emerged out of a problem posed by the oncologist Tillman Pearce. At the time, it did not occur to me to be a suitable subject for business, but I was intrigued by the problem.

When the subject was first broached, my thoughts went to the famous physicist, the late Professor Richard Feynman, who died from a rare form of cancer in 1988. It has been argued that his affliction could be traced directly to his work on the atomic bomb during World War II. Many of his colleagues at Los Alamos suffered a similar fate.

Freeman Dyson, of the Institute for Advanced Study in Princeton, New Jersey, called Richard Feynman 'the most original mind of his generation', while the *New York Times* in its obituary described him as 'arguably the most brilliant, iconoclastic and influential of the post-war generation of theoretical physicists'.

Feynman was one of the world's top authorities in particle physics, winning a Nobel Prize in 1965 with Tomanaga and Julian Schwinger for his work in quantum electrodynamics. His principal interest was in trying to understand the composition of matter by analyzing the collision of heavy particles at extreme high energies, but his biographies showed him to have been a compulsive problem solver with an insatiable curiosity.

There are many anecdotes of Feynman spending many evenings in cafés with his associates and students, covering the tablecloths with diagrams and figures as they amused themselves with all kinds of problem solving, both serious and non-serious. Such was his reputation for problem solving that when on 28 January 1986 the Challenger space shuttle accident happened, NASA asked Feynman to help with their investigations. Feynman figured out what was wrong: it turned out to have been a gasket material that had lost its resilience in freezing temperatures.

Feynman suffered from his cancer for the last decade of his life. It always struck me that with his brilliant mind he must have had many thoughts as to the explanation of cancer and the possibilities of a cure. Yet, there is no record of him taking any special interest in the causes and cures for cancer. These thoughts prompted me to think more deeply about Tillman Pearce's revelation that there were no really authoritative sites that covered all the possibilities of treating the various kinds of cancer. Surely, this must be frustrating and agonizing to all cancer patients and their families and friends.

As this interest prompted me to look further into the problem, I discovered that all the most recent advances in the treatment of cancer weren't available through prescribed treatment. Treatments have to be exhaustively tested and approved before they can be prescribed by physicians, a process that can take typically eight to ten years.

In effect, this disbars cancer sufferers from all recent medical advances. The only way a patient can receive up-to-date treatment is to take part in a treatment trial. This presents several problems. Firstly, the field is so vast that cancer patients wouldn't know where to start looking. Secondly, there are so many trials taking place that nobody has a complete record of them. Websites that try to provide information to cancer sufferers are overwhelmed by the scale and volatility of the information that needs to be processed.

In discussing this problem with patients, I found that besides the frustration of being confronted with vast amounts of confusing information, their problems were compounded by the fear of being used as guinea pigs, in trials that would be of little real benefit to them. This forced them to place implicit trust in their physicians.

The problem with this, as I discovered, was that most physicians are fallible. Like their patients, they are not able to have anywhere near the full knowledge that covers all the current research – even when limiting themselves to specialist areas. This has been why knowledge of cancer treatments has been used so often in this book: to illustrate the problems of information overload and data volatility.

Using a people space, where patients can meet other patients with a similar condition to discuss trials and treatments, seemed an obvious solution to this problem. From my own experience in researching for this book, I'd discovered that the best way to know what was going on in a particular area of technical complexity was to communicate with others who were trying to do the same thing. This shares the workload and brings up areas of investigation that a solitary searcher might not even have found to exist.

As I made further inquiries and met more specialists in the field of cancer, I discovered another problem area: an area where the same people space that could help cancer patients meet each other to exchange information could also help the physicians and researchers who were working on the cures.

The drug companies developing treatments needed to run many different kinds of trials. They start off a promising treatment with a small trial. If this shows positive results they will conduct a further larger trial. If this also shows benefits they will run an even larger trial. This series of trials can continue for several years, with each new trial getting progressively larger and closer to the stage where it can be safely authorized for general treatment.

This trial activity by the various drug companies involves finding hundreds of thousands of trial patients. Every trial requires the careful selection of people with exactly the right profiles. They have to have a specific type of cancer. The cancer has to be at a particular stage of progression or remission. The patients have to be in a particular age group. They can be selected only if they have, or have not, received particular types of previous treatment. Every profile drawn up for each trial contains a large number of specific requirements that describe a patient suitable for the trial.

This presents a huge problem for drug companies because to get patients for a particular trial they have to source a large geographic area. This necessitates using numerous clinics in all parts of the world which can each identify suitable candidates within their local areas. A typical drug trial might involve a hundred such intermediary clinics, which assist in carrying out these trials.

With many drug companies running hundreds of trials, needing thousands of clinics which would need to search for hundreds of thousands of specific patients – a formatted people space would be an ideal structure to reduce their costs. This saving could be used to finance the setting up and running of a people space for the patients, who would need to be part of it for the benefit of the researchers and physicians.

It was the perfect situation. The profits made by the drug companies could be used to finance a free and valuable service for the patients because it was in their interests to do so. This then constituted the basis for a valid business opportunity – a business where everyone could benefit and everyone would have an incentive to take part.

Discussing the idea with various doctors, oncologists, clinicians and patients, there was overwhelming enthusiasm. But would it form a basis for a viable and stable business? I had to subject it to the rules.

checking against the rules

Throughout this trilogy of books on e-business, I've consistently criticized the concept of a business plan. To my mind, the idea that you can plan or predict what is going to happen in a complex and dynamic environment is ludicrous.

This viewpoint has been met with fierce resistance, even hostility and scorn. 'How can you run a business without a business plan?' everyone would ask. Perhaps this section will explain. It is not about planning or prediction; it is about having knowledge and experience of natural, self-organizing systems. It is not about regulation and control; it is about keeping to the rules.

Let's go through each rule in turn. This process replaces the concept of a business plan used in more conventional, Industrial Age businesses.

1   **The business should take advantage of a system's natural tendency to self-organize.** The main lesson learned from the failures in the dot-com bubble was that the internet is a dynamic complex environment that is impossible to predict, control or regulate. However, as the successes of such phenomena as internet discussion forums, news groups, Napster and the open source movement have proved, the internet is self-organizing.

The ability to capitalize on this natural tendency for a complex system to self-organize was seen as the most important consideration when choosing a business. By using the virtual café software, bots and a stigmergic people space, a system for matching patients to suitable cancer treatment trials would be self-organizing.

The driving force behind this tendency to self-organize is that all participants can benefit and it will be in everyone's best interest to take part.

2   **The business should not rely on an ability to determine future profitability.** By choosing to use a self-organizing system, all running costs, development and expansion must be financed out of actual rather than anticipated income because the future is unpredictable. In this situation, the concepts of determining future profitability and aiming for predetermined sales targets are not even applicable.

3   **The business must be capable of starting with a small amount of capital and be able to generate enough of an immediate revenue stream to make further progress.** Using founder assets, most of the necessary software is already prototyped. The system does not require elaborate hardware or server-side organization, so start-up costs will be relatively small. Low overheads equates with low burn rate. This removes the necessity of having to have a large amount of capital to finance the business during the start-up period.

Being modular in nature, the system can begin operating with just a single trial or a small niche area in cancer research. It doesn't need to

NOTE Income is expected to come from drug company contributions and a variety of other kinds of funding (see below), but these will manifest only as a direct response to the operation of the system: not through persuasive sales techniques. This is the principle of stigmergy.

attract the whole spectrum of cancer patients and treatment trials to be viable, especially in the early stages of growth.

4 **The business must be able to provide value right from the start.** From the moment it begins, a people space can provide benefit to the participants: simply though the value of being put in contact with each other. This benefit may be small at first, but the nature of stigmergic growth is such that benefits rapidly escalate as participation increases.

There is an exponential at work here. It is like the telephone network. If only one person has a telephone it is a completely useless device. As soon as a second person has a telephone it acquires value. This value increases exponentially as more and more people acquire telephones and can join the network of connectedness.

5 **The business must be such as to be able to solve immediate and real problems.** The business would help drug companies find clinics. It would help clinics find drug companies which will be conducting the trials. It would help clinics find trial patients. It would help patients find trials. It would allow patients with similar conditions to communicate and share knowledge of various types of treatment and trials. These are real and immediate problems that a stigmergic people space can solve.

6 **The business must be chosen such that it makes full and appropriate use of the founder's assets.** In an earlier chapter, mention was made of Bill Gates' own explanation as to why his company had achieved success. He told a UK television audience that his company had created and explored a computer environment and in so doing had developed many useful techniques and tools. He'd simply used that learned knowledge, and the tools that had been developed, as the basis for his business.

In this instance, I'd explored the environment of humans linking to each other through computers, while writing *Lingo Sorcery* and *Magical A-Life Avatars*. I gained many valuable insights and developed some useful techniques and tools (i.e. the virtual café; bots and digital agents; using databases to create formatted space; etc.). It is on the basis of this knowledge and those tools that this cancer treatment trial business is being formed.

7   **There must be enough suitable contacts, direct or indirect, available to cover all aspects of the chosen business situation.** During the writing of my books, I'd used the virtual café as the basis for developing relationships with a variety of people in all kinds of business environments and from many different countries. Together they provide strategic links into most of the areas of knowledge and specialization that will be needed for this cancer treatment trial project.

Most of these contacts consist of people who have many valuable contacts of their own. This represents a dynamic, human information network that reaches far and wide, particularly into the world of information technology.

8   **All employees must be revenue producing and fully covered by a stable and reliable income.** With a business based upon a low overhead system, which is self-running, self-organizing and self-evolving, very few employees would be needed. Further need for employees would come only as a result of organic growth and would be financed through increases in the revenue stream.

By having a system that can grow from a small base, there is no need for any large investment funding or support from a venture capital company. This removes the necessity for an expensive, high-profile, top-management structure.

Investors need to have confidence that their investments will be used wisely. They can be convinced (rightly or wrongly) only if there is a strong and provably successful management team running the business. They'll need details of how their money is to be spent and they'll need to be assured, by the presence of provably successful executives, that targets will be met.

Such management and executives do not come cheaply. They will be used to having secretaries and assistants; they will want to create management hierarchies. They will need to be rewarded with high salaries, bonuses, perks and stock options. A self-organizing business doesn't need all this, but fortunately it also doesn't need investors or venture capital companies.

9   **The product or service should be sufficiently distinctive to be able to take advantage of viral marketing.** The stigmergic approach to dealing with volatile data is itself of novel interest. Together with the concept of a people space, it will provide a low-cost environment for people trying to find others who have a special interest in a particular narrow area of knowledge. Such a system has many possible applications and will be of interest to many people, even outside of the field of oncology. This novelty is sufficient to spread knowledge about the existence of the project.

There are many internet discussion forums and newsgroups devoted to the subject of cancer. Via these communities, any new approach to helping cancer patients is rapidly propagated throughout the internet. From these internet communities, information is passed on to people who are not connected to the internet. It is likely to be propagated to most places where the treatment of cancer is discussed: hospitals, clinics, surgeries and even social events.

There are numerous specialist journals dealing with oncology. There are many conferences and seminars where information relating to various forms of treatment are discussed by specialists. There is a two-way exchange of information between these off-line centres of information and the internet communities: a valuable positive feedback loop that can accelerate the spread of information.

There is every reason to expect that should this stigmergic people space start to work, word will spread quickly. This will cost nothing and will be far more effective than any expensive advertising or marketing campaign.

The proviso is, of course, that the system can operate effectively. However, as yet, there is no low-cost system that provides cancer patients with up-to-date information on cancer treatment trials, particularly with the rarer forms of cancer. This suggests that there is every chance that the system will take off as expected.

10 **The critical mass must be easily adjustable,** and

11 **The essential infrastructure required must be such as to entail very low overhead costs.** These two rules are grouped together because they are inextricably linked. The lower limit to which the critical mass can be shrunk is dependent on the lowest the overheads can be reduced to without losing efficiency.

As discussed above, by making use of an organic, self-organizing system that can grow from a small base, there isn't a need for large amounts of investment capital. This means that this cancer trial treatment business doesn't have to carry the costs of a high-profile, cosmetic management structure. The employee base can be kept small and efficient, greatly reducing the burden of overheads.

The fundamental structure of a people space is a server and a low-cost database that simply hold lists. The functional components are client-side software that, once designed, involve no running costs. At any time, the business can be quickly reduced back to a basic, low-cost system without affecting the quality of the service.

Additional overheads, over and above the basic system, would be incurred only to provide customer liaison and further system development. These overheads can be scaled up or down according to actual business activity and in line with current cash flows.

12 **The business should have a lower critical mass than its competitors.** By utilizing a low-cost, low-overhead, self-organizing system that relies on organic growth and word-of-mouth advertising, there is very little leeway for competitive businesses to have a lower critical mass.

Competitors using large amounts of investment capital will be handicapped with an inherently larger critical mass.

13 **There should be no substantial development or pioneering costs.** The basic simplicity of the proposed system, and the fact that much of the essential software has already been prototyped, will ensure that

initial costs will be orders of magnitude smaller than any conventional approach to the problems to be solved.

The ability to grow organically, starting from a small base, will remove the need for expensive development costs. The pioneering will automatically occur as part of the self-organizing process as the system evolves its own path towards efficient operation. Such evolutionary development is financed, controlled and limited by the extent of the inward revenue – so there is no need for this to be funded out of capital.

14 **The business environment must be such as to allow switches in direction without too much disruption.** The modular nature of a people space provides ample opportunity for switching into different subject areas should any become too competitive or too crowded. For example, the areas dealing with the most common forms of cancer might be crowded out with different alternatives offered by big businesses that have large marketing budgets.

However, the limitations imposed by the need to achieve critical mass will prevent these companies using mass marketing techniques in the smaller areas of the less common forms of cancer, or with the more specialist cancer treatment trials.

A low-cost, highly adaptable system can pick and choose in the niche areas and fear no competition from the larger companies which will be handicapped by their higher critical mass.

15 **The business environment should offer ample scope for evolutionary growth and expansion.** Again, the modular nature of a people space is highly conducive to organic growth. Starting with perhaps a few niche categories of types of cancer, or specialist trials, more can be added, one by one, as different areas of interest open up. The very fact that categories are not specifically chosen in advance allows such areas of interest to manifest randomly.

16 **There must be a variety of funding possibilities available.** A people space that covers the various needs of so many people and so many

different businesses and organizations involved in the treatment of cancer provides a wealth of different sources of funding.

The modular structure and the organic growth allow areas of interest to manifest anywhere at any time. These can be initiated and sponsored by small amounts of funding so that any interested party can promote and develop the area that is of particular interest to them.

If drug companies need patients for a particular type of trial they can promote the appropriate categories. Similarly with trials clinics. Physicians and consultants may want to promote categories that concentrate information and patients around their particular area of speciality. Even patients, their relatives and friends will have strong motivations for promoting niche pockets of interest.

There are ample opportunities for government funding and grants. Charities also will have an interest in this project as it can help them to help cancer sufferers.

Even from outside of the cancer treatment area there will be many opportunities for funding because the basic idea of a stigmergic people space with client-side input and control has a wealth of different applications.

The equivalent of funding will also be readily available from university students who might decide that this area of technology would make a suitable subject for a thesis. Such student interest and participation can provide valuable contributions to system development.

conclusion

The conclusion reached, after two years of work on these three books on e-business, is that the dot-com bubble was a result of trying to apply the thinking and the business models of Industrial Age businesses to the Information Age.

The internet is predominantly a medium for communication, but this does not mean that it is confined simply to exchanging information. It is much more than this: it is a highly complex environment that allows human activity to be computer enhanced in ways that have no 'bricks and mortar world' equivalent. It is in these esoteric areas of communication enhancement that real advances can be made, with the potential to provide limitless opportunities for creating products and services that are as yet beyond the imagination. That these will emerge is beyond doubt.

The example provided here, of a business based on cancer treatment trials, did not arise out of using the internet to help solve the problems involved in cancer treatment. It arose out of an exploration of the unique environment of people using computer-enhanced methods of communicating and then looking for a way in which this knowledge could be applied. That I happened to decide upon applying what I'd discovered to the area of cancer treatment trials is almost a random outcome. I could just as easily have applied this same thinking to a host of other problem areas. It just happened that an oncologist came up with this particular problem at an opportune time.

epilogue

PROOF OF CONCEPT

Many of the ideas covered in this book can be seen on the website:

http://www.cancertreatmentworld.com

This site was constructed after the book was finished. The explanation on the home page reads:

Cancer treatment world is a virtual world, consisting of many different virtual countries. In every country, a specific type of cancer is the sole topic of interest.

In every country there are many towns, each dealing with a different variation of the type of cancer the country is concerned with. In each of these towns there are many different buildings, where each building is dealing with a particular aspect of the variation. In each of these buildings, there are meeting rooms set aside to concentrate upon particular finer details.

Patients, friends and relatives of patients, physicians, consultants, trial treatment clinicians, oncologists and drug company researchers can enter this virtual world; visiting any country and town that is of specific interest to them. They can go into the buildings and enter the meeting rooms to join discussion groups, discover where the latest information can be found; hear about the latest research and developments, learn of current and proposed treatment trials.

It is of course a people space. There is no information on this site. It is a place for people to meet others who have a similar interest in a particular niche area of knowledge, where they can share experiences and information with each other.

Of particular interest: all activity and organization happens on the client side. There is no server-side database. There are very few web pages. The whole system is run by the users themselves.

Further examples of stigmergic systems will be published on the website:

http://www.petersmall.net

… as and when they happen.

INDEX